THE ASHANTI WAR

A NARRATIVE

Mampong
20th Oct. 1873.

To His Excellency,
Governor in Chief of Her Majesty,
Fort

Sir!

I have received those two letters which you sent to me in order to send them to the King of Ashantee. For what purpose I came here is that:— Assin, Dankra, Akyen Wassaw. Those four nations belong to the King of Ashantee, and they refused to serve the King, and they escaped away unto you, if the King sends his servants to or to buy something at Cape Coast they catch them and plundered their good to. And those nations ordered the King of Ashantee that he may come to fight with them. Therefore I said they are not a friends with the King, on account of that

I shall come down here to catch those four thieves who ordered the King of Ashantee to come to fight with him; And they fought with me six times and I drove them away and they escapped to be under you. But the King did not send me into Cape Coast, and then you delliver Assin, Dankra Akyen and Fassaw unto me, I shall bring unto the King there is no any quarrel with you.

I send My love to You,

I am yours
Amanguatia

THE ASHANTI WAR

A NARRATIVE

PREPARED FROM THE OFFICIAL DOCUMENTS BY PERMISSION OF
MAJOR-GENERAL SIR GARNET WOLSELEY
C.B. K.C.M.G.

BY

HENRY BRACKENBURY
CAPTAIN ROYAL ARTILLERY
ASSISTANT MILITARY SECRETARY TO SIR GARNET WOLSELEY DURING
THE WAR, AND FORMERLY PROFESSOR OF MILITARY HISTORY
AT THE ROYAL MILITARY ACADEMY OF WOOLWICH

WITH MAPS AND PLANS COMPILED FROM THE STAFF-SURVEYS, REPORTS OF SPECIAL
COMMISSIONERS TO NATIVE KINGS, AND OTHER OFFICIAL SOURCES
BY HARRY COOPER, LIEUT. 47TH REGT.
Sometime Adjutant of Transport in the Campaign

IN TWO VOLUMES

VOL. I.

WILLIAM BLACKWOOD AND SONS
EDINBURGH AND LONDON
MDCCCLXXIV

All Rights reserved

Printed and bound by Antony Rowe Ltd, Eastbourne

Dedicated

TO MY COMRADES

OF THE

HEAD-QUARTER-STAFF MESS

IN REMEMBRANCE OF

OUR UNBROKEN GOOD-FELLOWSHIP

FROM THE FIRST TO THE LAST DAY

OF THE

ASHANTI EXPEDITION

PREFACE.

THIS is not an official history. I alone am responsible for its contents. Neither Sir Garnet Wolseley nor any member of his staff has seen a word of the book in manuscript or in proof; and I have not received directly or indirectly from the Major-General any suggestions as to the matter or manner of the work.

But I claim for my book all the accuracy of an official account. Sir Garnet Wolseley did me the honour of placing at my disposal all the official documents of the campaign, without reservation; and they form the basis of this narrative. The account of Captain Glover's expedition is taken entirely and solely from the letters which passed between Sir Garnet Wolseley and himself. The missions of Captain Butler and Captain Dalrymple have been described from their own letters.

For some valuable information as to the medical arrangements for the campaign, I am indebted to Deputy Surgeon-General A. D. Home, V.C., C.B.; and for the statistics of the campaign, to Surgeon-Major W. A. Mackinnon, C.B. Lieutenant-Colonel Colley most kindly furnished me with a memorandum on the transport operations; Captain Rait, R.A., was so good as to lend me his journal; and Lieutenant-Colonel Festing and Captain Gordon drew up for me some notes on the operations preceding Sir Garnet Wolseley's arrival on the Coast. I have also to acknowledge my obligations to Major-General M'Dougall for having, with the permission of the Secretary of State for War, placed at my disposal all the sketches sent home by the survey department during the Expedition; and to the Secretary of State for the Colonies for having allowed me to examine the despatches received from the Gold Coast since the departure of Sir Garnet Wolseley for England.

Considerable experience in the study of military history has taught me that the greatest obstacle in the way of its successful pursuit is the difficulty of obtaining sufficiently detailed accounts of operations in the field. I have therefore, at the risk of being tedious to the ordinary public, given all such details as seemed to be necessary for a complete military study of this war. I am well aware that these details may seem trivial to those accustomed to studying the great wars of the Continent. But the wars of England are generally little wars; and it is by the study of details as well as of great principles that success in war, great or small, is attained.

PREFACE. ix

While I have supplemented the official papers by a personal narrative of the doings of the headquarter staff, taken from my private journal, I have not in any way attempted to compete in descriptive writing with the numerous civilians who are writing, or have written, books on the war. I must have failed in such a competition, for I am limited to the facts as told in the official documents. My plain narrative rests its claim to attention on its strict accuracy as regards facts, and on my knowledge of the springs of movements.

No one can be more aware than myself of the literary defects of this book. But it has been written in six weeks, immediately following a five months' campaign on the Gold Coast; and I have preferred placing it in its present state before the public while the interest in the campaign is fresh, to polishing it up at the expense of delay.

HENRY BRACKENBURY.

LONDON, 23d *May* 1874.

CONTENTS OF THE FIRST VOLUME.

CHAPTER I.

OUR EARLY RELATIONS WITH THE ASHANTIS AND THE PROTECTED TRIBES, AND THE CAUSES OF THE LATE WAR, . . 1

CHAPTER II.

EVENTS FROM THE COMMENCEMENT OF THE WAR TO THE DATE OF SIR GARNET WOLSELEY'S ARRIVAL AT CAPE COAST, . 53

CHAPTER III.

THE DESPATCH TO THE GOLD COAST OF THE EXPEDITIONS UNDER CAPTAIN GLOVER AND SIR GARNET WOLSELEY—INSTRUCTIONS ISSUED BY THE GOVERNMENT, ... 104

CHAPTER IV.

CONDITION OF AFFAIRS ON ARRIVAL OF SIR GARNET WOLSELEY —MEASURES ADOPTED UPON ARRIVAL—THE ACTION OF ESSA- MAN, 14TH OCTOBER, ... 144

CHAPTER V.

EVENTS CONTINUED TO THE BREAKING UP OF THE ASHANTI CAMP AT MAMPON, 25TH OCTOBER, ... 186

CHAPTER VI.

EVENTS TO THE RE-CROSSING OF THE PRAH BY THE ENEMY—THE MARCH TO ASSANCHI—ACTIONS OF ISCABIO—DEFENCE OF ABRAKRAMPA — RECONNAISSANCES — ACTION OF FAISOWAH—FLIGHT OF THE ASHANTI ARMY ACROSS THE PRAH, . . 235

CHAPTER VII.

PREPARATIONS FOR THE INVASION OF ASHANTI—THE ROAD TO THE PRAH—CAMPING-GROUNDS FOR EUROPEAN TROOPS—SANITARY PRECAUTIONS—HOSPITALS AND TRANSPORT FOR SICK AND WOUNDED—THE TRANSPORT QUESTION GENERALLY—ARRIVAL AND DESPATCH TO SEA OF THE EUROPEAN TROOPS—ORDERS FOR THE MARCH AND FOR THE FIGHT—THE MAJOR-GENERAL'S PLAN OF INVASION, ... 308

CHAPTER VIII.

CAPTAIN GLOVER'S OPERATIONS TO THE END OF DECEMBER 1873, ... 376

APPENDIX, ... 425

LIST OF MAPS TO VOL. I.

FACSIMILE OF LETTER FROM AMANQUATIA, . . *Frontispiece.*
SKETCH TO ILLUSTRATE THE ACTION AT ESSAMAN, *To face page* 184
MAP TO ILLUSTRATE OPERATIONS UP TO THE REPULSE OF THE ASHANTIS FROM ABRAKRAMPA, ... ,, 306

MAP OF THE GOLD COAST,
MAP OF THE THEATRE OF WAR, } *In pocket at end of* VOL. II.

THE ASHANTI WAR:

A NARRATIVE.

CHAPTER I.

OUR EARLY RELATIONS WITH THE ASHANTIS AND THE PROTECTED TRIBES, AND THE CAUSES OF THE LATE WAR.

THE known history of the Ashanti nation shows us a powerful, warlike, disciplined, though barbarous race, ever marching seaward in pursuit of conquests and of trade, thrusting out and driving before it its rebellious tributaries and the weaker tribes who vainly strive to oppose its progress, and at last, when the ocean barrier closes their path, reconquering them and subjecting them to its sway. Not till the white man intervened was this career of victory rudely checked, nor till the present war had sufficient force been put forth to teach this warlike savage people that they must once and for ever bow to that mysterious strength which the arts and sciences of civilisation confer upon the nations of the Western world.

There have not been wanting writers who have traced the early history of the Ashanti monarchy through the dim regions of myth and legend; it needs not that we should follow them ; but, if a clear understanding is to be obtained of the causes of the recent war, remote as well as proximate, it is necessary that we should glance at the mutual relations which have existed for the last century and a half between the Ashantis, the coast tribes, and the European nations who established settlements on the Gold Coast.

The earliest event which bears directly on the recent cause of quarrel is the conquest in 1719 by King Osai Tutu, the founder of Coomassie, of the kingdom of Denkera, a rich and powerful state lying to the southwest of Ashanti. Here, as at Troy, a woman was the cause of quarrel, though there is little doubt that the jealousy of two great powers, long smouldering, needed but a breath to be fanned into the flame which should light the torch of war. The King of Denkera had sent, in a somewhat boastful spirit, an embassy of his wives to compliment the King of Ashanti. Treating them with all courtesy, and loading them with presents, King Osai Tutu sent them back ; and not long after sent an embassy of his own wives to Bosiante, the King of Denkera. On one of these Bosiante, a young and valiant prince, looked with too loving eyes ; and counting the world well lost for love, forgot her doubly sacred character of ambassadress and wife, and wooed and won her to his arms. In vain did he offer gold, in vain try to pacify the injured monarch and husband. Osai Tutu prepared for war ; nor did even the death of Bosiante during the course of the preparations appease him. Sweeping down with a vast army, he defeated the Denkeras in two great battles, overran the country, and forced into exile all whom he did not slay or lead into slavery.

At the time of this invasion the Dutch were the possessors of several forts on the Gold Coast, and carried on a brisk trade in slaves. Mr Bowdich tells us, in his work written in 1819, that the King of Denkera, Intim Dakarey, "was so considerable a trader in slaves, that the Dutch Governor-General paid him a monthly note from his own purse, and assisted him with two or three small cannons, and a few Europeans, on the eve of the Ashanti invasion."* This fact is of considerable importance; and we shall find later on, when the cession of the Dutch territories to the English comes in question, that the King of Ashanti appears to have received the subsequent payments on account of this "monthly note," by virtue of his right of conquest over the King of Denkera. The three small cannons were taken as trophies to Coomassie.

The Ashantis appear to have annexed and occupied the greater part of Denkera, depopulating the country by fire and sword, while the surviving portion of its inhabitants were driven to the south-east. There they have since remained. The present capital of the state of Denkera is Jooquah, near the Sweet River, and the king's authority is limited to a small tribe, and a small extent of territory.

Osai Tutu also carried his victorious arms into Akim, a small but vigorous state lying south-east of the Ashanti kingdom, whose ruler had joined cause with the Denkeras. Besides being compelled to pay a heavy fine, the King of Akim was reduced to the condition of a tributary. But the chiefs of Akim refused to accept the terms of peace, and on a renewal of the war, the

* Mission from Cape Coast Castle to Ashantee, by T. E. Bowdich (London, 1819), p. 233.

Ashantis suffered a great defeat at Acromantee or Cormantee. The king was slain, and his body not recovered; many great chiefs shared his fate; and the army returned in wrath and gloom to Coomassie, not, however, till it had rased Acromantee to the ground, and sacrificed the whole of the Akim prisoners as an offering to the slain king. This occurred in 1731.

The conquered tribes now threw off the yoke; but the successor of Osai Tutu again occupied Denkera, subdued Akim, and thoroughly reduced Assin, a nation at that time living on the northern bank of the river Prah. This second conquest of Akim gave into the hands of Osai Apoko, the King of Ashanti, certain "notes," concerning the exact origin of which there is some little doubt. These "notes,"* or undertakings on the part of the issuers to pay to the chiefs to whom they were delivered a certain annual sum, had been issued by the English, Dutch, and Danes to the chiefs on whose ground stood the forts belonging to these respective nations at Accra; but whether as rent for the ground, or as a stipend to secure friendly relations, it is difficult now to say. These "notes" appear to have been in the first instance captured by the Akims from the Accras, and other coast tribes; and the Ashantis now claimed payment by right of capture, just as in the case of the Denkera "notes" they claimed payment from the Dutch.

We may pass over the reigns of Osai Apoko and that of his brother Osai Aquasi, notable only for an unsuccessful war with Dahomey, and so reach the reign of Osai Cudjo, who came to the throne in 1752.

* Journal of a Residence in Ashantee, by Joseph Dupuis (London, 1824), p. 234. See also Bowdich, p. 234.

By him the northern portion of the Wassaw territory was overrun and depopulated. Wassaw, Assin, Aquamoo, and Aquapim, were subjected to Ashanti during this reign; and the Akims were again conquered after a new revolt by Cudjo's successor, Osai Quamina. This king was deposed in 1797, and succeeded by his brother Osai Apoko the Second, who, during his short career, waged successful war with Gaman, a state lying to the north-west of Ashanti. Dying soon after his great victories, this monarch was succeeded, in the year 1800, by his brother Osai Tutu Quamina, whose earlier years upon the throne were marked by successful invasions of Gaman, and the countries lying between Ashanti and the Volta.

The year 1807 brings us to a more notable point, the first invasion by the Ashantis of the Fanti territory, and the first collision of the great inland kingdom with the British occupants of the forts on the seaboard. At this time the state of Fanti had no such homogeneity as the Ashanti kingdom, nor was it ruled by an absolute monarch. At least two kings exercised authority, and many chiefs, each claiming virtual independence of the kings. The origin of the Fantis is doubtful; whether, as appears from the similarity of language, they were emigrants from the Ashanti people, or a weaker tribe driven out by the stronger race, has not been clearly proved. At all events, they were, now that Ashanti had conquered Wassaw, Assin, and Akim, the only tribe remaining between the southern boundary of Osai Tutu Quamina's kingdom, and that great goal of the aspirations of all inland nations—the sea-coast.

The British forts on the Gold Coast were held, at the time we have now reached, by the "African Company," established under a royal charter for purposes of trade. The forts were at Dixcove, Secondee, Commendah, Cape Coast Castle, Annamaboe, Winnebah, and Accra. The system in force of payment by "notes" to the chiefs owning the adjacent territories has already been described.

A dispute between the Ashantis and the Assins had resulted in the defeat of the latter, the rout of their army, and the flight of the two great Assin chiefs southwards into Fanti territory. Refusal by the Fantis to deliver up these chiefs, or allow the Ashantis to pursue them, with insults offered to the king's messengers, brought the Ashantis down with fire and sword into the heart of Fanti land. Destroying Abrah, the victorious army marched on, burning and slaughtering, to Annamaboe, whither the Assin chiefs had fled, destroying Cormantine on their road, and taking possession of the Dutch fort. The Assin chiefs fled to Cape Coast Castle. The inhabitants of Annamaboe crowded into and under the walls of the fort, the Ashantis pursuing them, killing and carrying them off from under the very walls, silencing the guns of the fort by their fire upon the embrasures, and even assaulting the gate. The fort itself was in sore strait, when orders arrived from the Governor-in-Chief at Cape Coast Castle to hoist the white flag. This was succeeded by the delivery to the king of one of the Assin chiefs; the other had made good his escape from Cape Coast. Colonel Torrane, the Governor-in-Chief, waited on the king in his camp at Annamaboe (the king having refused to come to Cape Coast), made him handsome presents, and concluded a peace. The terms of this peace were, if Mr Dupuis is to be believed, "a formal and solemn acknowledgment on the part of the Governor, that by right of conquest, Fanti, including Cape Coast and every other town in the neighbourhood, belonged exclusively to the empire of Ashanti, with the reservation of a judicial authority to the Company over such towns as stood in the vicinity of any of the castles; and in confirmation or ratification of these terms, the Governor expressly admitted the king's title to those deeds, called notes, upon which he paid him the arrears then due, and a tribute, called perhaps a present, which was demanded of the Cape Coast people."*

Thus, then, in this first meeting of the Ashantis and the British, the victory, military or diplomatic, was not on our side. We had given in to all the demands of the king—had acknowledged him the lord of Fanti—had consented to pay him rent or tribute for our forts—had yielded up to him to be tortured a prisoner who had sought our protection. Well might the King of Ashanti say that he took the English for his friends, as he "saw their object was trade only, and they did not care for the people."† A sorry beginning of negotiations for the nation whose creed is philanthropy!

The actual pressure of the invasion being removed, the Fantis resolved to punish Elmina and Accra for not coming to their aid; and this brought down the Ashantis again in force. On the one side the Ashantis and Elminas were successful; on the other Akim and Aquapim rebelled, and drew off the Ashanti troops destined to assist the people of Accra.

In 1816 and 1817 the Ashantis again overran the whole Fanti territory. Thousands were butchered in cold blood, thousands more dragged away into slavery

* Dupuis, p. 262. † Ibid., p. 263.

or to the stool of sacrifice. Famine followed in the train of the invader. British interference resulted in the blockade of Cape Coast Castle, and the war was only ended by the payment of a large sum of money by the Fantis, advanced to them for the purpose by the English Governor.

Thus, for the second time in ten years, the Ashantis were to all intents and purposes able to dictate terms to the British Governor on the Gold Coast.

Disturbed and alarmed by these occurrences, the African Company despatched an embassy to Coomassie, "to deprecate these repeated calamities, to conciliate so powerful a monarch, and to propitiate an extension of commerce."* The mission started in April 1817; Mr James was its leader, and he was afterwards replaced by Mr Bowdich. The following paragraph of the instructions to Mr James will be read with interest by the light of recent events: "You will particularly explain to the king the ill treatment the people of Cape Coast have received from those of Elmina, which has added very much to the distresses they have for some time suffered from the extreme scarcity of provisions; and there is reason to believe that this unjust persecution has been induced from their presuming on their connection with the Ashantis. Being perfectly aware that it has been done without the concurrence of the king, I have no doubt but he will, by a proper representation of the affair from you, exert his influence and prevent what is at present to be apprehended, and what the Elminas are endeavouring to provoke—a war between the two people."† Here, then, is direct evidence, fifty-five years old, of the hostility between Cape

* Bowdich, p. 4.   † Bowdich, p. 12.

Coast and Elmina, and the influence exerted over the latter by the King of Ashanti.

At an early stage of the negotiations, difficulties arose as to the payment of the "notes." The king accused the English of cheating him, by not having paid the monthly stipends which were due for the forts, and had been formally made over to him by the Fanti chiefs, whereas the Dutch paid him regularly. This was settled by the distinct recognition of the king's rights; and a sum of 6 ounces of gold per month was promised as a regular payment at the Castle. The king also raised a discussion as to the conduct of the Commendahs, in reference to a quarrel between them and Elmina. The Commendahs acknowledged their fealty to the king, and paid 120 ounces of gold. Mr Bowdich then signed a treaty of perpetual peace between Ashanti and the British subjects, as well as all nations residing under the protection of the Company's forts and settlements on the Gold Coast. It was agreed that neither party had any claim upon the other; but who the protected nations were was not defined. It was agreed that, in case of any aggression by the natives under British protection, the king should complain thereof to the Governor-in-Chief to obtain redress, and should not resort to hostilities without endeavouring to obtain an amicable arrangement. The King of Ashanti guaranteed the people of Cape Coast from the hostilities threatened by the people of Elmina; and agreed to accept a British resident at his capital. In return, the Governor promised to protect the Ashantis resorting to the coast. The treaty was signed in September 1817.*

* Compare the versions of this treaty in Bowdich, p. 126, and Dupuis, Appendix, p. cxix.

The Home Government, desirous of cultivating the harmony now existing, despatched Mr Dupuis to the Gold Coast, with a commission as Consul to Coomassie. He arrived at Cape Coast in January 1819, and found that the late resident at Coomassie had returned to Cape Coast, having been recalled by the Governor. The King of Ashanti was on the point of making war with Gaman; and one of his captains was living at Cape Coast, virtually in the capacity of resident representative of the Ashanti interests. The people of Cape Coast were not sparing in their wishes for the defeat of the Ashantis, and circulated reports of heavy losses and defeats. The Commendah people, urged on by this, insulted some messengers from the king who thereupon sent to claim the protection and interference of the Governor, by virtue of Mr Bowdich's treaty. The king added that if the Governor did not do justice, he should send troops to enforce it on the natives.

Unfortunately, the Governor's answer was a defiance of the king. The Cape Coast natives commenced to intrench their town, and all trade came to an end. But the king sent another messenger in September with a large retinue, who insisted on the treaty being read, claimed satisfaction under its clauses, and said that if redress were not granted, he should leave the treaty, and war would be declared. However, the announcement of Mr Dupuis' appointment by the Home Government procured a delay; and early in January 1820, another embassy arrived, escorted by 1200 armed men. The king claimed a fine of 1600 ounces of gold from the Cape Coast people, and the same from the British Governor for his breach of the treaty, threatening war as the alternative of compliance with his demand. An unqualified refusal to pay any fine to the king was made by the Governor; and war must have resulted, but for the acceptance by the Ashantis of Mr Dupuis' mission. He started for Coomassie early in February, and was favourably received by the king. The demand for a fine was given up, and Mr Dupuis concluded a new treaty, signed in March 1820.

In this treaty the sovereignty of the king over Fanti was acknowledged, the king, however, agreeing to acknowledge the natives residing under British protection as entitled to the benefit of British laws. The king swore allegiance and fidelity to the British Crown, undertook to support trade and British interests, and would in future address complaints to the Consul only, and on no account make war with the natives at any of the English settlements, without first giving the Consul an opportunity of adjusting the differences. The king was to keep half the path from Coomassie to the sea well cleared. On the other hand, the Consul guaranteed protection to Ashanti subjects on the Coast, promised to keep the other half of the road clear, and to take on himself the payment of the "notes" for the future, thus preventing exorbitant prices being charged for the articles given in payment.*

Had this treaty been approved and faithfully kept on our side, it is probable war with Ashanti might long have been warded off. The Fantis would have assumed their natural position of subject tribes, the Ashantis would have held free access to the coast, and commerce might have been freely carried on. But the local authorities, and subsequently the Home Government, refused to ratify the treaty, on the ground that it transferred

* See original treaty in Dupuis, Appendix, p. cxx.

the Fanti territory to the King of Ashanti; and the local authorities decided to discontinue paying the "notes."

Bearing in mind that the king viewed Mr Dupuis as the ambassador of his sovereign, and that his own dealings with us had been always fair and straightforward, it is not difficult to see that he must have looked on the repudiation of this contract as a deliberate breach of faith on the part of the British; and it is difficult to conceive a more unwise policy than that adopted by us—a policy more likely to bear bitter fruit in the form of future mistrust, fatal alike to commerce and the progress of enlightened civilisation.

The friendly treaty so happily made being thus nullified, the King of Ashanti adhered to his previous demands, though he did not take immediate steps for enforcing them.

In the year 1821, Parliament passed a bill to abolish the African Company, and to transfer its forts and possessions to the Crown. Sir Charles Macarthy, whose wise rule at Sierra Leone had gained him golden opinions, was appointed Governor of the Gold Coast, and arrived at Cape Coast early in 1822. He found Cape Coast blockaded by an Ashanti force, and all trade gone into the hands of the Dutch. Sir Charles adopted a policy the exact reverse of that of Mr Dupuis. He held the Fantis free from Ashanti rule; he sent no embassy to the king, such as the courtesies of the country demand; and he virtually defied the king, who was still hoping for good news of Mr Dupuis' treaty, to enforce his claims.

It was not long before hostilities commenced. A sergeant of the British service was carried off from the square at Annamaboe, on the ground that he had spoken disrespectfully of the King of Ashanti, and publicly executed. The king, finding no steps taken in revenge, sent a message to Sir Charles that he would make his head into an ornament of the royal death-drum; still, he attempted to negotiate through the Dutch Governor of Elmina, but this failing, he sent a large army into Wassaw, and drove before him the allied forces of the Wassaws and the Denkeras.*

The result of Sir Charles Macarthy's expedition against the enemy is well known. Gifted with indomitable energy and self-reliance, the unfortunate Governor crossed the Prah into the Wassaw country with a mere handful of men on the 13th January 1824, and advanced beyond Assamacow to the banks of a stream called the Adoomansu, on which he had induced the retreating allies to halt. On the 21st he was attacked by the enemy. His ammunition failed; thousands of Ashantis outflanked his force. Deserted by the Wassaws, separated from the Denkeras, he and the few white men who clave to him were, with three exceptions, slain and beheaded.

In this unhappy battle the main portion of the force which Sir Charles might have employed was not engaged, but, under the command of Major Chisholm, was absent from the field towards which Sir Charles had hurried without giving time for its arrival. It fell back upon Cape Coast, and when the Fantis had been beaten again in April and pursued to near Cape Coast by the enemy, it attacked the Ashantis in May, and an action ensued without decisive result, owing

---

* The events briefly related in the remainder of this chapter will be found more fully stated in the first two chapters of 'Fanti and Ashanti,' by the author and the late Captain Huyshe. Blackwood & Sons, 1873.

chiefly to the desertion of the Fantis. Cape Coast itself was now so closely threatened that the men were landed from the fleet for its defence. Another general action ensued in July, after which the Ashantis retired further from the coast, remaining, however, in the Fanti territory till sickness caused them to recross the Prah in the year 1824.

Strange to say, on the very day of Sir Charles Macarthy's unhappy defeat, the king Osai Tutu Quamina was gathered to his fathers. He was succeeded by his brother Osai Okoto.

Once again a large force of Ashantis advanced towards the coast, and on the 19th September 1826, was defeated and routed at Dodowah by a force of native allies and the Royal African Corps under command of English officers. Rockets were used in this action for the first time on the coast; and there seems little doubt that the moral effect which they produced aided materially in the victory. The Akims seem to have behaved well, penetrating to the very centre of the enemy's camp, and capturing much booty.

Whatever we may think of the conduct of affairs by the British up to this time, whether they had behaved justly and wisely towards the kings of Ashanti or not, they had, until this action, always had the worst of the argument whenever the Ashantis had chosen to invade the friendly territory. But now modern inventions in war had made their mark, and a message was received in September 1827 that "the King of Ashanti found it was no use fighting against white men, and wished to make peace, and be subservient to them." Negotiations were entered upon. A draft treaty was drawn up, but though agreed upon, not finally adopted.

In 1831, however, a treaty of peace was concluded by Governor Maclean.

This officer had been sent out in 1828 by the company of African merchants to whom in that year the Government, weary of perpetual failure, had transferred the rule over the Gold Coast settlements, withdrawing altogether from responsibility. His name is now held in special esteem in the country, as a wise and able governor, who did much to restore fallen commerce, and ruled with a firm and equable hand.

In the pavement of the courtyard of Cape Coast Castle are many stones which mark the resting-place of European victims to that deadly climate. Among them are two graves that never fail to attract the notice of the new-comer. One bears the initials G. M., the other the initials L. E. L. Not side by side, but yet not far apart, lie the famed Governor, George Maclean, and the far more famed poetess, his wife, Letitia Elizabeth Landon. The dark mystery that enshrouds her fate is never likely to be cleared up; and the feet of thousands of native carriers and soldiers are fast wearing away the stones whose inscription will yet perhaps outlive her memory.

The treaty made by Governor Maclean on behalf of the King of England, and the Kings of Ashanti, Cape Coast, Fanti, Annamaboe, Denkera, Tchuful, Wassaw, Assin, and all other chiefs in alliance with the King of Great Britain, contained the following clauses :*

Renunciation by the King of Ashanti of all right or title to any tribute or homage from the kings formerly his subjects; obligation on the Fantis not to molest the people of Ashanti, or in any way insult the king; and

* The treaty is given in full in Appendix I.

agreement that any dispute between the kings was to be referred to the British Governor for arbitration, the kings pledging themselves not to make war upon each other.

An era of peace followed this completion of the treaty of 1831, and in 1842 a committee of the House of Commons recommended the resumption by the Crown of the government of the West African settlements, acting on the report of a commissioner who had been sent out by Lord John Russell, and who considered that the existing system of government favoured the continuance of the slave-trade. In 1843, the government of the forts on the Gold Coast was resumed by the Crown; and in 1844 a treaty was signed between Governor Hill and the Fanti kings and chiefs of Denkera, Abrah, Assim, Donadie, Donomassie, Annamaboe, and Cape Coast, by which they acknowledged the power and jurisdiction of her Majesty, and consented to the customs of the country being moulded according to the principles of British law. At the same time a judicial assessor was appointed to administer justice among them.

Osai Okoto had died in 1838, and was succeeded on the throne by Osai Quaku Duah, whose relations with the British continued on a very satisfactory footing.

In 1848, Governor Winniett went to Coomassie, where he held a most friendly interview with the king, who assured him that the number of human sacrifices in his kingdom was being reduced. The abolition of these sacrifices had been the object of the Governor's mission.

From the year 1852 dates the first positive and definite recognition of the right of the Fanti tribes to protection at the hands of the British Government. In that year a general meeting was held of all the

THE ASHANTI WAR.

chiefs of the Protectorate, and it was resolved that the meeting constitute itself a legislative assembly, with power to enact laws. The assembly "having taken into consideration the advantage of British protection, considered it reasonable that the natives should contribute to the support of the Government," and a poll-tax was agreed to. This ordinance for the poll-tax received the sanction of the Home Government, and it may thus be said that the native tribes had now from this day a distinct right to British protection. They had undertaken to pay a tax in consideration of that protection, and any doubtful obligation which may formerly have existed on our part had now become written and distinctly acknowledged.

The treaty of 1831, with the unsigned treaty of 1827, and the bond between Governor Hill and the Fanti kings of 1844, formed, together with the new ordinance of 1852, the documents which defined the position of the British Government, Ashanti, and the Fanti tribes.

A new difficulty sprang up in this year, 1852, between Great Britain and Ashanti. A chief of Assin, of the name of Cudjo Chibboo, had received bribes from the King of Ashanti, and had promised to bring his people under the rule of that monarch. He had also committed some other offences, and defied the authority of the British Government. He was apprehended, and tried before a native court, under the Governor's presidency, convicted, sentenced to imprisonment for life, and confined in Cape Coast Castle. Governor Hill, writing home at this time, says that there was a strong war party in Ashanti, and that the Ashantis could not forget their former sway over the whole of the Fanti settlements, and the large revenue extorted from these unfortunate Fantis; and he considered that it was only the peaceful disposition of the reigning king that prevented immediate collision. At the urgent request of the chiefs, Governor Hill soon restored Cudjo Chibboo to liberty; but he exacted hostages for their good behaviour from all the chiefs of Assin, required that all the Assins still remaining on the north bank of the river Prah should cross over to the south bank and live under the English rule, and insisted upon the Assins and Fantis making immediately a military road from Cape Coast to the river Prah—a stipulation which was unfortunately never carried into effect.

It appears that by native custom this Assin chief who had accepted bribes had brought himself under the Ashanti rule, and the Ashantis crossed the frontier early in 1853 to take away Cudjo Chibboo and another chief. Several excuses for the invasion were made by the King of Ashanti; but the chief in command of the body of men who crossed the Prah, acknowledged that the king's real design was to seize these chiefs. Cudjo Chibboo was brought into Cape Coast for safety, and a large Ashanti force was crossing the Prah; but a small force, which was sent under the command of Ensign Brownell—who had orders not to fire a shot except in self-defence, and to do all in his power to induce the Ashantis to retire amicably—was so well handled by that officer, that his efforts were successful, and the Ashanti troops, to the number of 7000, recrossed the Prah. Governor Hill feared the return of the Ashantis, and stated in his home despatches that he could place no reliance upon their promises. He wrote at this time that, "if it were not for the expense and exposure of a few white officers in this deadly climate, a contest with Ashanti, and the destruction of that power, would not only be a war of humanity and civilisation, but would open the interior of this country to mercantile enterprise, and enable those now shut out and under the yoke of that bloodthirsty people to enjoy the blessings of a mild government." He said, "It is revolting to humanity to know that, as a common average, at least 3000 persons are sacrificed annually to their superstitious rites; and on some occasions 3000 have been slaughtered on one royal grave."

From 1853 to 1863 there was peace; but in December 1862 there arose a difference between the King of Ashanti and Mr Pine, at that time Governor of the Gold Coast, causing the commencement of those hostilities which, it may be said, have never since ceased. In December 1862, the King of Ashanti demanded from Mr Pine the restoration of a runaway boy-slave, and also the delivery of an old chief of the name of Jennim, who was accused of appropriating some gold, the property of the king. Colonel Nagtglas, the late Commissioner of the King of the Netherlands on the Gold Coast, states in a letter dated February 1874, that "there is an agreement in existence between the local British Government and the King of Ashanti, either oral or in writing, that on both sides runaway prisoners for crime should be delivered, and that according to this agreement the King of Ashanti asked the Government to give up the runaway chief." The writer has not been able to find any trace of any such agreement, but there is no doubt that the King of Ashanti did make application for the delivery of these prisoners; and there is no doubt also that, as Colonel Nagtglas truly says, "the delivery of the chief would have been equivalent to his certain execution." There was no evidence offered against the chief. Governor Pine, almost unanimously supported at a very large meeting of his own chiefs and people, refused to give Jennim up, but told the king if he would send evidence of the old man's guilt he would surrender him. In a despatch to Governor Pine, the Duke of Newcastle thus expresses his opinion of his conduct: "I entirely approve of your having refused to surrender to the King of Ashanti the old man and boy who had been brought into British territory. No person once brought within the limits of a British possession can be then seized and handed over to a foreign power except with the sanction of the law of the colony; and no law should authorise such delivery to the authorities of a country in which justice is not fairly administered, except in the case of heinous crimes."

The King of Ashanti, however, had been entering into negotiations with the King of Elmina, had purchased large quantities of arms and ammunition, and replied to Governor Pine, complaining strongly of his conduct in this and in other matters where his complaints appear to have had no reasonable grounds. Parties of Ashantis commenced to overrun the Protectorate, and their commander sent a message making a new demand upon the Governor. He was to give up to them a certain king, Adgiman by name, who had on some previous occasion—so it was said—insulted and wronged the King of Ashanti's father. If this request were complied with, then the war, the Ashanti chief said, would be a short one; if not, the commander of the Ashanti forces would remain in the protected territory for years. At the time that this message was sent, the Ashantis had already pillaged and burned thirty villages, and slain several hundreds of Fantis.

In August 1863, Governor Pine refused to hold any further communication with the king till he should withdraw his troops and make reparation for these wrongs. Foreseeing the probability of a serious and lengthened war, Mr Pine made this proposition to the Home Government:—

"It is with the deepest regret that I find myself involved, in spite of all my precautions, in a serious, and, I fear, lingering war; but such being the case, I will not conceal from your Grace the earnest desire that I entertain that a final blow shall be struck at Ashanti power, and the question set at rest for ever, as to whether an arbitrary, cruel, and sanguinary monarch shall be for ever permitted to insult the British flag, and outrage the laws of civilisation.

"This desirable object can be attained only by the possession of such a force as I fear the Governor of these settlements can never hope to command, unless your Grace should be pleased to urge upon her Majesty's Government the policy, the economy, and even the mercy, of transporting to these shores an army of such strength as would, combined with the allied native forces, enable us to march to Coomassie, and there plant the British flag.

"To a stranger, the course I point out may appear a visionary one; but I am convinced that, even with all the disadvantages of climate, the expedition would not be so dangerous, so fatal, or accompanied with such loss of life as have attended expeditions in other and apparently more genial climes; and with 2000 disciplined soldiers, followed by upwards of 50,000 native forces, who require only to be led and inspired with confidence by the presence of organised troops, I would undertake (driving the hordes of Ashanti before me) to march to Coomassie.

"As the case now stands, the most I can hope is, to drive the Ashantis from the Protectorate, without the chance of administering that chastisement, or demanding that retribution, which is so justly due to its inhabitants,—and remain in constant dread of subsequent incursions of a powerful enemy."

Such an expedition as the Governor had demanded required permission from home; but, to his great disappointment, that permission was withheld. He wrote that "the protected tribes had wellnigh lost their confidence in British protection;" and he found it necessary, in order to restore their confidence, to take some decisive measures. In December 1863, he caused a body of troops to advance towards the Prah, with a view of their encamping there, in the hope that their presence on his frontier would induce the King of Ashanti to make peace. The Ashantis having withdrawn into their own territory, at the latter end of December some companies of West India troops were marched to the Prah, and there encamped under shelter-tents on wet ground. At first the novelty and interest kept the men up, and the season was dry; the soldiers were reported as being in good spirits and in fair health, busily employed in erecting stockades, building huts, and constructing a bridge. Their condition continued good until the beginning of March 1864; but no sooner had the rains set in than work became impossible; and the combination of wet with inaction, that most deadly foe to men in hot climates, did its work—depression set in, and the men became ill. By the 31st of March there were 80 to 90 men in hospital out of the force of 360. The hospital accommodation was very bad, the men lying on the ground surrounded by pools of water. Three out of six companies were now withdrawn to Cape Coast. Early in June the detachment at Prahsu was reduced to 100 in strength, of whom more than half were sick; the camp was flooded by rain; and on the 13th June they were all withdrawn to Cape Coast. For five months they had been encamped on the river, three months of which were in the rainy season. These troops, so say the medical reports, were bad subjects; they had been attacked by fever and dysentery immediately on their arrival at Cape Coast in March 1863, and were not wholly recovered when marched up country. But without such special cause, it may be safely said that no troops can bear to be encamped in the rains in the middle of an African forest.

The great loss of officers and men in this detachment exercised a powerful influence on the minds of the authorities at home, with regard to the possibility of ever carrying on hostilities in the Ashanti territory; but, as subsequent experience has shown, it would have been far less risk to have carried out, at this time, the active aggressive movement which Governor Pine had recommended, which the Duke of Newcastle conditionally sanctioned, but which his successor in office refused to approve. In this unfortunate expedition not a shot had been fired; and on leaving the Prah, the bulk of the ammunition had been destroyed, and the guns either buried or thrown into the water. Strange to say, although there are now several officers on the Gold Coast who took part in this invasion, not one of them was able to give information to us in 1873 as to what had really been done with these guns.

This abortive expedition, in which no strength had been shown, but rather an appearance of weakness and proof of inability to conduct military operations in the African forest, was succeeded by insubordinate conduct on the part of some of the chiefs in the Protectorate. The Government treated these chiefs with a high hand. In 1865, Aggery, the King of Cape Coast, claimed jurisdiction over some ground within a few yards of our fort, and became insulting and offensive when his claim was resisted by Colonel Pine. The Government refused to recognise him any longer as king; and Colonel Conran, who succeeded Governor Pine in the administration of the Government, arrested Aggery, and sent him off to Sierra Leone. Colonel Conran reported that Aggery "evidently desired, not only to make himself independent of the Administration of the Gold Coast, but chief of the whole Protectorate; in short, paramount to the Queen's representative."

Aggery's deposition was approved of by the Government, and from that day there has been no king of Cape Coast.

Colonel Conran appears to have proclaimed that peace was concluded between the Government and the King of Ashanti, after the withdrawal of the troops from the Prah; but this peace was never really concluded. No treaty was ever made; and although, at comparatively rare intervals, Ashanti traders have visited Cape Coast, it cannot be said that any real peace has existed between the British Government and the King of Ashanti, since the Ashanti invasion of 1863.

In 1850, the British Government had purchased from the Danes all their forts on the Gold Coast; but there still remained, interspersed amongst the British forts, others in possession of the Dutch; different customs-duties were levied by the Dutch and by ourselves; tribes round the Dutch forts were under Dutch protection; tribes round the English forts under English protection. Broils constantly arose between the Dutch and English protected tribes: the English were zealous to put down slavery; the Dutch virtually encouraged slavery by a system which was called the enlistment of soldiery for service in Java. Slaves were sent down to the Dutch possessions by the King of Ashanti, paid for by the Dutch, and shipped off under the name of soldiers to Java. As the trade in slaves is one of the chief sources of revenue to the Ashantis, it will easily be understood that the king was more friendly to the Dutch rule than to the English.

In March 1867, a convention was concluded between the Queen of England and the King of the Netherlands, by which the Dutch ceded to us all their possessions east of the Sweet River, and we gave up to them all our possessions west of the river. By this treaty, which came into effect on the 1st January 1868, the British handed over Apollonia, Dixcove, Secondee, and Commendah; and received Moree, Cormantine, Apam, and Dutch Accra. Her Majesty's Government also relinquished to the Dutch the Protectorate over Eastern and Western Wassaw, Apollonia, and Denkera. The object of this treaty, so far at least as we were concerned, was to prevent the constant broils between the various Dutch and English protected tribes, and to facilitate the collection of customs-duties; but the treaty appears to have been effected without any consultation with the tribes whom it concerned. The people of Commendah, loyal to the English, refused to accept the Dutch Protectorate; and having attacked a boat's crew of the Dutch navy, had their town destroyed by the Dutch for this insult. The people of Dixcove also objected to be transferred to the Dutch. It seemed, then, that the previous complications were increased, rather than diminished, by the new treaty; and the Dutch entered willingly into negotiations with the British Government for the transfer to her Majesty of all the Dutch settlements and forts on the Gold Coast. From this transfer our Government anticipated great advantages. All the tribes would now be under the same protection, and the same system of government could be applied to them all; one uniform system of customs-duties could be established along the whole coast, and the influence exerted by the British in the direction of civilisation could be brought to bear on these tribes, among whom the Dutch had hitherto not exercised even moral interference.

But at the very outset of the negotiations there arose difficulties which it is necessary to analyse with some care. A mutual hatred had existed between the Fantis and the Elminas for long years. The Elminas had always held most friendly relations with the Ashantis, with whom the Fantis had been constantly at war; and now the Fantis, looking upon the Dutch and the Elminas as one power, retaliated upon the Elminas, whom they regarded as " the instigators and abettors of the destroyers of their houses and homes," for the destruction of the Fanti town of Commendah. Moreover, the Fantis had another cause of grievance against Elmina. Akyempon, an Ashanti chief, had marched with some hundreds of followers from Ashanti, through Fanti, committing great atrocities on the road, devastating the country, killing many people, and sending away numbers of slaves; and he was now, at the end of 1869 and beginning of 1870, living quietly at Elmina with his people, aiding the Elminas against the Fantis, and drawing subsistence from the Dutch Government.

The Fantis, aided by the Denkeras, on these grounds invaded the Elmina territory, destroyed some sixty villages west of the Sweet River, taking the whole of the crops, and actually blockaded the Dutch in their forts at Elmina.

At this point we must notice two important matters. First, in 1869, one Adoo Boffoo, a chief of the Ashanti kingdom, had inveigled into his power some European missionaries and others, from their settlements on the Volta, and carried them off as prisoners to Coomassie. There were two Germans, Messrs Kuehne and Ramseyer, the latter having his wife and child with him; a Frenchman named M. Bonnat; and a native of Accra, Mr Palmer by name. These prisoners had not been fighting; they had committed no act of hostility. The Ashantis took the missionaries away from their peaceable homes on the Volta, under the pretence that Adoo Boffoo wished to see them and speak with them, treated them shamefully and cruelly on the road, and dragged them to Coomassie.

The other point to be noticed is, that a party of small

speculators and traders had formed a so-called Fanti confederation of the various Fanti tribes, had taken steps to appoint a president, and had drawn up a constitution, known as the Mankessim Constitution. This movement appears to have had its origin in the attempt made by the Government to stop supplies of arms and ammunition to the Fantis, in hopes of thus putting an end to the Fanti invasion of Elmina. The administrator of the Government, Mr Salmon, viewed this matter very seriously, and consigned to prison the three officials of the so-called confederation who brought the rules of the constitution to him at Cape Coast, charging them with conspiracy to subvert the rule of her Majesty on the Gold Coast.

Thus at the beginning of the year 1870 this was the condition of affairs :—

There had been no peace since 1863. Ashanti is allied with and is aiding Elmina, Akyempon with a number of his men being actually present in the town. Elmina is invaded by the Fantis, who are bitterly hostile to Ashanti; and the Fantis are at the same time shaken in their allegiance to the British, by the evil influence of a number of agitators working for their own purposes, endeavouring to raise this so-called confederation, in order to get into Fanti hands the monies collected by way of customs-duties, with the evident object of endeavouring to make that money change hands as soon as possible. The Assins are closing the road to the coast against the Ashanti traders. This was the state of things while negotiations were going on for the transfer of all the Dutch possessions to the English.

It is impossible to read the correspondence between

Sir Arthur Kennedy, at this time Governor-General of the West African settlements, and the Dutch Governor, or the orders received by Sir Arthur Kennedy from home, without seeing the careful determination on the part of the Government of Great Britain not to effect the transfer of the Dutch forts, if it was likely to cause any trouble with the native tribes; it is equally difficult to avoid seeing the strong desire of the Dutch to effect the transfer. Sir Arthur Kennedy was led to believe that if the Elminas were subsidised they would offer no opposition to the transfer. He was distinctly told by the Dutch Governor, Colonel Nagtglas, that the Elminas had no treaty with Ashanti, and that the King of Ashanti had no recognised claim over the territory or people of Elmina. Towards the end of 1870, it was notified to Colonel Nagtglas that this country would not complete the transfer while an Ashanti force remained in the territory to be ceded; and Mr Ussher, Administrator of the Gold Coast, wrote to the King of Ashanti, saying that he ought to give up the captive missionaries, to remove Akyempon from Elmina, and Adoo Boffoo from the Volta, before any amicable solution of our difficulties could be attained. At the same time Mr Ussher issued a proclamation to the Elminas, promising, in the event of the transfer taking place, to respect their feelings as much as possible, to protect them against their enemies, and to give them even justice. He offered them the protection of the British flag, and showed them how helpless they would be if left alone, should they refuse to accept that protection.

On the 24th November 1870, the King of Ashanti, Koffee Kalkalli, the successor of Quaku Duah, who had died in 1868, wrote, objecting to the transfer of Elmina to the English, claiming it as his by right, and saying that it had from time immemorial paid annual tribute to his ancestors.

"I beg to bring before your Excellency's kind consideration regarding the Elmina, if it is included in the change. The fort of that place have from time immemorial paid annual tribute to my ancestors to the present time by right of arms, when we conquered Intim Gackidi, King of Denkera. Intim Gackidi having purchased goods to the amount of nine thousand pounds (£9000) from the Dutch, and not paying for them before we conquered Intim Gackidi, the Dutch demanded of my father, Osai Tutu I., for the payment, who (Osai Tutu) paid it full the nine thousand pounds (£9000), and the Dutch delivered the Elmina to him as his own, and from that time tribute has been paid to us to this present time. I hope, therefore, your Excellency will not include Elmina in the change, for it is mine by right."

On receipt of this document, Mr Ussher made a distinct statement to Colonel Nagtglas that the British Government "could not and would not purchase forts from the Netherlands Government which lay under the suspicion of being feudatory to a powerful native prince, the traditional enemy of its protected tribes." The Dutch Governor then gave a distinct denial to the King of Ashanti's claim; he said "that the £80 yearly was paid not as a tribute, but more as a present to keep on friendly relations of trade." He said that "the West India Company, to whom the forts had belonged, had granted an annual payment to the King of Denkera, not as a tribute, but as a gift, to promote the trade with the natives of the interior. That on the invasion of Denkera by the Ashantis, this pay-note had fallen into their hands, and that the Government had continued to pay it, as before said, not as a tribute, but more as a present to keep on friendly relations of trade." He declared that "neither the King of Ashanti, nor his ancestor, have any right over the forts." He said that "the King of Ashanti had no recognised claim upon the territory or the people of Elmina." That he "had given himself much trouble to search the records of past years, and had never found the slightest proof that the prince of Ashanti had any claim of sovereignty on the Dutch forts; that the money had always been paid to him as subsidy." He could readily understand that the King of Ashanti would be very much annoyed by the transfer of these possessions to the Queen of England, and believed he was endeavouring to throw difficulties in his way, and prevent it. He ended his letter by saying that the alleged claim of the King of Ashanti was "entirely without foundation."

Still the British would not treat till the Dutch had placed their title beyond all doubt, and as the first step to this, Akyempon's expulsion from Elmina was insisted upon: it was said that no treaty would be made while such a claim was in force, backed as it apparently was by the presence of Akyempon and Ashanti troops in Elmina. To prove their view of the case, the Dutch arrested Akyempon on the 14th April 1871, and refused to pay any further stipend to the King of Ashanti until he withdrew his claim to Elmina. Akyempon was released in May, on his swearing the king's oath to return to Coomassie within 30 days, but was reimprisoned in June for not having fulfilled his oath.

The convention for the transfer had been signed at the Hague on the 25th February 1871; but in consequence of these doubts, the ratifications of the treaty were not exchanged till a year later.

On the 20th May 1871, the King of Ashanti writes to Mr Ussher: "From the ancient up to this time Elmina Castle is mine, and living with them as friends, and they also paid yearly tribute to me; but having understood that it is going in exchange to your Excellency's protection, I do not understand."

In consequence of the King of Ashanti's apparent obstinacy, the Dutch sent one Henry Plange, a native of Elmina, to Coomassie, to bring round the King of Ashanti; and the result was the transmission of the following most remarkable document to Mr Ussher by Colonel Nagtglas:—

Certificate of Apology.

"1. These are to certify that the letter addressed to his Excellency H. T. Ussher, the Administrator of her Britannic Majesty's Settlements on the Gold Coast, dated Coomassie, 24th November 1870, by me, Coffie Calcalli, King of Ashanti, residing at Coomassie kingdom, was totally misrepresented on the part of the parties intrusted with the writing and dictating.

"2. I, therefore, do solemnly declare, in the presence of your Excellency's ambassador, Mr H. Plange, profession writer of the Government Office at St George d'Elmina, and my chiefs, that I only meant board wages or salary, and not tribute by right of arms from the Dutch Government.

"3. On account of circumstances relative to my ancestor, Osai Tutoe the First, having conquered Intim Gackadi the then King of Denkera, a friend or kind of commission agent of some transactions for his Netherland Majesty's Government on the Gold Coast, to the amount of £9000, my said ancestor was caused to make it good by the said Dutch Government; and in virtue of which the custom pay-note of the said Intim Gackadi was transferred to my said ancestor, who enjoyed it in times immemorial, and became heritable to his heirs the kings of Ashanti, who now hold the said custom pay-note in possession to this present moment.

4. " The said £9000 was paid to insure friendship and good will or feeling towards the Dutch Government on the Gold Coast Settlement in Elmina Fort, castle or fort.

"5. Tradition tells us that Ashanti and Elmina are relatives; offspring of one mother; they are brethren; also, they are not to have hostilities against each other by oath of allegiance.

"6. In conclusion, I must acknowledge that the aforementioned letter, dated Coomassie, 24th November 1870, about my communication to his Excellency H. T. Ussher, concerning Elmina Fort, is a vague, formal, or nominal expression, the sentiments of which I therefore must now write that the whole is a mistake.

" Signed in the presence of the ambassador and the chiefs.

"COOMASSIE, 19th *August* 1871.

"COFFIE X CALCALLI (his mark),
King of Ashantee,
reside at Coomassie Kingdom.
H. PLANGE, *Ambassador*.

Chiefs.—TUSUASI POKOO X (his mark).
BOOACHIE TINTSIN X (his mark).
TORNO NYCHWIE X (his mark)."

This letter was openly and solemnly affirmed by the

king's ambassador named Effrifa in the presence of the king, his chiefs, a numerous attendance of natives, and the Ashanti prince, Ossoo Ansah, at Elmina. The ambassador declared "that the King of Ashanti has not any claim on Elmina; that the people of Elmina are a free people, and are not the slaves of Ashanti." The ambassador renounced all rights to the Dutch forts on the coast, and the Dutch Government now released Akyempon.

It has been asserted that this certificate of apology was a purely "got up and illusory document;" it has been called "the interpolated copy of a Dutch composition of an Ashanti explanation;" and it has been alleged that "no one that has read the papers through can rise from them ready to attach any relative importance to this so-called retractation." Be this as it may, the transfer was effected on the strength of this document, which must be accepted as genuine, or the Dutch Governor must be convicted of forgery and gross falsehood.

Lord Kimberley now wrote "that the Elminas were to be informed that on the departure of the Dutch, British protection would be extended to them, and the Fantis would be desired to desist from making any further attacks upon them." The English were quite willing to pay even a higher sum to the King of Ashanti than had been paid by the Dutch, but not as a tribute. Lord Kimberley writes that "it is to be paid him as an inducement to maintain peace and to encourage trade, under such conditions as might be required for the security of the inhabitants of the coast." It was to be paid as an annual gift, which would be kept up so long as his conduct was peaceful, and otherwise satisfactory to her Majesty's Government. According to Colonel Nagtglas, these are exactly the terms on which the payment was formerly made, that officer himself having on one occasion told the king that he would stop his pay the first time the Elmina people were ill-treated in Coomassie.

On the 12th January 1872, the King of Elmina protested to the Netherlands Government against the transfer, professing his desire to remain faithful to the Dutch flag. But the Dutch had decided to withdraw. The renunciation procured by Mr Plange satisfied the English Government, and ratifications of the treaty were exchanged on the 17th February 1872. The Dutch ceded the whole of their forts and possessions on the Gold Coast to the English, who paid for the stores in the forts the sum, fixed by valuation, of £3790. The British Government, however, refused to complete the transfer till Akyempon was removed; and accordingly, the Dutch sent him away in a man-of-war to Half Assinee, where it was supposed he would do no further mischief.

Mr Pope Hennessey was now sent out from England to effect the transfer of the Dutch forts. He was instructed that the transfer was agreed to "in reliance on the Dutch power to transfer them peacefully and without giving rise to any acts such as had taken place in 1868."

The following is an extract from Mr Hennessey's instructions :—

"The objects which her Majesty's Government have throughout had in view in negotiating this treaty, are not the acquisition of territory, or the extension of British power, but the maintenance of tranquillity, and the promotion of peaceful commerce on the coast; and nothing could be farther from their wish than that a treaty made with these objects should be carried into effect by violent measures. At the same time, they trust that, by judicious and cautious management, the excitement which may possibly arise upon an event of so much importance as the retirement of the Dutch from the coast, may not lead to any serious difficulties; and I need not say that they would greatly regret that arrangements which they believe are calculated to be of much benefit to the whole population, by putting an end to old feuds and difficulties, inseparable from the division of authority which has hitherto prevailed on the coast, should be frustrated by the jealousies of the native tribes.

"But you will on no account employ force to compel the natives to acquiesce in the transfer of the forts; and if you find that the attempt to assume possession of the forts on the part of the British authorities would probably be followed by resistance on the part of the surrounding native tribes, you will not accept the transfer of the forts, but will report the circumstances to her Majesty's Government, and await further instructions."

Mr Hennessey arrived at the Gold Coast on the 2d April 1872, and held a conference on the 4th with the native chiefs at Elmina. The transfer took place on the 6th without disturbance. The King of Elmina was present, and the other chiefs who had in January opposed the transfer. Each tribe separately was called upon to state if there was any objection to the transfer, and each chief rose and announced, publicly, the agreement of his people to it. A detachment of the 2d

West India regiment was landed and relieved the Dutch troops; and by the 10th April, Axim, Dixcove, and Secondee were all garrisoned by our soldiers.

We must now revert for a moment to the direct relations between the British on the Gold Coast and the King of Ashanti. On the 1st September 1871, only a few days after the issue of the certificate of apology, the King of Ashanti had written to Mr Salmon, the acting Governor, urging certain claims of the Elminas on the Fantis, and making other complaints. Mr Salmon answered in December to the effect that the king must not meddle with the chiefs of the Protectorate; that, as regarded the Elminas, that was an affair for the Dutch; and further, that until peace was made between Great Britain and Ashanti, the king could not be allowed access to Elmina through the Protectorate. Mr Salmon professed himself most anxious for peace, and proposed an arbitration; but he said that, as a preliminary to all negotiations, the German and French captives must be sent back. The king had promised to liberate them on the return of Adoo Boffoo to Coomassie, but he did not keep his promise; and Mr Salmon informed him that this breach of his word inspired general distrust. The king replies that he wishes for peace: he has heard that the passage of munitions of war to his kingdom has been stopped; and he desires to give explanations on several minor points. Mr Salmon answers, that the only obstacle existing to peace was the continued detention by the king of the captive missionaries. Mr Salmon said he would prevent the Akims from annoying the king, but until there was a lasting peace he could not allow the transport of munitions of war to Ashanti. "As soon," he said, "as peace is concluded, then unfettered trade may commence." Before any reply could be received to this letter, Mr Salmon closed the road to the coast against Ashanti traders. He told the Governor-in-Chief that he was afraid that the Fantis would, out of their covert hostility to the efforts to effect peace with the Ashantis, and their jealousy at seeing Ashanti traders pass to Cape Coast, cause Ashanti traders to be molested, and he wrote to the king as follows :—

"I have had no opportunity before this of sending your majesty word that, for the present, until your majesty had finally decided upon making a lasting peace with us, it was necessary for me to close the frontier to your majesty's traders.

"The reasons for my doing this will be obvious to your majesty, and will at the same time give your majesty another proof of my friendship, and my confidence in your majesty's good and peaceful intentions to this Government and the people under it.

"When the trade was at first opened, it was the general belief of the people that peace would speedily be made. Nine months have elapsed since that time, and we are not much further advanced. Under these circumstances, doubts have arisen in many people's minds.

"Your majesty will be assured that, from the commencement, the Government here have believed that your majesty intends peace. We have also often heard that your majesty wishes, above all, the good of your people, and we know that peace is the best way to obtain that good.

"The Government have had some little troubles here, now happily settled. On account of these troubles, I could not be quite assured of the safety of your people travelling. They might have been annoyed on the road, and I should have been responsible for the wrong done them.

"Under these circumstances, I decided to stop the traders coming until peace was declared by your majesty, and the white captives sent to me, as I have already asked your majesty. This being done, I shall be justified in opening the road to all; and if any harm be then done to any of your people, I shall be able to punish the guilty according to our laws."

It can hardly be doubted that this step, however righteous the motive which prompted it, would scarcely be viewed by the King of Ashanti as another proof of friendship.

The king took time to deliberate on his answer to this letter; and on the 20th Feb. 1872, he wrote that he had requested his chief, Adoo Boffoo, to hand over the prisoners for transfer to the Governor, his friend, but that Adoo Boffoo refused to give them up, except on payment of 1800 ounces of gold.

"Respecting the release of the Europeans, I requested Adoo Boffoo (through my linguists) to hand them over to me to send them to the Governor, my friend. Adoo Boffoo refused to give them to me, and said he has fought with his powder and guns, and has made great war expense and caught them: therefore I (Adoo Boffoo) will not give them to you without selling or asking a ransom for them. The prince (your messenger) asked what will be the ransom, that he may have something to inform your Excellency; Adoo Boffoo said, he will take 800 peregens (1800 oz.) for the ransom of the Europeans.

"Your Excellency's messenger asked to know from me concerning other matters of the peace, and when peace shall be finally settled; my answer to him is, 'Tell the Governor that I and my great chiefs have decided this: after the ransom is paid to Adoo Boffoo, then peace between us shall be finally settled, and not before.'"

This letter is of great importance, as no further correspondence passed till after the Dutch forts had been transferred to the English.

We are now, therefore, in possession of the ultimatums of Mr Salmon and the King of Ashanti respectively, at the date of the transfer—namely, the 6th April 1872.

On the 20th April the Dutch Commodore wrote to the king, sending him some presents, informing him of the transfer, and asking him to give up the white captives to the English; at the same time Mr Hennessey wrote, sending a present of gold-embroidered silks, announcing also the transfer, and telling the king that, to show his friendship for his majesty and the Ashanti nation, he had ordered all the trading communications with Ashanti along the British frontier to be reopened, and offering to pay the king double the sum paid yearly by the Dutch. In this letter he did not touch on any of the causes in dispute. The most extraordinary fact, however, is, that he chose as a messenger to carry this very present the same Mr Plange who had previously been Dutch envoy, and had procured from the King of Ashanti the so-called certificate of apology; and this although, in the previous October, Mr Salmon had thus written to the Dutch Governor: "It seems that the young man, Plange, your Excellency deputed to pass to the King of Ashanti, did not confine himself to messages from your Excellency, but entered into local questions between Fantis and Elminas, respecting which, up to the present time, neither this Government nor that of your Excellency has taken any official cognisance. This conduct of Mr Plange has had an ill effect upon the people here in regard to their willingness to allow messengers to pass between Elmina and Coomassie, more especially as I assured the Fantis that Mr Plange was your Excellency's messenger only, and would carry no messages to the king from the chiefs or people of Elmina, or the Ashantis established there. In consequence of Mr Plange's representation on behalf of the chiefs and people of Elmina, the King of Ashanti has made demands on this Government respecting delivery over to him of certain Elminas stated to have been captured, together with a considerable amount of property, by the Fantis in the recent wars." Amongst the presents sent from the Dutch Government, by the hands of Mr Plange, was a large mirror, whose movement along the bad road was a matter of great difficulty. It appears never to have gone further than Karsi, a village some miles on this side of Coomassie, where it was found by the British troops on the 4th Feb. 1874.

On the 22d April, Mr Hennessey wrote a second letter to the king, saying that it would be a good omen of his future friendship if he would send the captive missionaries to Elmina. Mr Hennessey was now absent at Lagos for a short time, and on his return received a letter from Prince Ossoo Ansah, nephew of the king, to the effect that the only question now remaining to be settled in order to insure peace was the ransom of the captive Europeans. He said that such a ransom had been promised by former British envoys, and that the king expected the promise to be fulfilled. Mr Hennessey replied to the king on the 4th June, saying that he could not even speak of exchanging Europeans or men for money, but that he wanted the king to send the prisoners, and he would consider if the German Missionary Society (to which Messrs Kuehne and Ramseyer belonged) might properly send to Coomassie the actual expenses incurred by Adoo Boffoo, as stated in the king's letter. Some time after writing this, Mr Hennessey actually released Opoku, Adoo Boffoo's son, who had been taken prisoner and brought into Cape Coast, and paid all his expenses back to Coomassie, although at this very moment the King of Ashanti was claiming money for Adoo Boffoo's expenses in capturing and retaining the German missionaries. The superintendent of the Basel mission does not seem to have been favourably impressed with Mr Pope Hennessey's suggestion that he should pay a ransom for the captive missionaries, and said (let the reader judge if he was right) that it was unjust for our Government to call on him to do this, while we were releasing Ashanti prisoners free. Mr Hennessey now informs the king that the mission would undertake to pay any sum not exceeding £1000 for Adoo Boffoo's expenses, and that the amount should be paid if his majesty would send the captives down to the Prah. So confident was Mr Hennessey that his diplomacy had been successful, that on the 8th June he wrote to the Government that "the anticipation of hostilities with Ashanti no longer exists."

Plange's journal written during his stay at Coomassie is in the writer's possession. It appears that the king was at first quite willing to accept the £1000, but said it must be sent to Coomassie. He complained bitterly of the conduct of the Assins in molesting his people passing to and from the coast. He objected very much to the cession of Elmina to the British, but said, as it was deemed advisable by his Excellency for the bringing about of peace, he would not find fault with it, as what was done could not be undone; but in a number of subsequent interviews, at which Adoo Boffoo's son and other relations were present, they declined to accept any such small sum as £1000.

The following extract from Mr Plange's journal may not be without interest:—

"MONDAY, *September* 2, 1872.

"This morning 10 o'clock I was called by his majesty the king to appear before the chiefs in his palace. I went accompanied by Mr F. Ramseyer, Mr J. Kuehne, and Mr J. Bonnat. In the king's palace were assembled, viz., the great chiefs from various great towns surrounding Coomassie, also King of Beckwhy, Duabbin, Mampon, Cokofoe, and Fommanah, &c., also the chiefs, linguists, and principalities, inhabitants of Coomassie, &c.

"I am requested by the linguist to near them—also the white men.

"His majesty began to inform them (his great chiefs) all the contents of the several letters his majesty received from the coast; first, his majesty informed them the kind attention his Excellency Governor of the coast has paid to him for the messages he sent to the coast, and the transfer of the Elmina to the British Crown, of which his Excellency the Governor of the coast has promised to carry on the same friendly policy towards his majesty and Ashantee nation, as the late Dutch Governor of Elmina was pursuing. The Governor request his majesty to reduce the ransom money to be £1000 or £500, as the Basle missionaries will be able to pay for their white brethren.

"If you cannot believe what I told you just now, I beg Affilfa to come forward and explain to you as he came from the coast.

"*Affilfa.*—I was told by the Governor to come and beg his majesty, that his Excellency desires to have peace with the king, but if these white men still in captives the peace cannot be established, so therefore his Excellency begs the king to let his Excellency pay amount of £1000, for the redeeming of the white men.

"*King.*—I beg the linguists present here to inform this matters to the representatives of Adu Boffoe, what the Governor requested him.

"*Bwaachi-tintsin, step-father of the king.*—I beg the son of Adu Boffoe to bring his opinion in this matter.

"*Adu Boffoe's Son.*—This is only play of the Governor with us; we have asked £8000 as ransom of the captives white men, and if the Governor likes to buy them, and not able to pay such sum, he should begs to reduce them to be £6000; but all at once his Excellency cast £7000 in his pocket; no! my father cannot accept this, as he had much trouble of the white men to brought them here.

"*King.*—I beg you will go to counsel first before you should tell something about this matters.

"*Adu Boffoe's families from counselling.*—Our opinions are about these matters, we will accept no less or no more than 600 prayquen, equal to 1350 oz. or 21,600 dols. as the head money of the white men.

"*H. Plange.*—I beg the king, the great chiefs, and the king's mother, to give ear for my opinion. Governor of the Gold Coast, he asks only for peace, so his Excellency promised to pay to the Kings of Ashantees double stipend every year as the late Dutch Government on the coast hitherto has paid. I testify that the English Governor on the Gold Coast will do so good to the Ashantis, I daresay more than the Dutch has done. As far as the ransom affairs are concerned, Governor has to pay that £1000—as his Excellency has written to his majesty as promised made; but after all, the Basel mission will pay back to the Governor, which money belongs to God, it was taken by poor and rich men from all the corners of the world (as tax); I beg the king to bring it into consideration, that there is no fault on behalf of these white men, because they are not enemies against the Ashantees; only what they do to preach the Gospel and teach the small boys to do good. His majesty says that the money of £1000 does not come to him, but to pay as Adu Boffoe's trouble; of course Governor has to do with the king; but whereas the king said so, his Excellency cannot alter it, and at all event it must go through his majesty and come to Adu Boffoe; the same I beg that the king may give his opinion and bring it in reasonable terms for the purpose to maintain peace with the coast.

"*King.*—I have heard the goodness of the Governor towards me and the Ashantees, therefore I beg Adu Boffoe's families to reduce the said 600 praquen to enable me to answer the Governor.

"*Adu Boffu's families.*—He ask Affilfa again, can't

Governor not to pay any money more than the £1000, he said or what?

"*Affilfa.*—So far I know Governor begs the king as a good friend to let him pay only £1000 as recompensation of Adu Boffu.

"*Achampon, King's Steward.*—This £1000, only we cannot understand why king asked £6480, and now Governor promised to pay £1000, keeping rest in his pocket: Governor thought that we are fool!

"*King of Beckwy.*—If we do not accept the £1000, and not agree to let these white men free to go to the coast, what will come?

"*H. Plange.*—Nothing will come; but the friendship will not increase as before, because it will pains the Governor.

"*King of Duabin.*—Then war will come, but remember that from time memorial or from ancient time you never heard that the Fantees declared war against Ashantees, but always Ashantees against the Fantees; and how is it? These white men we sell them for gold: if Governor agree the price, he can buy them; if not, we will keep them for curiosity. Another thing, if the Governor has not money to pay the amount we ask, let him give back the Assins, Ackims, and Dencirras, in the place of these white men, and we will give them up to him (Governor), but not any less money.

"*H. Plange.*—I am not sent to decide old matters which I don't know; but this point I will not be scruple to answer you; the Assins are refugees, and Governor cannot give them to you as you wish; no, never.

"*King.*—Put this aside and let we manage the money matter. Arthur (Plange), what you say about the money?

"*H. Plange.*—My master, the Governor, wrote a letter to his friend, while I am already here, sent it by Affilfa, request the king to pay that £1000, even £500—the Basel missionaries are able to pay, as I told you before: Governor offered this £1000 to his majesty for the purpose to maintain peace; but for any money more beside the £1000 Governor will not pay.

"*King.*—Can't Governor pay any money more than the £1000?

"*H. Plange.*—As it was in the letter.

"*King of Fommanah.*—Governor has only pinching us with the £1000 to hear some word from us, and that is all. Governor will hear is a war; and seeing I am the King of Fommanah, even I am the smallest king, I know that the Governor will not able to come to me.

"*King's Mother.*—You think also that I am woman; it is so, but my right arm is strong enough to meet unnumbered Fantees, whoever likes to declare war against the Ashantees.

"*Ammanquateah.*—If lice or louse are too much in the hair and troubles you, should better to shave the hair and get rest.

"*H. Plange.*—Have I spoke any bad words to caused you to anger? How you mean by these?

"*King.*—Governor wants really to have war with me but not for peace, reason why instead he has to pay the half of the amount 600 praquen £4860. The chief, Adu Boffu, asked only sent a letter to pay £1000. For fight affairs I am not afraid; if you like I can show you my magazine, to see so much quantity of ammunition I have, that you may tell the Governor and the Fantees. So far I know that the white man never agree with raining and sunshine as we can bear.

"*H. Plange.*—I am not sent to make declaration of war, but I was sent as messenger of peace; and if you mean to declare war with the coast as you are hooting at it now, I daresay if it is so I will never cross the Prah before the roads will be shutted; and not this I am going to write to my master about it—if I do so the matter will be spoiled.

"*All the chiefs.*—Do so, war we never afraid; if you boast us with war affairs we not afraid, &c.

"*H. Plange.*—I beg the King of Mampon to speaks with the king and chieves to be quite, and I beg to know something to enable me to inform my master, as the period of the affairs.

"*Adu Boffu's families.*—After our opinions are not to be blamed the king on the coast, as the coast men will talk bad against our king, so we let the amount comes to £4000.

"*King.*—Governor messenger, Arthur (Plange), has to write a letter to the Governor just now, and that, as for my side, I am willing to let these white men go to their country free, without ask any cent, but the chiefs sticks upon the said money, and I beg the chiefs are here present, that as I wish to have peace with the coast, the amount of £4000 you said to be reduced as to come to the amount of £2000.

"*King of Fommanah.*—I beg the messenger Arthur not to write Governor about these affairs, that we may settle these affairs quitely.

"*King.*—Do not mention this, because it shows that you are afraid. I wish the messenger write the Governor so."

The limits of space forbid further extracts from this remarkably interesting journal, which bears evidence that it was written at various times. The journal shows that Plange had several private interviews with the king, who had already, while these negotiations were going on, sent a force to Apollonia at the request of King Amakie, and received applications for aid from the King of Elmina, who had sent his brother to Coomassie. It was, says Plange, openly said at Coomassie at this time, that the king would declare war against Fanti; and the chiefs would in no way abate their insolent demand for the ransom of the missionaries. It was equally well known at Cape Coast, and Mr Salmon mentions it in his despatches at this date, that the king had long been collecting munitions of war. All his interviews with Plange, if truly reported, show a hesitation between bravado and desire to make peace. Had he been left alone, it is possible, even probable, that peace might have been made; but he was perpetually urged on by his chiefs and the court flatterers, who told him of the glorious warlike deeds of his ancestors, and made him believe himself superior to every other monarch, even to the white men. His boast as to the quantity of ammunition in his magazines, and his assertion as to the white man's inability to bear rain and heat, show the working of his mind. His chiefs were ripe for war. There can be no doubt that he himself wanted but little urging;—the Assins and Akims had annoyed his traders, and sent him more or less insulting messages. The arrest of Akyempon by the Dutch was, rightly enough, attributed to English interference, and the result was the resolution to make war. But when an Ashanti king has resolved to make war, his policy of cunning teaches him to profess peaceable intentions; and accordingly we find that the king consented to the Governor's terms, and agreed that the £1000 should be accepted, but asked for it to be sent to Coomassie. A somewhat remarkable letter accompanied the king's acceptance of the money offered. It was written by the missionaries, and says that, according to their opinion, the king is very much in the hands of his chiefs. Mr Salmon replied to the king that the money was lodged in the hands of Mr Grant, a coloured merchant at Cape Coast, as agent for the king, and should be paid over to the king's envoys upon the arrival of the prisoners at Cape Coast. On the 9th of November the king acknowledges the letter of Mr Salmon, and says that he is sending down the prisoners to Fommanah, whence they will be sent on, if the money has been paid over to his envoys at Cape Coast.

Colonel Harley had now arrived at Cape Coast and relieved Mr Salmon as Governor. A Legislative Council was held on the 26th November, and it was agreed not to pay the money until the captives arrived at Cape Coast. A letter was written informing the king of this decision, and was sent to him by the hands of a Mr Dawson, a native interpreter, of whom we shall hear much more in the course of these volumes. It was at the same time decided to send back the notorious Ashanti chief Akyempon to Coomassie, paying his expenses and giving him safe conduct. He had been found to be fomenting strife in Apollonia between Kings Blay and Amikie, and inciting the Dutch settlements in that neighbourhood to disaffection to the English; he had therefore been seized there in October 1872 by Colonel Foster, inspector-general of armed police, under orders of the Administrator, Mr Salmon, and conveyed to Cape Coast Castle, where he was lodged in prison. He left Cape Coast on the 12th December, was escorted to Prahsu by armed police, and conveyed across the frontier on Christmas-day. The Abrahs stopped him at Darman, and the Assins refused to let him pass; but, on the remonstrance of the Governor, he was allowed to proceed on his journey. He did not receive any ill treatment; and the assertion that his being plundered and ill treated on the road was a cause of the Ashanti invasion, is sufficiently proved false by the fact that the enemy's troops had actually marched to invade the Protectorate before he left Cape Coast.

The last letter written by the King of Ashanti had been an undertaking to accept £1000 for the prisoners; and they had actually been sent down as far as Fommanah in company with Plange, who, writing from Fommanah on the 17th November 1872, said distinctly that he had no confidence in, and could not trust the Ashantis, and thought it quite possible that after the king had received the money he would detain the prisoners. These prisoners were still at Fommanah when Dawson arrived there on his road to Coomassie; Akyempon, with his people, had not yet started for Coomassie, though he had been promised safe conduct there, and to be sent, with all his expenses paid, in a manner becoming his rank; and yet Dawson, writing from Coomassie, which he reached on the 14th December, informs the Governor that as early as the 9th a force of the Ashanti king had marched to invade the Protectorate.

Documents exist amply sufficient to prove that the king had long been contemplating this invasion; that he had been collecting arms and ammunition for some time. The negotiations about the missionaries were only entered upon with a view to delay. The sending them down to Fommanah was truly, as Dawson says, only "fool-trapping" the British Government. At Fommanah they were plundered of all their property, and Plange was severely beaten and put into irons. No pretext was alleged, no cause given for the invasion at this special time, except the most extraordinary one which appeared in March in the king's letter, to be given in the next chapter. Dawson states that the king had long been preparing for the war; and that already before his arrival at Coomassie in December, captives had been sent in by the force which had invaded Akim. A force had, as already said, been sent down to Apollonia long before; and now, on the 22d January 1873, without warning given to the Governor of Cape Coast, in the midst of peaceful negotiations which were going on at the time when payment of the ransom had been promised, and when Akyempon with his followers had been released and sent back, an Ashanti army, estimated at many thousands of men, crossed the Prah at Prahsu, and invaded the Protectorate.

CHAPTER II.

EVENTS FROM THE COMMENCEMENT OF THE WAR TO THE DATE OF SIR GARNET WOLSELEY'S ARRIVAL AT CAPE COAST.

THE news of the Ashanti invasion first reached the Administrator at Cape Coast in a letter from Amfoo Ottoo, the King of Abrah, written from Abrakrampa on the 29th January, to the effect that Inkie, one of the two kings of Assin, had sent him messengers carrying the head of an Ashanti, and bringing word that the Ashantis had crossed the Prah, and that their armies had taken possession of seven towns. The Administrator at once assembled the Legislative Council and informed them of what had occurred; and it was decided on his recommendation to issue a proclamation, and despatch the whole of the available Houssa police to Dunquah. A proclamation was at once issued to the kings and chiefs of the Fanti territory and despatched to them by special messengers; and Dr Rowe, the colonial surgeon, who placed himself at the Administrator's disposal, was sent to them as a special commissioner. Arrangements were made for the issue of arms and ammunition in small quantities to the kings, and the Governor urged upon them the necessity for co-operation in this emergency, as there could be no doubt that all their efforts would be taxed to arrest the hordes of their ancient and barbarous enemy. Colonel Harley reported to the Administrator-in-chief (Mr Pope Hennessey) that a sort of enthusiasm pervaded all classes of the natives, and that a body of 250 volunteers had paraded at Cape Coast for his inspection. The Kings of Abrah, Denkera, Mankessim, and Assin, had applied to him for assistance in arms and ammunition; but the amount of assistance he was able to render in arms would only be very limited, as he considered that something like 60,000 men in the Protectorate would be more or less actively engaged in the coming struggle, and were all prepared to demand Government aid. He recommended that a reinforcement from Sierra Leone should be sent to strengthen the small garrison on the Gold Coast, numbering only about 160 officers and men all told, and occupying four posts 160 miles apart. Colonel Harley said that he had only 381 flint-guns and 190 Enfields available for issue to the native tribes, and he recommended that 300 Snider rifles should be sent from Sierra Leone to the Gold Coast for the purpose of re-arming the Fanti police and Houssas. The arms and ammunition were sent from Sierra Leone to Cape Coast Castle on the 10th March, and a detachment of 100 men of the 2d West India regiment arrived there on the 20th. The War Office, on receipt of these despatches, sent at once to Cape Coast Castle 700 M. L. rifles and 210,000 rounds of ammunition, which arrived towards the end of April.

The instructions given to Dr Rowe stated that the despatch of 50 armed police to Dunquah was not in any way to be regarded otherwise than as a mere demonstration in favour of the Protectorate, though they were of course to defend themselves in case of attack. Should there be any chance, however, of their being outnumbered and attacked by a force too strong for them to repel, they were at once to fall back on Cape Coast Castle. A rough estimate of the Fanti force was made by Colonel Harley as under :—

ROUGH ESTIMATE OF THE FANTI FORCES.

Districts.	Kings.	Number of men available.
Assin	Inkie & Tchiboo	say 2,000
Akim (E. and W.)		,, 10,000
Denkera	Quachie Fram	,, 6,000
Abrah	Anfoo Otoo	,, 3,000
Akoomfie	Akinney	,, 5,000 or 6,000
Goomwa	Tando	,, 15,000 to 20,000
Wassaw		,, 10,000
Cape Coast, &c.		,, 3,000
Annamaboe	Amoanoo IV.	,, 2,000 to 3,000
Anyan		,, 2,000
Ajimacoo	Moquah	,, 2,000
Inkooso Kroom & Brobor		,, 3,000

Total, 63,000 or 70,000

On the 1st of February 1873, information was received at Cape Coast that the Ashantis had advanced a day's journey from the Prah; that the inhabitants were retiring before them, and would retire further. The Ashantis had burned the villages, sparing the plantations for their own use. Nothing definite could be ascertained as to their numbers. The King of Elmina was said to have made a fetish oath with the King of Ashanti to join with him for offence and defence against the Fanti tribes and the English Government; and Amakie, King of Apollonia, was known to have asked the Ashantis to help him six months ago. Dr Rowe reported in a day or two that the Ashantis had crossed the Prah in force, in three divisions; that one had gone to Denkera, another to Akim, and that the third, or main division, was advancing down the main road from Prahsu. Seven captains were said to have accompanied this latter, the whole of it being under the command of Prince Mensa, the king's brother. There was no remaining doubt that the Ashantis meant war; and an Assin, who had been at the Prah when the Ashantis crossed ten days before, reported them to have so large a force that it took them five days to cross the river, by two ferries of two boats, about 30 men crossing at once in each of the boats, which made four trips an hour. In this way it was estimated that in five days something like 12,000 men had crossed the Prah. Ashanti captives said that the king was going to take the fort at Elmina, which belonged to him, from the British, and that he also intended to take back the Assins, his subjects; that all Coomassie had come out; that only the king and Akyempon were left behind; and that the fighting men had brought their women, children, and slaves.

How completely the Administrator of Cape Coast was taken by surprise is shown by his report of this invasion, in which he says: "I need scarcely convey the profound astonishment with which I have received these tidings, as nothing but the most amicable relations have existed between this Government and Ashanti for some time; and assurances of lasting peace and good will have been sent down by the king ever since my assumption of the government." Commodore Commerell and Mr Pope Hennessey, however, considered that the affair was very much exaggerated; and even after these reports Mr Hennessey wrote, "I do not believe that this is an Ashanti invasion, or the prelude to an Ashanti war."

Early in February Mr Keate arrived on the coast, relieved Mr Hennessey as Governor-in-chief, and proceeded to the Gold Coast. He reported his opinion that the English could only hold their forts on the defensive, and that the natives must defend themselves in the field; and he drew the attention of the Home Government to a despatch from the Secretary of State for the Colonies, in which the principle is expressly laid down with respect to the Protectorate chiefs, that " the wars in which they engage are their wars, and not the wars of Great Britain; that they must rely upon themselves for success in their wars; and that the British Government is unable to make itself responsible for their defence in case they should prove unable to defend themselves."

On the 11th February, Colonel Harley, who had from the first viewed the invasion in its true light, reported that the Ashantis were then only twenty-four hours' march from Cape Coast; that they had received no check whatever to their advance since they had crossed the Prah, and that they had swept away by fire the several villages they had passed through. The Assin kings, he said, had at length mustered their fighting men and taken up a position two or three hours' march from the Ashanti camp, but he was satisfied that they could not, unaided, repel an attack of the enemy. However, Dr Rowe had induced them to hold their ground, while he was endeavouring, by every effort he could bring to bear, to induce the Fantis to move up to their assistance. He had issued ammunition and lead to the kings and chiefs, and had received a promise from Mr Bentil of Mumford to turn out 20,000 men. His great difficulty, he feared, would be a want of unity on the part of the Fantis.

A postscript was added to this despatch to the effect that the Assins were now in full retreat, a battle having taken place at Yancoomassie Assin. Still the Fantis had not yet advanced, notwithstanding all the efforts made, and the Administrator anxiously looked for reinforcements. A proclamation was now issued embodying a volunteer company at Cape Coast, and another prohibiting the importation and sale of arms and munitions of war.

The advance of the Ashantis was slow. The Assins fell back to Mansu, where the King of Abrah joined them with a small force which he had originally assembled at Dunquah. Then they retired together to Yancoomassie Fanti, followed by the enemy. A body of 100 Houssas, who had been sent from Lagos at Colonel Harley's request, was at once sent forward to join the detachment of 50 already at Dunquah. Lieutenant Hopkins, of the 2d W.I. Regiment, took the command of the Houssas and volunteers. He was ordered to act in the way he might deem best, with the view of giving every moral aid to the Assins and the Fantis in resisting the progress of the enemy; and if he should find himself in a position to do so, to aid and succour the Assins, drive back the Ashantis beyond Mansu, and hold that place. Meanwhile, Mr Thompson, a Government interpreter, was sent to rouse the Fantis to action. He reported that, in his opinion, they were determined to unite and drive the Ashantis away, but that "delay was the evil: they would not go to fight and drive the king away; they said, let him come and we will fight him."

On the 1st March, Lieutenant Hopkins proceeded to Yancoomassie Fanti, with a company of Houssas. He assembled the kings and chiefs, and desired them to clear the bush in advance of their lines, and to form three lines 500 yards apart. They complied to a very great extent with his request. "They were," he says, "working with a will, and had formed an extensive camp in lines, on the right and left of the road, in advance of Yancoomassie." He was now enjoined by the Administrator at Cape Coast to make no movement with the Houssa troops, endangering their safe and direct concentration, in case the Ashantis should make a further advance towards Cape Coast. The important object of his command was, he was told, to cover Cape Coast from any sudden attack by the Ashantis. Steps were also taken, to some small extent, to clear the bush and make other arrangements for the defence of Cape Coast.

On the 10th March, a battle was fought at Yancoomassie Fanti. Part of the Fanti army had advanced to attack the Ashantis in front of their camp, but not succeeding in meeting the enemy, they returned, sending forward a few scouts. They were preparing their morning meal in camp when they heard shots, and had scarcely time to take up their arms when the Ashantis were upon them in a great body. The Mankessim detachment, under King Adoo, fell back at once, and the Ashantis thus got in rear of the Cape Coast people, who retreated, as did the Abrahs, and apparently all the tribes except the Assins and Denkeras. These also subsequently retired; and Lieutenant Hopkins, considering that his special duty was to cover and protect Cape Coast from any sudden attack—which consideration he held, according to his orders, to be paramount over any other—when he found that the natives were retreating at such a pace, fell back to Cape Coast. A report was made that the Assins had taken the Ashantis in rear, and captured 2000 prisoners; but on investigation this number had to be divided by 1000, only two prisoners having been taken.

Great complaint was made by the Fanti kings and chiefs of the inaction of the Houssas in this battle, and accordingly they were sent back to Dunquah, together with all the available Fanti police, armed with Sniders; the Cape Coast companies and the volunteers were also sent back to Dunquah. One insuperable difficulty appeared to be the reckless waste of ammunition by the natives, making it almost impossible to keep them sufficiently supplied. Colonel Harley, however, drew from the imperial magazine, and further supplies were despatched from England with the utmost rapidity. There seems to have been most remarkable variance of opinion as to the actual number of Ashantis present in this action. On the 31st March, the Administrator officially expressed his own impression that the Ashantis had never had more than 4000 men, while at the present time the Fantis and their allies in arms could be little short of ten times that number, there being as many as 25,000 then present at Dunquah, at which place the tribes were again assembling, having been supplied with considerable quantities of ammunition. Lieutenant Hopkins again encountered the old difficulty in stirring the native chiefs to action; he was very anxious to form a great camp in two or three lines, with space well cleared in front; and a definite place was allotted to each tribe. He found, however, that Mr

Bentil, with the Goomoahs, and the Assins under Inkie, were especially dilatory; and he with difficulty succeeded in "shaming them into immediate co-operation." The allies alleged as an excuse for not attacking that they could not advance to attack the Ashantis till the camp was completely formed from left to right, as their defeat in the action of the 10th had been owing to the existence of a gap in the line, into which the Ashantis had penetrated. The Cape Coast people were especially slow in their movements. Mr Hopkins soon abandoned the idea of forming a camp of more than a single line, as he believed that the number of men in the Fanti camp was insufficient to cover the Ashanti lines. He continued strongly urging upon the chiefs the necessity of advancing and attacking the enemy. Bush was being cleared away, and scouts sent out, and the natives promised to attack on the 4th April. Then they postponed the attack to the 5th, when, weary of the perpetual non-fulfilment of promises, Mr Hopkins marched his Houssas and volunteers to the front, as if to attack the enemy, without waiting for the allies; but he had scarcely proceeded beyond the outposts, when several of the chiefs—prominent among them being Attah, of Cape Coast,—begged and implored him not to proceed further, solemnly assuring him that no longer delay would take place, and that in two or three days they really would attack.

Still they did not advance, and on the 8th April Colonel Harley wrote that they could not be induced to attack, and that their whole conduct might be summed up in the Spanish phrase, "Manaña" ("to-morrow"). He said that the Fantis were in force and spirit, but that they could not be induced to advance and attack the enemy, though he had little doubt they would act vigorously in the defence of their country, if themselves attacked. At the very time that Colonel Harley was writing, the Ashantis were taking the initiative, and themselves attacking the Fantis. About seven o'clock on the morning of the 8th April they attacked the Fanti camp along its whole front, said by Mr Hopkins in his report to extend for a length of six miles. The bulk of the loss on the side of the allies fell upon the Fantis, though the Houssas had some seventeen killed and wounded, and the Cape Coast volunteers also suffered slightly. The Fantis held their position at every point—the first instance in their history, Colonel Harley reports, of their having successfully resisted an attack by the Ashantis. Ammunition was again as recklessly expended as before. After five hours' fighting, Mr Hopkins had again to ask for more ammunition for his Houssas and volunteers, although they had entered into action with sixty rounds per man, and a reserve. Mr Hopkins urged the people to follow up their success on the next day; but, repeatedly as he impressed upon them the necessity of taking the offensive, and often as they promised to do so, they never would advance, but awaited another attack.

On the 13th April 1873, before any more fighting took place, great excitement occurred in the Fanti camp in consequence of an accusation of treachery made against Mr George Blankson, a native of Cape Coast, and a member of the Legislative Council. He was accused, upon sworn evidence, which, however, was only hearsay and second-hand, of holding communication with the enemy, and sending them supplies of ammunition, and of having advised the king to invade the Protectorate. The kings and chiefs present in camp requested the Governor to arrest and imprison Mr Blankson; and in order to save his life from the excited natives, Dr Rowe claimed him as bound to answer these charges to the Governor, and removed him from the camp to Cape Coast under escort. It may here be noted that the investigation of these charges against Mr Blankson was wisely postponed until the excitement caused by the war should be over; he was, at his own request, released on bail shortly after the arrival of Sir Garnet Wolseley in the following October, and was still under these charges when the Major-General left the coast in March 1874.

On the 14th April the Ashantis again attacked the Fanti camp along its whole length, and the fight continued without any decisive result from eight in the morning till seven in the evening, when the chiefs sent messengers to Dr Rowe, expressing their intention of sleeping on their respective war-paths, and prosecuting the fight on the following morning. Ammunition, however, again ran short, and their supplies were nearly expended. Mr Loggie, Acting Inspector-General of Police, and formerly in the Royal Artillery, did excellent service with his rockets on this occasion. But for them, Mr Hopkins was of opinion that the centre of the position would have been lost. Still, although the Fantis had thus held their ground well, at no time during the action could they be induced to make an advance, or do more than fight on the ground on which they stood. The Cape Coast people appear to have shown in this action the same cowardice for which they were subsequently conspicuous. Mr Loggie says that they would not advance, although there were nearly 3000 men;

that he and Dr M'Kellar had to act as drivers of several hundreds of them; and that at times means the reverse of gentle were used to make them return towards the front. "I regret to say," he adds, "it was the most fatiguing part of the day's work acting as whipper-in to these people."

On the following day a great quantity of arms and ammunition was sent by the Administrator to the camp; but the Fantis, in spite of their previous day's success, retreated *en masse*. The retreat commenced with Mr Bentil and the Goomoah people, and before long the whole of the tribes were in full retreat to the coast, regardless of all the efforts of Mr Hopkins and Dr Rowe. Mr Hopkins withdrew his Houssas and volunteers, in rear of the panic-stricken host, to Cape coast. Bound to allege some cause for this panic and dispersement, the Fantis threw the whole burden of the blame on Mr Blankson, and said that they could not fight the enemy when there was treachery in such a quarter. This retreat was the more lamentable, as it was ascertained from captives subsequently taken that the Ashantis had suffered so severely in the fight, and were so astonished at not defeating the Fantis, that they had themselves actually commenced to retreat, and destroyed many of their things, when intelligence was brought that the allies were running away. Dr Rowe estimated the Fanti force present in these actions on the 8th and 14th April at 56,500, of whom on the 8th alone 221 were killed and 643 wounded. The fighting ground of this last action was a deep and thickly wooded valley, into which the Ashantis poured in swarms from their camps, the Fantis advancing to meet them across the open ground cleared in front of their camp.

This break-up of the whole of the Fanti army seems to have caused considerable consternation at Cape Coast, and the Administrator requested Commander Stubbs, the senior naval officer, to send a gunboat immediately to Elmina, as there was every reason to believe that the Ashantis would take every opportunity of advancing and taking possession of the place. Commander Stubbs was himself of opinion that a simultaneous attack would very shortly be made on Cape Coast and Elmina, and that they were both "in the most critical position possible." Colonel Harley showed less fear for the consequences to Cape Coast and Elmina, and contemplated the formation of another camp; but Dr Rowe advised him that it would be impossible to unite the whole of the Fanti tribes in one camp until after the close of the rainy season, although something might well be effected in uniting those who were near to each other, or whose interests were especially common, in larger bands than they would otherwise form. By this means he hoped to prevent the ravages of small bands of Ashanti plunderers, though not to prevent the approach of the Ashanti army.

On the 21st April, Colonel Harley was obliged to write home that for the present defensive operations on a large and combined scale were at an end, as the Fantis had dispersed to their homes sadly demoralised, and that even the Houssas and volunteers required time to rest and recruit, many of them being foot-sore and knocked up. Measures were taken to carry out Dr Rowe's suggestion for the formation of small camps. Mr Loggie, with sixty Houssas, was sent to Annamaboe to form the nucleus around which the Annamaboes, Cormantines, Saltponds, and Winnebahs, should be induced to rally. The Assins, Abrahs, and Akims collected in small numbers at Assayboo, and the Cape Coast people promised to join them. Around Elmina was drawn a cordon of the lesser chiefs, who promised to oppose any advance of the Ashantis; and the King of Commendah promised to resist the enemy should they advance in his direction.

The condition of affairs at this time was indeed lamentable. Dr Rowe speaks of the people "as a heap of scattered fugitives at the mercy of a pitiless and bloody foe, whose delight is to torture, and who will drive them by thousands into slavery, and slaughter all the weak and sick." Colonel Harley, while expressing no apprehension whatever for the safety of Cape Coast and Elmina, the two points of immediate possible attack, felt that the sad spectacle of the people being "dragged by thousands into slavery by a savage and relentless foe, such as the Ashantis, while the sick and weakly would be mercilessly butchered, was a thought too terrible to dwell upon;" and feared that the Ashantis would make their cruelties felt in the districts away from the immediate neighbourhood of the forts, and that the country, "overrun and depopulated, would show traces of suffering and misery for years to come."

The Ashantis did not advance upon Cape Coast or Elmina, but concentrated their forces at Dunquah. A week after the last fight, repeated statements were made by prisoners captured by the Fanti scouts to the effect that the Ashantis were very much alarmed by the withdrawal of the Fantis from Dunquah; that they were very anxious to return to their own country, but feared that the Fantis had moved to their rear, between them and the river Prah; and were afraid to return by the road along which they had come. The Ashanti camp was reported to be in a most wretched condition, containing great numbers of wounded. Small-pox and other diseases were said to have broken out among them, and provisions were very scarce. Plantains, the price of which was usually about 2d. per dozen, were now fetching from 2d. to 3d. apiece. Several men deserted from their camp in the hope of getting food, and reported the camp to be in a foul condition, with an abominable stench from dead bodies scattered through the bush in all stages of decomposition. Small parties of the Ashantis were discovered foraging at long distances from the camp, and the King of Aquafoo complained that a considerable body of Ashantis had entered his territory. On the 15th May the Administrator wrote to Lord Kimberley as follows : " The position of the Ashanti force at the present time is indeed very critical : they are at least 15 miles from their base of supplies, with a swollen river, the Prah, in their rear ; in a hostile country with no provisions left, and with the rainy season now set in. In any other country in the world under the same adverse conditions to the enemy the Fanti forces would take advantage of it, but they seem indifferent. I do not hesitate to assure your lordship that the coast people, who have been maintained in comparative ease by a pampered indulgence for so many years, are almost worthless ; while the bush tribes, retaining the courage of a savage freedom, have shown a determination and bravery unknown to the coast people, possibly from the latter knowing that they are protected by our guns ; but, my lord, it is a very trying position to be placed in the midst of them, all absolutely like children looking up for protection and guidance, and yet, when they are afforded both, flying from their own responsibility and self-defence." Still, critical as to the Administrator's eye the position of the Ashantis was, so fertile was the country, and so demoralised their enemy, that they were able to remain in it, as we know, for more than half a year longer. As one camp became denuded of provisions, plantains, yams, and ground-nuts, they had only to remove to another and extend the area traversed by their foragers. Their method of making war reminds one of the earlier wars of the middle ages; the object being not so much to defeat the enemy's army in pitched battle, as to ravage his country, destroy his towns, and feed upon his crops.

Towards the middle of May the Ashantis broke up their camp at Dunquah, and moved at a leisurely pace in an easterly direction into the Denkera country. There is little doubt that the punishment of the King of Dunquah, his capture if possible, or at all events the destruction of his chief towns, was one of the objects of the Ashanti invasion; and it is also quite possible that it was the intention of the Ashantis to return from Denkera by the Wassaw country, instead of by the Prahsu road, where they feared being attacked in their retreat by the Fantis, and where also their own ravages would have created a scarcity of provisions. It was reported that the Ashantis were about to move by way of Abrakrampa upon Effootoo and Denkera; and the Denkeras applied for assistance in arms and ammunition, and requested the Government to compel the Abrah people and those of Cape Coast to move to the Denkera camp and force an engagement with the Ashantis. Dr Rowe was now despatched to the Denkera country, and the kings and chiefs along the coast lying to the eastward were summoned to support the Denkeras and the Abrahs. But the King of Abrah, considering that Abrakrampa, his own capital, was threatened, would not leave it to join the Denkeras at Jooquah; and the King of Annamaboe, although his country lay so far away to the eastward, replied that, hearing part of the enemy was still at Dunquah and on the Annamaboe road, he intended waiting for a few days to watch their movements before he would join the Denkeras. This want of unity of action among the Fantis, whose blind selfishness in action can only be compared to that shown by the Bavarians and Badensers in the war of 1866, was of course fatal to successful action against the enemy. Dr Rowe found the Denkeras full of complaint that the Cape Coast people and the Abrahs would not come to help them. The Cape Coast people, the Abrahs, and others assembled at Abrakrampa, were dissatisfied with the assistance given to them by the English Government. The merchants and traders of Cape Coast were dissatisfied with the steps taken by Colonel Harley for the resistance of the invasion, and accused him of expressing in his despatches to the Home Government a confidence and a feeling of security which did not exist in their minds. The situation was a most difficult one; there was no nucleus of trained and disciplined troops upon which to rally the disunited kings and chiefs. Rumour perpetually changed the intentions of the Ashantis. At one time they were about to advance on Cape Coast, at another to attack Abrakrampa, at another to march into the Denkera country. Then they were said to be in three divisions, one directed against Denkera, one against Accroful, and another against Abrakrampa.

At last the King of Annamaboe moved to Dunquah, and on the 24th May the kings and chiefs assembled at Abrakrampa and solemnly promised Dr Rowe to march the following day to Jooquah to assist the Denkeras, against whom it was now evident that the main force of the Ashantis was moving. It was considered most important to hold Jooquah, from its proximity to the Elmina villages, and the fact that its possession by the Ashantis would give them a close approach to Elmina itself, and to the villages on the coast, from which they could obtain any quantity of supplies. On the 4th June, the Fantis and their allies concentrated a considerable force near Jooquah and the adjacent villages. They were reported as being amply supplied with ammunition, and ready to make a stand against the enemy. The Cape Coast volunteers had joined them in their camp, and the camping ground was being cleared. The Ashantis were known to be close at hand, to the number, as reported by their prisoners, of about 30,000, who had determined, so it was said, to fight to the last, and either kill all the Fantis, or be themselves all killed.

There was some desultory fighting on the 3d and 4th June, and on the 5th the Ashantis made an attack in force, and completely defeated and routed the Fantis and their allies, by whom scarcely any resistance was made. One of the first to quit the scene was Quasi Kaye the King of Denkera himself; and when the tribes who had come to his aid and had made some stand against the enemy inquired for him, he was not to be found.

That afternoon was seen the terrible sight of the whole people flying in panic for many hours. All the afternoon the roads and thoroughfares leading into Cape Coast were crowded by masses of people, men, women, and children, flying panic-stricken into the town. The alarm and terror at Cape Coast was such as can scarcely be described. All through the evening and night of the 5th these fugitives continued to come in, the kings and chiefs being amongst the most demoralised. At dawn on the 6th, a report was circulated that the Ashantis were at the Sweet River, five miles from Cape Coast.

On the 7th, a muster of kings and chiefs was held at the Castle. They exhibited the greatest terror and alarm that their towns would be destroyed by the Ashantis, and their women and children taken for slaves. It was a pitiable spectacle; and the Administrator impressed upon them the absolute necessity for further and continued effort on their part to defend their country. He said that the Government was still willing to help them, and that if they would decide upon forming another camp, and would really resolve to fight, he thought that something might yet be done. A legislative council was then held, and the steps which had been taken for the defence of Cape Coast and Elmina were explained at this council. Captain Blake, the senior naval officer on the station, and Captain Brett of the 2d West India Regiment, the officer commanding the troops, were present.

The commandant at Elmina now applied for assistance, saying that the king's party at Elmina had turned traitors. Daily alarms took place in Cape Coast; the Ashantis were said to be rushing into the town, and the postmen sent from Cape Coast to Elmina returned reporting the road stopped by Ashantis. Such was the condition of affairs when on the evening of Saturday 7th June, H.M.S. Barracouta, Captain Fremantle, steamed into the roads with a detachment of 110 Royal Marines, under the command of Lieutenant-Colonel Festing of the Royal Marine Artillery.

On the receipt of Col. Harley's despatches narrating the retreat of the Fantis, after the battle of the 14th April, her Majesty's Government had immediately decided to send out an additional ship of war with a detachment of marines. They were embarked on board H.M.S. Valorous at Portsmouth on the 13th May, and proceeded to Lisbon, where they were transferred to H.M.S. Barracouta, and conveyed to Cape Coast Castle. The Admiralty had selected Lieut.-Colonel Festing of the Royal Marine Artillery to command, as an officer in whom they had entire confidence. He was instructed to act in concert with the Administrator and the senior naval officer, though virtually under the command of the latter. The senior naval officer was informed that a detachment of marines might be landed for the occupation or defence of Cape Coast or the other forts; but if no such necessity existed, it would be better to retain them on board the ships of the squadron; and it was impressed upon him that the Lords of the Admiralty most strongly objected to any of the marines or seamen of the squadron advancing inland, unless they should be required for any special operation, or for repelling any attack within such a distance of the forts as would avoid any necessity for encamping.

On the 9th June, the marines under Colonel Festing were landed at Cape Coast Castle, the enemy being at this time at Jooquah and Effootoo, and having command of the provisions of the whole of the Denkera country, and of the villages near and to the westward of Elmina. Colonel Festing now assumed the command of the troops on the coast. On the 10th, Captain Fremantle, Colonel Festing, and Dr Rowe, proceeded together to Elmina, which they had agreed should be, in the present position of affairs, used as the base of operations. They found that the inhabitants of the king's quarter of the town of Elmina, which is separated from the loyal part of the town by the river, were disaffected, and were supplying the Ashantis with stores of various kinds by way of Saltpond. On the 12th, a legislative council was held at Cape Coast, Captain Fremantle, now the senior naval officer on the station, and Colonel Festing being present. After consultation, it was unanimously decided that martial law should be proclaimed in the town of Elmina and in the surrounding districts entered by the Ashantis, and that the people should be summoned to give up their arms; and Colonel Festing marched with a small force at midnight of the 12th for Elmina, carrying with him the documents for the proclamation of martial law, his plans having previously been arranged with Captain Fremantle.

The disaffected western portion of the town of Elmina stands on a narrow peninsula, of which Fort St George forms the eastern extremity, the small river Beyrah the north side, and the sea the south side. It was arranged that the river should be guarded by a string of boats, and that the ships should prevent any escape by the sea, while Colonel Festing with his marines should man the guns and reinforce the garrison at Elmina, and a force of Houssas should guard the exit to the west of the village. At about half-past five in the morning the operation was effected, the boats of H. M. ships Barracouta, Druid, Seagull, and Argus being employed. A proclamation of martial law was immediately issued, followed by two others, the first requiring the delivery of arms in two hours, and the second, issued at half-past ten, giving one hour for the removal of women, children, and unarmed men; after which, should the arms not be given up, the town would be bombarded. Many armed men were seen in the town, and some of the chiefs came with excuses to gain time, but no arms were given up; and at a little past noon, the Houssas having been reinforced by some marines from the boats and some men of the 2d West India Regiment, so as more effectively to guard the narrow neck of land to the west of the village, the bombardment commenced from Fort St George and the boats, and was continued for about twenty minutes. The town was set on fire in several places by rockets, and a large number of armed men were seen to be escaping through the Houssas to the west of the village by making for the bush through the prickly-pear scrub. Orders were sent to the Houssas and marines to follow them. The Elminas commenced firing upon the troops, and some skirmishing ensued. About this time, movements of armed men were discovered at various parts of the surrounding hills; and from the commanding position of Fort St Jago, a large body of Ashantis, probably 2000 strong, was seen streaming along the side of the bush to the west of the town, and extending their right rapidly towards the sea. Colonel Festing now resolved to take the field with all his available force, and Captain Fremantle placed himself and his men unreservedly under

Colonel Festing's orders. Colonel Festing advanced along the beach, and as soon as it was practicable, extended and advanced, driving the enemy away in the utmost confusion and disorder, though they had at first held their ground, keeping up a hot, spirited fire. The enemy having been pursued for nearly three miles, the halt was sounded, and the troops returned to the fort. The loss of the enemy was estimated at between twenty and thirty men, while that on our side was only one killed and three wounded out of a force of more than five hundred.

The troops were now allowed to rest and dine, when a report arrived that the Ashantis were advancing in force from a northerly direction upon the loyal quarter of the town. Colonel Festing having satisfied himself that the Ashantis were in force close to the garden outposts, troops were marched towards that point. Most of the boats of the squadron had returned to their ships; but those of the Barracouta remained, and their men were landed under Lieutenant Wells, R.N., and placed at Colonel Festing's disposal. The enemy advanced boldly along the plain, over one of the few pieces of open ground that we ever saw on the Gold Coast; and the Houssas under Mr Loggie were directed to advance against them, supported by the marines and the 2d West India Regiment. The troops were greatly outnumbered by the Ashantis, who, estimated at between 2000 and 3000 men, were massing their main body on the plain, while their skirmishers were hotly engaged in front. They were outflanking the right of our troops; but at this opportune moment, Lieutenant Wells, advancing on the extreme right, rushed upon some of them who had entered a large garden, drove them out of it, and from the shelter of the garden wall poured a heavy fire of Sniders into their skirmishers and main body. The enemy was outflanked and staggered under this unexpected attack; and seeing his flank to be secure and the enemy thus shaken, Colonel Festing ordered the advance of the whole line, and drove the enemy back with great loss. A running fight ensued across the plain, the enemy actually attempting to make a stand, but being completely defeated and driven into the bush, leaving some 200 dead upon the field. Their retreat was at first conducted in an orderly manner, and they made a stand at the edge of a thick bush, some three miles distant from the town, where they were mown down, till they rushed away in full retreat and confusion. A halt was now sounded and the troops marched back to the Castle. In this engagement, out of a force of about 330 on our side, only one man was killed, and one officer and three men wounded. There is no doubt that the Ashantis suffered severely; but in no action of the war did any officer in command of troops get so splendid an opportunity of punishing the enemy as did Colonel Festing on this occasion. It is the only time on which the Ashantis were ever encountered on open ground, where the enormous superiority of the Snider had full opportunity of displaying itself; and one almost wonders that during an action lasting on open ground for some hours, not more than 200, out of the reported 3000 engaged, should have been placed *hors de combat*.

The effect of this action was excellent, so far as preventing effectually any renewal on the part of the Ashantis of attack upon our forts; but as the enemy had not been pursued into the bush, the Ashantis retained the opinion, which they were known previously to possess, that the European troops dare not advance after them into the bush.

It was not without reason that the town of Elmina had been bombarded. The disloyalty of the king had long before become apparent. On the 12th March, the oath of allegiance of the British Government had been tendered to him, but he had refused to swear, and said that he had taken the fetish oath to oppose the English Government coming to Elmina. He had then been arrested, and some little time afterwards was conveyed as a prisoner to Sierra Leone, where he remained throughout the war. At the same time that the king had thus refused his allegiance to her Majesty, three of the most important Elmina chiefs had signed; and two of them, Esservie and Andooah, rendered the most admirable and faithful service to the English throughout the whole of the campaign. Both of them showed loyal courage in action. They were present with us in our first fight at Essaman on the 14th October, and accompanied us to Coomassie.

The King of Elmina was known to have sent his brother to Coomassie to communicate with the King of Ashanti. It was asserted that he had gone there as one of Plange's hammock-bearers, and had told the king at Coomassie that he and his people were cowards for not coming to fight for Akyempon, and to take the British flag off the Castle of Elmina. In February a proclamation had been issued by Colonel Harley to the Ashantis in Elmina and the adjacent territories, warning them to depart from out of the Protectorate with their goods and effects, or to remain within it at their peril. It would probably have been better had stronger measures been taken, and the whole of these Ashantis been made prisoners; but up to the very last, even to the day of our leaving Coomassie, the enemy was treated with a forbearance that is seldom seen in European war.

While these military events had been going on, Mr Keate, who, as already said, had been appointed to succeed Mr Hennessey as Governor-in-Chief of the West African Settlements, arrived at Cape Coast Castle on the 7th March, found Colonel Harley ill with fever, and Mr Chalmers administering the government. Colonel Harley shortly recovered, but Mr Keate fell a victim to anxiety and the terrible climate. He died on the 17th March, and is buried at Cape Coast. Colonel Harley was now sworn in as Administrator-in-Chief, by virtue of a dormant commission given to him before his leaving England.

On the 16th March, an outrage of a most cruel and savage character had occurred in the town of Cape Coast. Five Ashantis who were living in the house of Prince Ansah had been seized by a mob, who had dragged them to the beach and cut off their heads. Ansah sent to ask for protection, as his life was in danger; and a party of police arrived just in time to save him from being murdered. His house was completely wrecked; and the wife and child of Kotiko, one of the three Ashanti envoys who were still remaining at Cape Coast, and who was lodged in the Castle for safety, were with difficulty rescued from the mob, and brought to the same place. Prince Ansah was shortly afterwards sent to Sierra Leone for safety.

On the 12th April, Colonel Harley had received the

following letter from the King of Ashanti, together with letters from Dawson, and extracts from his diary :—

"COOMASSIE, 20*th March* 1873.

"SIR,—His majesty, Kalkaree, sends his best respects to your Honour, also to Messrs Ossoo Ansah, and G. Blankson.

"2. His majesty states that, he being the grandson of Ossai Tutu, he owns the Elminas to be his relatives; and, consequently, the fort at Elmina and its dependencies being his, he could not understand the Administrator-in-Chief's sending Attah, *alias* Mr H. Plange, to tell him of his having taken possession of them for Quake Fram, and notifying him also that in four months he, the Administrator, would come to Ashanti to take away power from him.

"3. He states that he has been made angry by this, and it was this which led to his sending his great captains and forces to bring him, Quake Fram, of Denkera, who dares to take his Elmina fort, &c., and also the Assins and Akims, who are his own slaves, and who have united with the Denkeras to take power from him.

"4. His majesty further states that your Honour's restoring him these tribes—viz., Denkeras, Akims, and Assins—back to their former position as his subjects, and also restoring the Elmina fort and people back in the same manner as they were before, will be the only thing or way to appease him, for he has no quarrel with white men; but should your Honour come in to interfere, as he hears you are, that you have not to blame him, because he will then start himself.

"5. That his majesty having heard of some false

information being brought to your Honour respecting your messengers and the white captives, he has requested their attesting this letter with their own signatures of their being in health.—We have, &c.,

"For his Majesty,
(Signed) KOFI KALKAREE.
Linguist, YAWOO NANKWI, X his mark.
AKWESSI APPEAR, X his mark.
KOFI BUAKI, X his mark.
JOSEPH DAWSON, the writer.
FR. RAMSEYER, for himself, his wife, and child.
G. KÜHNE.
M. J. BONNAT, sen.
H. PLANGE, to testify my being alive.

"To his Honour,
Colonel ROBERT WILLIAM HARLEY, C.B.,
Administrator of her Majesty's Forts, &c.,
on the Gold Coast."

The accusation made against Plange had been, says Dawson, "the cause of great irritation in the mind of the king." Whether Plange had ever made any such statement it seems difficult to ascertain. It seems hardly likely that the assertion could have been pure invention on the part of the king, and yet in Plange's diary there is nothing to lead to the belief that any such statement was made. Dawson says that the king "spoke awfully bad of Plange, and put him down as the causer of the existing irritation;" and the chiefs generally united in denouncing Plange. The king called him a rogue, and said that all the evils of the war were upon his head; and it may be observed that in the first letter received by Sir Garnet Wolseley from the king, the accusation against Plange was renewed.

THE ASHANTI WAR.

The only other events of any importance previous to the action of Elmina which have not been touched upon, were the resistance of the Wassaws under Apecoon to a body of Ashantis who had penetrated into their territory, and the march of the notorious chief Akyempon, the same who had very lately been liberated and sent up with all due honours to Coomassie, with a force of 3000 men into Apollonia, for the purpose of invading the western district of the Protectorate, and co-operating with King Amakie against our most loyal and faithful ally, King Blay. In consequence of this movement of Akyempon, a man-of-war had been sent down to the windward. The fleet on the station had been greatly increased between March and June, her Majesty's ships Seagull, Bittern, Coquette, Decoy, Argus, and Barracouta, being present in the latter month. On the 3d April the Legislative Council passed an ordinance prohibiting the importation of munitions of war into the ports upon the Gold Coast, and the navy were active in blockading the coast and preventing the landing of the forbidden munitions.

The latest reports of the position of the Ashantis continued to be, as usual, conflicting; but it was generally supposed that they were concentrated at Effootoo, and parties of them had been seen at Simeo, Beulah, and Napoleon. Captain Fremantle was in favour of an advance to attack them at Effootoo, even without waiting for the expected arrival of the headquarters of the 2d West India Regiment; but pointed out the absolute necessity of some systematic method of sifting the information as to the enemy's movements, and remarked that hitherto there had been no thorough attempt made to discriminate between truth and falsehood. Small-pox had broken out at Cape Coast Castle; 140 patients were now in the small-pox hospital, and there was great distress in the town owing to the crowds of natives who had fled there for refuge. A sanitary commission was formed by Colonel Harley, with orders to act also as a relief committee; while supplies of rice were issued to the kings and chiefs for distribution among the people, from a quantity which had been sent out by the Government in anticipation of its being required. At Elmina, also, thousands of people, including those of the disaffected quarter, fled to the castle for protection on the 13th, and were taken in for some days. They were in great terror, reports of a renewed attack being prevalent; but in a week's time the fear had abated, and the castle was almost cleared of natives.

On the 21st June, information was received from a prisoner that the Ashantis were preparing to attack Cape Coast on the 28th; and that they had received plentiful supplies of arms and ammunition. So circumstantial was the statement, that Colonel Festing repaired to Cape Coast to make preparations against attack. On visiting the different forts he found the stores in a wretched condition, quantities of Snider and other ammunition being quite unserviceable. At Connor's Hill, the first cartridge he put his hand on in one of the gun-limbers was so sodden, that water could be squeezed out of it like a sponge. A considerable number of cartridges for the 6-pounders there were quite unfit for use, and one limber contained a well-organised ants' nest. Arrangements were now made for the organisation of a larger volunteer force of the Cape Coast people, and for their being regularly mustered and drilled. On the 25th, Colonel Festing held a field-day of all the available troops at Cape Coast, and employed them in a sham defence of the town.

For some time the health of the white troops remained good. On the 20th June, Captain Fremantle reported to the Admiralty that "at Elmina yesterday there was not a single marine of Colonel Festing's detachment on the sick-list;" and he preferred to leave some men from H.M.S. Druid permanently on shore to running the risk of wetting them in landing, if called upon suddenly, as on the 18th; but, towards the end of June, sickness broke out amongst the marines and sailors, and especially among the former; and the Druid had 35 seamen and marines on the sick-list. On the 1st July, her men were all re-embarked. Colonel Festing's detachment of marines, although they had not many very serious cases, showed a great sick-list; dysentery began to show itself; and on the 30th June the first man died from this disease. The real rainy season had begun about the middle of June; the heavy rains continued without intermission; several officers were sick; and it was decided to embark on board ship all the sick men.

On the 5th July, Commodore Commerell arrived in the Rattlesnake from the Cape of Good Hope, finding the Barracouta, Druid, and Merlin in the roads, and the Argus at Elmina. On the 6th July, the Himalaya arrived with the headquarters, 13 officers and 360 men, of the 2d West India Regiment, who had been ordered from Barbadoes at the same time that Colonel Festing's detachment of marines had been sent out from England. They had embarked at Demerara on the 29th June. Lieutenant A. H. Gordon of the 98th Foot, having volunteered for active service, came in the Himalaya attached to the 2d West India Regiment; and on the 10th July he was appointed Commandant of Houssas and Adjutant of Armed Police. On the 9th, the headquarters and 160 men of the 2d West India Regiment landed at Cape Coast; and Lieutenant-Colonel Wyse of that regiment assumed command of the troops, although in such ill health that practically the arrangements for disposing of the men remained in the hands of Lieutenant-Colonel Festing. Colonel Festing took with him the marines from Cape Coast to Elmina, so as to make room for the 2d West India Regiment, and also to have all the marines together in one place. On the 11th, the remaining 200 of the 2d West India Regiment were landed at Elmina, and quartered in houses in the town. The sick-list of the marines had now very much increased; and on the 12th July, when Colonel Festing ordered a march in the evening, their weary condition was most conspicuous. Colonel Wyse was before long invalided to England.

It may be well at this point to sum up the numbers and condition of the troops now on the coast. Of the detachment of Royal Marines at Elmina, numbering in all rather more than 100, a very large number were on the sick-list. The 2d West India Regiment had parties at Axim and Accra—the bulk of the men being at Elmina and Cape Coast Castle. The Houssas, numbering 210 of all ranks, had 32 in hospital, 52 at Elmina, and 126 at Cape Coast. The corps had not been well looked after for some time. Lieutenant Hopkins, their former commander, had been ill for a long time, and Captain Brett had taken temporary charge of them; but with his duties of assistant magistrate and staff station-officer, he was unable to give them much attention. Their arms and accoutrements were worn out; the men were slack and slovenly in their drill, and had suffered from being sent out on picket in the heavy rains without the protection even of greatcoats. The vastly changed condition in which those men were found by Captain Glover on his arrival, was due to the unremitting care and attention bestowed upon them by Lieutenant Gordon, who raised them before the end of September to a strength of 300. This officer also took command of the Cape Coast Volunteers, and assembled them daily for drill, under non-commissioned officers of the 2d West India Regiment. Although the corps mustered 250 men on its roll, for which number arms and ammunition had been issued, only 70 or 80 used to attend drill; and when afterwards embodied, about the 1st of August, only 120 men joined. In addition to these troops, the marines and seamen of the fleet, to the number of some 400, might be counted on in case of emergency for the defence of the forts.

All the troops suffered much in consequence of the rains, which were unusually heavy this season, and much sickness was introduced by the same cause amongst the natives. In the town nearly all the houses were crumbling. Even the ramparts of the castle began to fall in, carrying the platforms and the guns with them in two places. There was the utmost want of hospital accommodation. On the urgent advice of Dr Home, C.B., V.C., who had volunteered for service on the coast during this emergency, and had arrived on the 28th June, a hut for hospital purposes was erected at Connor's Hill; and Colonel Harley placed the drawing-room wing of Government House at the disposal of the medical authorities.

As regards the Ashantis, no further movements were known to have taken place: they were in constant communication with Elmina, from which they drew supplies, and Col. Festing held repeated meetings with the second king and others with a view to inducing them to put a stop to this. Every movement of the troops was at once known in the Ashanti camp, the arrival of the troops in the Himalaya having been made known to the enemy even before they landed. The only information of any value was derived from the prisoners, for the native scouting-parties lied freely. There is no doubt that the opinion expressed by Commodore Commerell on his arrival was perfectly correct, that three-fourths of the scouts lay down in the bush and never went near the Ashantis at all, but returned to Cape Coast Castle with such information as they considered would best suit. Chief Attah of Cape Coast was employed to send out scouting-parties, which he afterwards made an excuse for demanding money, on which he used to get drunk; while these scouts seldom went further than a mile from the town, where they remained till they had finished their provisions.

On the 16th July, Lieutenant Gordon marched with 60 Houssas from Cape Coast to Elmina; and on the 17th he marched northwards on a reconnaissance, with Lieutenant Jones of the 2d West India Regiment, 100 Houssas, and 50 Aquafoos. His instructions were to ascertain the strength and position of the Ashantis at Sanka, then said to contain 600 of the enemy, and any other information he could procure without bringing on an engagement. He approached Sanka, and occupied it, finding only a few sick left behind. From them he learned that the Ashantis had been there that morning, but that intelligence had reached them from Elmina that a white man was coming, and so they had all decamped. Sending out patrols that night, Gordon marched on the following morning towards Essaman, but had to return, as the water on the road was so deep as to wet the men's pouches. Colonel Festing had sent out a detachment of 32 West Indians and 30 Aquafoos at four o'clock that morning to carry provisions to Gordon's force, and prevent their being cut off. An Ashanti prisoner, captured on his road to Effootoo, stated that the bulk of the Ashantis lay about Effootoo and Mampon, and that constant intercourse was maintained with Elmina through the neighbouring villages, where the Ashantis were always welcomed. On the evening of the 18th, Gordon's party returned to Elmina. It had been impossible for them to reconnoitre towards Effootoo, in consequence of the very heavy rain. They had found no trace of Ashanti encampments.

On the 21st, in consequence of the receipt of despatches from Axim, Dixcove, and Secondee, reinforcements of Houssas were sent there. The reports represented the Ashantis to be in force in Apollonia under Akyempon and Adoo Boffoo; and King Amakie, of Apollonia, who had recently taken the oath of allegiance, was said to have joined them. They had destroyed two towns belonging to the loyal King Blay, and Dixcove and Secondee were threatened. A detachment of 100 of the 2d West Indians was also embarked in the night for the windward coast, and Commodore Commerell accompanied them in the Rattlesnake. About 50 of these were left at Secondee, and the remainder returned to the Rattlesnake on the 24th. On the 28th, Colonel Festing, having been requested by Colonel Harley to transfer his headquarters to Cape Coast, endeavoured to proceed there by land, but was unable to cross the Sweet River, no canoe being forthcoming for the passage. On the 29th he transferred his headquarters to Cape Coast.

On the 26th July, only 44 men were effective out of a force of 104 marines landed on the 9th June, and it was decided to embark the whole detachment on board the Himalaya, and despatch them to England, especially as the principal medical officer said there was every occasion to believe that all the men as yet unaffected would sicken, while relapses were to be dreaded in the cases of those already suffering from the dysentery or remittent fever induced by the climate. Dr Home was of decided opinion that the force of marines would not be efficient for further military duty in the command during the present season. About 87 marines embarked for England in the Himalaya, 18 remaining on shore for service. 10 men of the marines died on the passage home, and 58 were admitted into hospital at Netley on their arrival.

On the 4th August, a conference was held between the Administrator, the Commodore, Colonel Festing, and Dr Home, as to what steps should be taken to dislodge the Ashantis from their position at Mampon. Dr Rowe and Major Russell of the 2d West India Regiment also attended by invitation of the Administrator. It was decided, on reading the instructions from home, that an effort for that end might be made; but Dr Home said that the weather would not be suitable for another fortnight for any troops, except Houssas, to move. It was therefore decided that a force of 100 Houssas, with 200 volunteers, should advance to the Sweet River at

Napoleon, and there throw up a redoubt and form an encampment, the object being to secure the safety of Cape Coast, to reconnoitre from this point so as to obtain better information of the enemy's position and strength, and to restore confidence. Colonel Harley contemplated striking a blow at the enemy's force from this point as soon as the season would admit.

On the morning of the 6th, Lieutenant Gordon with two subalterns of the 2d West India Regiment, 100 Houssas, and 100 labourers with tools, who for security had been lodged in the castle the previous night, paraded at 3 A.M. After waiting for more than two hours, only 20 volunteers arrived, and the reconnaissance started with only that number. In the course of the next two or three days other volunteers joined, making up the number to 120. It rained steadily the whole day. At 7 A.M. Lieutenant Gordon reached Napoleon, and after posting pickets, selected a position on rising ground commanding the ford, and turned out all hands, troops and labourers, to clear the bush. In the afternoon he traced an oblong redoubt, and commenced forming it, at the same time patrolling the roads two or three miles in each direction along the bank of the river. No map of the country of any description was procurable, and the first rough tracing of the country was made by Lieutenant Gordon. About a week was occupied in completing the redoubt and clearing the bush, during which time reconnaissances were made by a combined force of Houssas and volunteers, and the banks of the river were examined by means of a canoe procured from Cape Coast. It rained continuously. Lieutenant Gordon adopted a system of scouting of his own, having no confidence in the scouting-parties furnished by Chief Attah of Cape Coast. He took out from among the labourers and volunteers such men as knew the country well, gave them extra pay, and occasionally presents, and sent them out in parties of two or three in various directions, always sending one or two reliable Houssas with each party. The Houssas and Fantis, who could not communicate with each other, were afterwards separately examined, and their reports compared. Patrols were constantly sent towards Beulah up the Sweet River, and down the river northward towards Effootoo, and westward towards Aboo and the Sirowee. It was ascertained that no Ashantis crossed the Sweet River; that very few stragglers approached the banks; that the left of the Ashanti standing camp was at Effootoo, where their numbers were few; that great numbers were at Mampon, whence they extended westward towards Agoonah and Aquafoo; that a large body of them—probably several thousand—was at Simeo, where two scouts accompanied by Houssas crept so close to their camp that they could hear their conversation; and that they foraged for provisions in the gardens of deserted villages between Simeo and the Sweet River. It was ascertained to a certainty that they communicated with Elmina from Simeo. On the 7th, Colonel Festing visited Napoleon.

The immediate result of the occupation of Napoleon was that the villages between it and Cape Coast were reoccupied. Gordon established a market-place outside the fort which was much frequented, and under cover of his patrols many people came out from Cape Coast and foraged the ground about Effootoo and in the district between the Sweet River and the Sirowee.

On the 11th August, Colonel Festing summoned Gordon to look at the ground between Elmina and Mampon, with a view to erecting a similar redoubt to that of Napoleon; he was to accompany a reconnaissance from Elmina on the next day. Walking that night to Elmina, Gordon had to swim the Sweet River in the dark; and next day, the 12th, he accompanied a detachment of West Indians and Houssas, under the command of Captain Paterson. They marched with great caution towards Simeo. The path was much trodden, both by sandalled and naked feet, showing the amount of intercourse between the Elmina villages and the Ashanti camp. Simeo was found deserted, but a large encampment of some 1500 huts was there, and the marks of fires and the remains of food indicated that the camp had been deserted only two or three days before. Under these circumstances, instead of returning by way of Elmina and Cape Coast, Gordon and Paterson sought a road across country to Napoleon. Starting at 5 P.M., accompanied by 24 Houssas, they worked by compass and struck the Sweet River a mile below Napoleon at 7 A.M., having encountered no enemy. An excellent position for a redoubt, of great natural strength, had been found near Simeo, on the summit of a gentle knoll almost clear of bush, commanding on one side the Sirowee River, and on the other the junction of the roads leading to Elmina, Mampon, and Effootoo.

In the mean time further measures had been taken at home for strengthening the force on the Gold Coast. At the meeting held at the War Office on the 1st May, which had decided on sending out the marines in the Himalaya, and the wing of the 2d West India

Regiment from Barbadoes, it was also decided to despatch further supplies of military stores, including two mountain-guns, and camp equipment for two regiments of 500 strong. These had been sent out partly with the marines and partly by the mail-packet of the 18th May. Additional camp and hospital supplies, together with 10 per cent of hospital clothing for the whole force, were also sent out; and measures were taken to replace at Cape Coast Castle and Sierra Leone all stores issued from the imperial magazine for the use of the Colonial Government, so as to maintain this magazine unimpaired in case of future accident. Intrenching tools, camp-kettles, blankets, waterproof sheets and 30 tents, as well as 10 Norton's tube-wells, were ordered out. At a conference held at the War Office on the 15th July, it was determined to send out H.M.S. Simoom with 150 more marines, to be available for land service; while 50 were despatched to fill up casualties and vacancies among the marines and the ships of war. 240,000 rounds of Snider ammunition, 150,000 rounds of Enfield ammunition, and a quantity of powder and lead, were shipped on the 18th July, together with two 7-pounder mountain-guns and 300 rounds per gun. Two Gatling guns, with 10,000 rounds per gun, were also ordered to be got ready for shipment, and despatched on the 30th July by the mail-packet. At the same time a large demand for stores, which had been made by Commissary Marsden, immediately on his arrival at Cape Coast in the beginning of June, was complied with; and as, on the 30th June, the officer commanding the troops on the Gold Coast had reported that the water in the tanks was unfit for drinking, unless specially filtered, six of Crease's tank filters were at once sent off, and an equal number were held in readiness. In consequence, also, of a letter from Dr Home, in whose great sanitary experience confidence was justly felt, hospital stores were despatched for 20 per cent of the native troops and 45 per cent of the Europeans, with a reserve of 7 per cent. These were despatched from Liverpool on the 30th August.

On the 17th July the Simoom sailed with her 200 marines, and arrived at the Coast on the 9th August. She was ordered to remain on the coast as a hospital ship and to distil water. She also brought out a large supply of food, sent out by the Secretary of State for War to meet the enormous demands which were now being made upon the Administrator. In the months of July and August relief was issued to an average number of 980 persons daily by the Relief Committee. The marines remained on board the Simoom, and were not landed; and the 150 of them who had originally been sent out for land service were placed on the books of H.M.S. Simoom.

On the 7th a report had arrived from Dixcove that the Ashantis were trying to cross the Prah, two days' journey from its mouth, into the Wassaw country to the westward, to meet the Ashantis under Akyempon, and that they were together intending to attack Dixcove and Secondee. The Commodore, on receipt of this intelligence, sent the Argus to the windward coast, and on the 13th sailed himself in the Rattlesnake for Secondee. At 9 A.M. on the 14th he left with a number of boats armed and manned, in order to proceed to Chamah, with Captain Helden, the civil commandant at Secondee, and Commander Luxmoore of the Argus, to hold a palaver with the kings and chiefs of Chamah, hoping to obtain their assistance to drive the Ashantis from an island which they were said to be holding some miles up the river. The Commodore also proposed to ascend the river Prah and ascertain something of the locality in that direction, with a view to ultimately conveying a force in boats up the river to attack the flank of the Ashantis.

At ten o'clock, accompanied by Captain Helden and Commander Luxmoore, he proceeded unarmed, and with every friendly intention, and urged upon the chiefs to assist her Majesty's Government against the Ashantis. The chiefs denied that they had rendered any assistance to the Ashantis, and expressed their intention of remaining neutral in the war. The Commodore remonstrated with them, and asked the king to lend him two chiefs to accompany him up the river Prah, to make a survey of the river with his boats. This the king refused to do; but the palavering was so peaceful that the Commodore was not induced to discontinue his project. Embarking in his galley, a procession of boats proceeded up the river in the following order: Colonial steam-launch, under Sub-Lieutenant Cross of the Argus, with rockets on board, towing the Rattlesnake's galley with the Commodore and Captains Luxmoore and Helden on board, and followed by the steam-cutter of the Simoom, with rockets, towing the gig and whaler of the Rattlesnake. About 200 yards up the river the Colonial steam-launch broke down, and the gig remained with her, the Commodore proceeding in his galley in tow of the steam-cutter behind the whaler. The Commodore deemed it prudent to proceed on the Chamah side of the river, considering the inhabitants friendly, and that there might be marauding-parties of Ashantis on the other bank. The river was 70 or 80 yards broad, not less than six feet deep, with a current running about two miles an hour. All proceeded satisfactorily until, at about a mile and a half up the river, without warning, and without any enemy being seen, a heavy fire was poured into the boats from the dense bush on the Chamah side. The Commodore was shot down and badly wounded on the right side, and Captains Luxmoore and Helden were severely hit at the first discharge. The small-arm men in the boats opened fire, but the rockets could not be used, as the steam-cutter was towing the boats. The boats repaired to mid-stream, and a number of men being wounded, the Commodore ordered the expedition to return to the Rattlesnake. Himself prostrated by loss of blood, his orders were carried out by Captain Luxmoore, who, nearly fainting from his wounds, continued to direct the operations till the fire from the boats had driven the enemy out of the bush. Nearly all the officers had been shot in the back. Four of the gig's crew fell wounded from the thwarts, while two men were shot down in the whaler. The boats were towed down the river, and reached the Rattlesnake about 6 P.M.

While the boats were up the river, ten Fanti policemen were landed upon the beach, which was immediately crowded with natives, whose manner was most unfriendly. The cutter which had landed the police upset in the surf, and while the crew were engaged in endeavouring to right it, the natives fired at them, wounding several of their number. Sub-Lieutenant Draffen of the Rattlesnake endeavoured to protect the crew by the Fanti police, and succeeded in re-embarking in the cutter all except one ordinary seaman who was killed and decapitated by the natives. Two Fanti police and a Krooman were also killed. The boats from the Rattlesnake were at once sent to fire upon the natives, but they retreated to the bush and escaped without injury. On Commodore Commerell's return to his ship, it was cleared for action, and the town of Chamah was at once bombarded, and in two hours' time almost completely destroyed. In this most unfortunate affair 4 men were killed and 16 wounded, including 4 officers, 2 Fanti police, and 2 Houssas, of whom 15 had accompanied the Commodore. Commodore Commerell was so severely wounded that he was ordered by the medical officers to leave the coast; and he sailed for the Cape on the 22d August, leaving the command in the hands of Captain Fremantle, with orders which will be referred to in a subsequent chapter.

On the 14th August, Colonel Festing suggested to the Administrator that a camp of the native troops should be formed near Mansu; but the proposal was not adopted.

The Napoleon redoubt having been finished on the 15th August, Captain Lowry, 2d West India Regiment, was placed in command; and Lieutenant Gordon was ordered to move into the Sirowee valley, and erect a similar work there. It rained very hard the day and night of the 16th and 17th. The bridge across the Sweet River near Napoleon was carried away, and the river became 100 yards wide and 10 feet deep at the ford. Gordon's men, therefore, had to be moved across in a canoe; and during the operation a panic seized the

THE ASHANTI WAR.

Cape Coast Volunteers, officers and men believing they were being led to certain death. They begged Gordon not to go to Simeo, where they would certainly be killed. In vain did he reason with them, and think he had convinced them. When it became their turn to be ferried across, only half-a-dozen men obeyed the bugle-call; some threw down their arms and fled to Cape Coast, the remainder skulking into the bush, only one officer, Lieutenant Smith, whose conduct at this time and throughout the whole campaign was most admirable, giving any assistance. He assured Lieutenant Gordon that in their present frame of mind a single Ashanti would make all the volunteers run; and accordingly Gordon very reluctantly gave up the idea of marching on Simeo, and informed the volunteers that he would only go to Abbaye, three miles nearer to Elmina. They at once fell in and were ferried across. Abbaye was reached at dark, the roads occupied, and the villagers disarmed. On the 18th the redoubt was commenced; patrols were sent out to Simeo, Elmina, and Napoleon, two or three neighbouring villages examined, and their inhabitants disarmed. During the night war-drums were beating all round the camp, and at about 3 A.M. Gordon was awakened by Lieutenant Smith, who informed him that some of the volunteers had resolved to desert, and were tampering with the labourers to induce them to strike work in hopes that he would thus be compelled to retire. But he doubled the Houssa guards round the camp, and at early dawn paraded the volunteers and labourers. The latter promised to stick to him wherever he went, and kept their promise under most discouraging circumstances, never failing up to the moment when he finally handed them over to Major

Home at Mansu. He applied to Colonel Festing for a detachment of regulars to give the volunteers confidence; and Captain Matthews, with a detachment of 80 of the 2d West India Regiment, arrived in the course of the day, rested for a few hours, and then returned to Abbaye.

Gordon carried on a system of patrols and spies, and he daily captured Ashanti prisoners, who were forwarded to headquarters. Besides stopping the direct communication between Mampon and Elmina, the occupation of Abbaye restored large portions of fruitful land to the Fantis, and covered the lower Sweet River and Sirowee from the enemy. The Fantis came in thousands to secure the grain from 50 or 60 acres of Indian-corn just ripe, and which would otherwise have fallen into the hands of the Ashantis. On the 25th August, a reinforcement of 50 of the 2d West Indians joined the garrison at Abbaye.

Towards the latter end of August, Colonel Harley proposed to Lord Kimberley that if her Majesty's Government should decide upon offensive action against Ashanti, which he considered the only means of asserting once for all the sovereignty of England on the Coast, the measure should be carried out by the taking of Coomassie, which place, he said, "can be reached by a leisurely march in ten days from Cape Coast, *viâ* Dunquah, Mansu, Yancoomassie, and Prahsu."* He suggested for the invasion of Coomassie a force composed of 300 marines, 600 West Indians, a battalion of rifles not less than 800 strong, 200 volunteers, and 10,000

---

* Colonel Harley's despatch recommending this operation may be found in the Blue-Book, c. 891. Further correspondence respecting the Ashanti invasion, No. 2, presented to Parliament, March 1874, page 179.

native auxiliaries. He believed that the excitement of marching through a new and interesting country would keep up the European troops, and prevent sickness, especially during the month of November, when the rains were over, and the roads, he said, would be dry.

Colonel Festing's reply to this despatch, a copy of which was communicated to him, was most able. He pointed out that the distance from the coast to Coomassie was about 170 miles, and said,—" I am of course aware that extraordinary marches have been made on many occasions by troops of all nations; but I hear with the utmost surprise that a march of this distance could be accomplished in a leisurely manner in ten days, by an army moving along a single narrow track in an unmapped country, destitute of supplies, and covered with dense forest, where every morsel of food must be carried with the invading force from our base at Cape Coast or Elmina, and the climate of which all accounts agree in affirming to be baneful to the European." He expressed his opinion that such a march could not be accomplished, even if altogether unopposed, in much less time than a month; and that should they meet with any opposition, it would be impossible to lay down any time at which Coomassie could be reached. He said that he did not see his way to feeding 10,200 natives, and would look with apprehension to the impediment caused by the crowding up of the only line of communication, and that a single narrow track, by a totally unmanageable body of natives, " whose language we do not speak, and who are liable to panic-stricken terror." Without offering any suggestion of his own as to the number and composition of the force competent to make a successful invasion of the Ashanti country, and to seize its capital, he deprecated in the strongest manner any estimate which would leave it possible for a small band of weary soldiers to arrive in front of Coomassie. He ended his despatch thus : " As an officer writing with responsibility, I cannot permit myself to think lightly of an undertaking involving unknown hazards. That it is possible to assert the sovereignty of our country on this coast I fully believe ; but not, in my humble opinion, with the insufficient means proposed in your Excellency's despatch."

It will be sufficient to say that when this correspondence was laid before Sir Garnet Wolseley, after his arrival on the Coast, he wrote to the Secretary of State for War expressing in the highest terms his sense of the wisdom of Colonel Festing's conduct,—an opinion which was endorsed by Mr Cardwell.

We see in this an example of the evil of divided civil and military responsibility in war. It is impossible that thoroughly satisfactory relations can exist between a civil governor and a commander of troops, where the civil authority takes upon itself to propose military operations, and where the military commander is obliged to inform the civil administrator that he is not well informed as to the matter concerning which his proposals are made.

On the 25th August, a detachment of the 2d West Indians and Houssas was sent to Dixcove; and on the same day, Captain Thompson, of the 2d Queen's Bays, arrived on the Coast as a volunteer to serve under the Colonial Government, and took charge of the armed police of the settlement. Captain Lanyon of the 2d West India Regiment, who had been aide-de-camp to Sir Peter Grant at Jamaica, and had thrown up his appointment in order to serve with his regiment, also arrived, and was appointed to perform the duties of Colonial Secretary. On the 30th August, Colonel Harley, for the first time since his arrival, visited Elmina—the castle, not the town—and presented some silks and money to the second king and the chiefs who had sworn allegiance to the British Crown in June. The weather still continued very bad, and a great number of officers were sick. On the 2d September, Lieutenant Gordon was directed to march with the Houssas and labourers to work on the road between Cape Coast and the Prah : he reached Accroful on the night of the 2d, commenced on the 3d to work backwards towards Cape Coast, and by the 8th September the road was finished from Accroful to Assayboo. On the 5th, a council was held between Colonel Harley, Captain Fremantle, and Colonel Festing, which ended in Colonel Festing's agreeing to take the field for operations, provided that 5000 native allies were previously assembled at Abbaye, which Colonel Harley undertook to arrange. On the 11th of September the native tribes were commencing to assemble at Abbaye under Captain Thompson ; and Gordon had returned there with his Houssas, when the mail-packet arrived from England bringing Captain Glover, and letters from the Government, stating that Sir Garnet Wolseley was about to proceed to the Coast, and desiring that no extended operations should be undertaken pending his arrival. Colonel Festing then decided, in spite of the pressure which had been put upon him by Colonel Harley, not to go any further with the projected attack upon Mampon, and announced his decision at a council held on the 12th. Instead of the 5000 men who had been promised at

Abbaye, scarcely 100 had assembled; and the weather was still very bad. Colonel Harley having decided that his orders from England, which will be subsequently quoted, required him to hand over all the Houssas to Captain Glover, they were collected from their various stations at Cape Coast and embarked for Accra on the 15th. They had to be relieved by troops of the 2d West India Regiment, the regular force at Elmina and Cape Coast being thus enormously reduced. On the 22d September, the number of natives assembled in camp at Abbaye, including the Aquafoos, who had been present since June, was only 147. Lieutenant Gordon now returned to Accroful to continue making the road, and resumed work on the morning of the 23d, having only a guard of 20 Cape Coast Volunteers to protect his working-party. He therefore organised some new scouts, whom he kept along the banks of the Sweet River, so as to give him early warning of any Ashanti movements. When Sir Garnet Wolseley arrived on the 2d October, a road had been made to within a mile of Yancoomassie Fanti.

Rumours having reached Colonel Festing's ears about the 26th September that the Ashanti camp at Mampon was breaking up, and that the enemy were moving eastward, he had strengthened the camp of Napoleon by a detachment of 50 of the 2d West Indians, all that could possibly be spared, owing to the necessity for garrisons on the windward coast. On the 30th a fresh report arrived from Lieutenant Gordon, derived from his scouts at Abrakrampa, to the same effect; and on the 2d October, Colonel Festing sent to Accroful a detachment of 50 of the 2d West Indians, who were immediately pushed on to Dunquah by decision of Sir Garnet Wolseley on his arrival.

The reader will not fail to have appreciated the great difficulties under which resistance to the Ashantis had been carried on up to this time. Unable to use the marines and sailors for any operations beyond the immediate defence of the forts; terribly hampered in every military movement by the incessant rains which flooded the country and turned the streams into rivers; underhanded in officers; without any staff to assist him; obliged even to copy his own letters; harassed with incessant office-work and correspondence, both with the civil Government and the home authorities; not able to act entirely on his own responsibility, but compelled to defer his own judgment to that of others, and to give ear to the suggestions of the civil Administration, Colonel Festing had had a task which might well have appalled a man of resources and of energy less than those which he possessed. But he had proved well equal to his task, and had been most ably assisted by that invaluable officer, Lieutenant Gordon of the 98th, whose untiring exertions, coolness of judgment, and marvellous power of withstanding fatigue and exposure, had rendered him singularly fitted for the very difficult task which had been assigned to him. Colonel Festing, on giving over his command, brought this officer's services to the notice of the War Department, as did Sir Garnet Wolseley almost immediately after his arrival; and never was there a reward better bestowed than the promotion given to this most gallant officer. Houssa Gordon, as he was called, had not yet finished his work, but rendered services of the utmost value during the remainder of the expedition.

CHAPTER III.

THE DESPATCH TO THE GOLD COAST OF THE EXPEDITIONS UNDER CAPTAIN GLOVER AND SIR GARNET WOLSELEY — INSTRUCTIONS ISSUED BY THE GOVERNMENT.

ON the receipt of the news that the Ashantis had actually attacked Elmina, her Majesty's Government appear to have considered that the time had arrived for more decisive measures, such as would relieve the Protectorate from the presence of the enemy, and restore that prestige which we had undoubtedly lost by our inability to drive the enemy from the neighbourhood of our forts, or indeed to do more than protect those forts and the ground immediately surrounding them.

In July, Commander John Glover, R.N., who had formerly served as Administrator of the Government at Lagos, and whose influence with the native tribes and faculty for making them fight were well known, conceived and brought forward a proposal "to use the tribes of the eastern district of the Protectorate, in order to cause a diversion in the rear of the Ashanti army, and at the same time to threaten Coomassie." In a letter dated July 30, Captain Glover offered his services to carry out this proposal, pointing out his special qualifications for the service. He had met and defeated the Ashantis in action in 1870; he had acquired the confidence of the eastern tribes of the Protectorate;

he could enlist a hundred Houssas, where any one except himself would raise but five; numbers of Houssas were only waiting his arrival to enlist; and he felt confident that he could do good service to her Majesty's Government as Commissioner to the eastern tribes of the Protectorate. The particulars of the plan were submitted to his Royal Highness the Field Marshal Commanding in Chief.

Lord Kimberley having expressed his disposition to accept the offer, Captain Glover gave further details of his proposal. A depot was to be made at Addah Fork, at the mouth of the Volta, as a base of operations during the organisation of a force of 10,000 men to operate against the Ashantis; and a second depot in the neighbourhood of Pong, as a base from which to operate on the Upper Volta above the falls. European officers, stores, and equipments were to be provided, in order that the force under the kings and chiefs of the different tribes composing it might be capable of movement in three distinct divisions, a European officer being in command of each division. On the river Volta should be placed three steam-launches, with a flotilla of canoes, and a steamer when procurable. One thousand men of each division were to be armed with the Enfield rifle, on condition of submitting themselves to drill and to a higher organisation than those armed with a percussion musket. The Houssa police should be attached to the force, increased to a thousand strong, and placed under the command of Mr Goldsworthy, the collector of customs at Cape Coast Castle. Four 7-pounder mountain steel guns, rockets, and two Gatlings, were to be supplied. Captain Glover at the same time sent in a list of stores, arms, and equipments for his force, and applied that local military rank should be given to the officers serving with his expedition. He also applied for £6000 in florins and gold.

The officers originally applied for by Captain Glover were Mr Goldsworthy, as second in command ; Captain Sartorius, 6th Bengal Cavalry ; Captain Buller, 60th Rifles ; Lieut. Larcom, R.N. ; Mr Tatham, late Quartermaster 24th Regt. ; Dr Rowe, Surgeon-Major. Captain Buller being on the Continent was not communicated with, and the officers forming the expedition were ultimately as follows : Mr Goldsworthy, Dr Rowe, Captain Sartorius, Lieut. Larcom, Lieuts. Cameron and Barnard, 19th Regt. ; Mr Blissett, Deputy Commissary, and Mr Doorly, late Navigating Sub-Lieutenant in the Royal Navy. The War Office declined to entertain the proposition to give local military rank to any of these gentlemen.

While Captain Glover was still in England, and before he received his final instructions, the Government decided upon combining in the hands of a military officer of experience the command of her Majesty's land forces in Western Africa, and the administration of the government of the Gold Coast. Colonel Sir Garnet Wolseley, C.B., K.C.M.G., was selected for the command. His large experience of war, and his successful conduct of the Red River Expedition in 1870, were guarantees that, although still young, he possessed the necessary qualifications for a task likely to be one of great difficulty. In accepting the post offered to him, Sir Garnet Wolseley made but two important requests —first, that he should be given a force of European troops ; and secondly, that he should not be required to remain as Civil Governor of the Gold Coast after the close of the military operations. The latter request only was at once acceded to.

In making this appointment, and thus superseding Colonel Harley, the Government intended no withdrawal of confidence from the latter officer. He was officially informed of this by the Secretary of State for the Colonies; and while he was reminded that the Government fully appreciated his conduct in circumstances of no ordinary trial and difficulty, it was pointed out to him that, looking to the possibility that it might become necessary to engage in more extended operations against the Ashantis than had as yet been undertaken, her Majesty's Government were of opinion that it was essential that the chief civil and military authority should be vested in one person, who should be an officer of high standing and special qualifications; and that as the military command could not be exercised by Colonel Harley, there was no alternative but to relieve him from the active discharge of his duties. Sir Garnet Wolseley's appointment was notified officially to Captain Glover, Colonel Harley, and the officer commanding the troops on the Gold Coast, about the 18th August. The latter officer was informed that Sir Garnet's arrival might be expected about 1st October, and that he would hold the local rank of Major-General. "In the mean time," ran the despatch, "it will be unsuitable that operations should be undertaken which would involve the exposure of officers and men to the climate at the present season in the interior at any considerable distance from their own resources, and you will carry into effect such operations only as appear necessary or desirable in furtherance of the instructions which you had already received."

Captain Glover sailed for the Gold Coast in the mail-steamer on the 19th August. His instructions, dated 18th August, define with sufficient clearness the exact object of his mission, and the position which he was to hold in relation to Sir Garnet Wolseley. He was appointed under the royal sign-manual and signet to be "Special Commissioner to the friendly native chiefs in the eastern district of the protected territories near or adjacent to our settlement on the Gold Coast." The tenor of his instructions was to this effect: He was to be subject to the general control of the officer administering the government of the Gold Coast, to whom he was to address his reports, and with whom he was to correspond on all matters relating to the duty intrusted to him. He was, on Sir Garnet Wolseley's arrival, to communicate freely with him, and conform to all instructions issued by him or any officer who might succeed him in the government and chief military command. He would have under his orders the detachment of Houssa police in the settlement, and was to endeavour to raise their strength to the number of one thousand. He was to communicate with the chiefs in the eastern districts, especially at Accra, and should he find them ready to take part in the projected movement in the Protectorate, to furnish them with assistance in the way of arms and ammunition and such moderate sums of money as might be essential. He would be furnished with a steamer suited to the navigation of the Volta, and three steam-launches for proceeding up the river beyond the falls at Pong. The remainder of his instructions must be given in the actual words of the text.

"The general object which you will keep in view is,

to create such a diversion on the flank and rear of the Ashantis as may force them to retreat from the Protectorate, or at all events, to so far harass and alarm them as to enable an attack to be made on them in front with better prospect of success.

" 9. The facilities which are afforded by a river navigable, as the Volta is, to a long distance from the coast, for carrying the war into the Ashanti territory, are unquestionable; and it is stated that the country in the neighbourhood of that river is comparatively free from bush, and is therefore less unhealthy, and can more easily be penetrated than the district lying directly between the Gold Coast and the Ashanti country.

" 10. It would be impossible to suggest any particular line of operations. So much must depend upon the amount of support which may be afforded by the friendly tribes, the degree of opposition which may be encountered, the nature of the country and of the climate, the disposition of the populations of the districts to be traversed, and of the neighbouring tribes, especially of the Aquamoos, that it must be left to you to judge for yourself on the spot, according to circumstances, how far it may be prudent to attempt to penetrate into the Ashanti territory in the direction of Coomassie, and whether it may be practicable to march upon Coomassie itself.

" 11. You will, of course, bear in mind that the resources of the Ashantis are said to be very considerable, and that an advance to a great distance from the Volta must necessarily be attended with much risk, unless, indeed, you should succeed in obtaining assistance from the tribes in the eastern part of the Ashanti dominions.

"12. So little is known of that part of Africa, that opinions on this point amount to little more than conjectures. If it be true, however, that the population is, to a considerable extent, Mahommedan, decisive successes gained against the Ashantis might cause some disruption of the ties which unite it to the Government at Coomassie.

"13. But her Majesty's Government hope that even if you should be unable to penetrate far into the Ashanti country, the presence of a hostile force in the neighbourhood of the Volta will not fail seriously to alarm the Ashantis, and to make a powerful diversion in favour of the Protectorate; and they must not be understood as giving an opinion that a march upon Coomassie is an operation which it would in any case be prudent to attempt.

"14. It will be advisable that you should seize any opportunity which may present itself of opening communications with the tribes on the north of Ashanti.

"15. It is known that, from time to time, severe wars have been carried on between those tribes and the Ashantis, and news of an invasion of Ashanti from the east might possibly cause some movement to be made from the north.

"16. Lastly, I have strongly to impress upon you the necessity of using your utmost efforts to prevent the natives who take part in the movement from putting to death captives and unarmed men, and committing the other barbarities which are too often the concomitants of native warfare.

"Her Majesty's Government, when furnishing the tribes of the Protectorate with effective means to defend themselves against their enemies, have a right to require that those means shall not be used for purposes abhorrent to humanity and the usages of civilised nations."

Comment upon these instructions would be superfluous. It is patent that they indicate a general line of operations by the Volta to the Ashanti kingdom; that the chief object is to draw the Ashanti army from the Protectorate by threatening its rear; that a march upon Coomassie is suggested, but that the whole responsibility is thrown upon Captain Glover, whether or not to attempt such a movement. It was a roving commission, one thing only being quite clear, that Captain Glover's dealings were to be confined to the eastern tribes of the Protectorate. The cost of the expedition seems to have been but vaguely estimated. As late as the 1st September, the Treasury consented to an expenditure on behalf of the expedition of £27,000, of which £12,000, including the purchase of the Lady of the Lake steamer, had already been disbursed in England, Captain Glover being authorised to draw for the remaining £15,000, but not for any further sum, without fresh instructions.

Such was the origin of Captain Glover's expedition, and such the understanding upon which it started. The dread of exposing European life to the influence of a climate considered so deadly as that of the Gold Coast, led to very earnest hopes on the part of large numbers in England that the Ashanti war might be brought to a speedy end by this expedition, and that long before Sir Garnet Wolseley could employ any considerable number of Europeans on the coast, the few hardy, seasoned officers under Captain Glover, would have led a native force into the heart of the Ashanti kingdom, forced the Ashanti army to withdraw from the neighbourhood of Cape Coast and Elmina, and secured for us a peace which should render unnecessary the display of European force. But the task before Captain Glover was far harder of accomplishment than these had supposed; nor did they count on the energy which would enable Sir Garnet Wolseley, with a handful of white men, a few hundred recruits from various coast tribes, and the native levies who had fled before the enemy in April, to carry out a series of operations resulting in the defeat of the Ashanti army and its retreat across the Prah, before Captain Glover had been able to take the field.

The interval between Sir Garnet Wolseley's appointment and his departure for the Gold Coast, was occupied in making arrangements for the conduct of the expedition. Sir Garnet's appointment was no sooner made known, than he was besieged by applications from officers desirous of serving under him. The difficulties of the expedition were known to be immense; the dangers of the climate had lost nothing in the telling. Every day the newspapers were filled with letters portraying the country in terms of the most appalling nature. Yet the greater the difficulties and the greater the dangers, the more did the prospect appear to attract those officers of our army—and happily they are many—who look on the study of war in peace as only the means to an end, and desire to put the result of their peace studies into practice in time of war. Many officers resigned excellent appointments for the chance of seeing service under one holding so high a name as a practical soldier; and the only difficulty was to select from the large list of volunteers. There rallied round

Sir Garnet Wolseley his old comrades of the Red River; and no less than five members of the staff, including Colonel M'Neill, the second in command, and the senior control officer, Mr Irvine, were chosen from among them.

The original staff of the expedition stood as follows :—

Major-General Sir Garnet Wolseley, C.B., K.C.M.G.
Captain H. Brackenbury, R.A., Asst. Military Secretary.
Captain Hugh M'Calmont, 7th Hussars,   ⎱ Aides-de-
Lieut. Hon. A. Charteris, Coldstream Guards, ⎰ Camp.
Colonel J. C. M'Neill, V.C., C.M.G., Colonel on the Staff.
Major T. D. Baker, 18th Royal Irish, Asst. Adjt.-General.
Capt. G. L. Huyshe, Rifle Brigade, ⎱ D.A. Adjutants or
Capt. R. H. Buller, 60th Rifles,   ⎰ Quartermasters General.
Deputy-Controller, M. B. Irvine, C.M.G.

OFFICERS SPECIALLY EMPLOYED.

Bt. Lieut.-Col. H. E. Wood, 90th Light Infantry.
Bt. Major B. C. Russell, 13th Hussars.
Major R. Home, R.E.
Capt. G. A. Furse, 42d Highlanders.
Capt. A. J. Rait, R.A.
Capt. A. A. Godwin, 103d Fusiliers.
Capt. C. J. Bromhead, 24th Regt.
Lieut. R. W. T. Gordon, 93d Highlanders.
Lieut. J. F. Maurice, R.A., appointed Private Secretary to Sir Garnet Wolseley.
Lieut. R. O. Richmond, 50th Regt.
Lieut. W. F. Dooner, 8th Regt.
Lieut. H. F. S. Bolton, 1st W.I. Regt.
Lieut. A. F. Hart, 31st Regt.
Lieut. F. H. Eardley Wilmot, R.A.
Lieut. E. R. P. Woodgate, 4th Regt.
Lieut. A. J. Saunders, R.A.
Lieut. E. H. Townshend, 16th Regt.
Lieut. E. F. Lord Gifford, 24th Regt.
Lieut. J. W. Graves, 18th Regt.
Lieut. A. H. Eyre, 90th Light Infantry.

CONTROL DEPARTMENT.

Commissary C. D. O'Connor.
Commissary W. H. Ravenscroft.
Deputy-Commissary R. Walsh.
Assistant-Commissary E. Fitz Stubbs.
Deputy-Paymaster H. Potter.
Assistant-Paymaster C. Ward.

ARMY MEDICAL DEPARTMENT.

Surgeon-Major R. W. Jackson.
Surgeon C. A. Atkins.

Never, probably, has a commander about to undertake a military expedition striven harder than did Sir Garnet Wolseley to obtain information as to the nature of the country in which he was to operate, and the strength and position of his enemy; never, probably, has the effort been attended with less success. The Intelligence Department of the army, whose business it will in future be to have the latest information in reference to all our colonies and the bordering countries, had only just been created, and could give little or no help. Information must therefore be sought far and wide, and there was no known source which was not carefully explored. The few books descriptive of the country were obtained. Bowdich, Dupuis, Hutton, Ricketts, Beecham, Wilson, and all the other known authors, were laid under contribution. The official reports of previous expeditions inland were examined; Blue-books were waded through. Hours were expended in conversations with men who had served upon the Gold Coast in all capacities, and their various opinions were carefully collated and compared. Some few were found—as, for example, Major Bolton—who, having neither wish nor hope to further personal interests by their reports, spoke honestly their opinion that a military movement upon Coomassie was perfectly feasible if conducted with due precautions; but a very large majority displayed the gloomiest prospects, and pronounced the bush so deadly, that Europeans could not march through it and live. The military aspect of the question, also, was, according to most of these opinions, enveloped in immense difficulties. The natives of the coast tribes could not be made to fight the Ashantis; European soldiers alone could be counted on to stand before them. But, over and above the deadly nature of the climate, the bush, a home to the enemy, would be impenetrable to English soldiers. Our men would march into ambushes, whence there would be no escape. Surrounded on all sides, they would be shot down in the narrow paths upon which alone they could advance. Should the Prah be reached, its passage would be disputed. Every tree within reach would be full of armed men, and it would be impossible in their face to debouch from the track and cross the river. There was not one of these obstacles to success which was not put forward; and there is the very best reason to believe that one old resident of the Gold Coast, who had himself proposed to her Majesty's Government to conduct an expedition to Coomassie, wrote letter after letter to the leading journal, under a signature which conveyed the idea of special knowledge on his part, to prove the utter impossibility of such an undertaking, the moment it was known that the task was to be confided to Sir Garnet Wolseley.

Such were the opinions expressed by the majority of the witnesses; but through their evidence ran, for the most part, a tone which carried conviction that all must not be accepted as fact; and the strongest proof of the worthlessness of much of the evidence lay in the fact that the witnesses had themselves little or no knowledge of the country of which they so graphically described the terrors. Scarcely one had made any journeys inland; their experience was of the coast alone; they could give no information of the roads, the country, or the inland people; and except for some little information gleaned from the few survivors of the expedition of 1864, Sir Garnet Wolseley's sole knowledge of the country, when he started on his mission, was derived from works written more than fifty years ago.

From these ancient sources a map was prepared at the Topographical Department of the War Office, together with an itinerary and notes to accompany the map. But one single fact is pregnant with proof of the ignorance of the old inhabitants of the coast. It was almost universally represented that the first thirty miles inland were a dead level—a belt of swampy jungle; and that, this once passed, an entirely different nature of country would be reached. In reality, as was found out on arrival at Cape Coast, the country, from the very shore, consists of numerous small rounded hills, thrown together apparently without plan or system, and intersected by deep gullies; and the jungle or bush extends in one continued unbroken track, not only to the river Prah, but even to Coomassie itself.

After close investigation of all the circumstances of the case, Sir Garnet Wolseley arrived at definite conclusions as to the objects to be attained, and the means necessary for their accomplishment; and in order that the operations subsequently carried out may be fairly judged upon their merits, it is desirable that the problem, as it presented itself to him at the time, should be stated in his own words :—

"The first object to be attained, as I understand the circumstances existing on the Gold Coast at present, is to free the Protectorate of its Ashanti invaders; and secondly, having accomplished this, to advance into the Ashanti territory, and, by the seizure and destruction of Coomassie, strike a decisive blow at the Ashanti power, not only directly by the loss and severe punishment inflicted upon its Government, but, by the moral effects of a great victory, to destroy for ever its military prestige and influence over the neighbouring nations. It is its great military reputation—giving it so much power and influence, and causing it to be so feared by all the surrounding tribes—that we must break up; and this can only be effected by inflicting a severe defeat upon its armies, and leaving our mark of victory stamped in the country by the destruction of the capital, Coomassie.

"It has already been determined upon by Lord Kimberley to send Captain Glover up the river Volta, with a commission to raise a large native force, making use of a body of about 1000 trained Houssas as a nucleus for that purpose, and, proceeding up that river as far as he can in small steamers provided for the purpose, carry war into the Ashanti territory lying on the right bank of that river. If possible, he is then to advance westward in the direction of Coomassie. It is hoped that this operation may have the effect of causing the Ashanti force now in the Protectorate to fall back behind the Boosemprah, or at least act as a powerful diversion in favour of the force that is to advance from Cape Coast Castle, by drawing off, in the direction of the Volta, large detachments from the Ashanti army now in the Fanti country. I understand that Captain Glover's force is to be about 10,000 men, and that he takes out with him all the stores, guns, material, and munitions of war that he will require for his undertaking. I think it may be assumed that his expenses will be at least about £15,000 a-month; arrangements will therefore be required for supplying him with that amount from the treasure-chest at Cape Coast Castle.

"As this operation has already been determined upon, it is needless to discuss here its advisability in a military point of view, or to consider whether the best direction is thus being given to the best native troops (the Houssas) we have on the coast, and to the warlike tribes, the Accras and the Croboes, who in the present condition of affairs are the most easily available, if not the bravest, natives that could be obtained for direct military operations against the Ashanti army now threatening our posts on the seaboard. In framing a plan of operations for the attainment of the two objects before mentioned, it is necessary, therefore, that it should fit into this operation already determined upon. Let us therefore consider the effect that Captain Glover's expedition may be expected to have upon the first object in view.

"Captain Glover leaves England on the 19th inst., so he may hope to reach the Coast say on the 10th September; so it may be, I think, assumed that he will have reached with his force the point on the Volta by the middle of November, from whence he will begin his march by land towards Coomassie. Of course, if the rains are over early this year, as Lord Kimberley informs me may be expected, he will be able to begin his march before that date.

"It is to be expected that as soon as Captain Glover's force reaches Pong, an effect will be produced upon the Ashanti army now operating near Cape Coast Castle, rendering it perhaps possible to attack it with whatever native tribes and black troops there may be available at this time.

"Unless, however, the enemy's main body approaches near Cape Coast Castle, it cannot be hoped to strike any positively decisive blow at it until about the 1st December next; it would not, I think, be advisable to undertake any large operation until that date, for the climate and condition of the country after the rains would be very unfavourable. It would seem to me to be very important not to weaken our strength as regards Europeans by partial operations, returning to the coast after each, but to await our time until the conditions of the country and of the climate would admit of our advancing steadily day by day, with as great rapidity as possible, upon Coomassie.

"It may, however, be possible to clear the Protectorate of Ashantis at a much earlier date, and if that can be accomplished without undertaking any great operations in which Europeans are to be engaged, it should be done; for the final advance upon Coomassie would be immensely facilitated, if the Protectorate were freed from the enemy's troops for a few weeks before commencing an advance.

"The first object is therefore either to be accomplished soon, say about the beginning of November, by minor operations in which the friendly natives alone should be employed, assisted by the moral effect produced by the rumours of Captain Glover's movement on the Volta; or if the Ashantis are not shaken by his operations, and if they are found to be too strong to be dislodged by the native tribes in our pay alone, then the first object can only be attained by the final operation against Coomassie; in fact, in that case, the two objects must be considered together.

"In either case it will be necessary to have a force sufficiently strong to defeat in battle the combined armies that the King of Ashanti can bring into the field; and in the event of its being found possible to accomplish the first object before the final operations begin, that battle will take place north of the Boosemprah: but if the Protectorate is not cleared of the enemy before the final advance is made, the great battle will take place on the Cape Coast Castle Coomassie road, probably in the neighbourhood of Mansu.

"For this purpose, I think the following force would be required:—

	MEN.
2 Battalions of European Infantry of 650 men each, . .	1300
Detachment of Royal Artillery, with four mountain howitzers,	60
Detachment of Royal Engineers, ...	40
Administrative Services, ...	50
Total, . .	1450

This number to be exclusive of officers.

"To act in conjunction with these regular troops, there should be about 10,000 of the best natives we can obtain, using as many Houssas as possible, and, with the exception of these Houssas, and any other disciplined police that may be available, all to be under their own kings—one British officer only being sent with each king to keep him up to the mark, and to inspire his followers with confidence.

"If the enemy retire into their own territory early in November, it would be possible to have the bush cleared away at the various halting-places selected along the line of road from Cape Coast Castle to Prahsu for camping purposes, to sink Norton's tube-wells where required, and to make other arrangements for water-supply. Huts, which can in this country be constructed in a few hours, might also be erected.

"It might also be possible, under these circumstances, to form a large depot of stores and supplies at Mansu (about 34 miles from Cape Coast Castle). If this were possible, the European troops might march the very day they landed. Under any circumstances it would not be advisable to land the Europeans until every arrangement that it was possible to make beforehand had been completed.

"I may perhaps here remark that the composition of this European force is a point upon which too much stress cannot be laid. To detail any two battalions in the army for the service would not answer the purpose required, as it is essential that every officer should be carefully selected for such a service, as peculiarly suited for the work both physically and mentally; and to take any non-commissioned officer or private, unless of the best constitution, would be merely to increase the difficulties of the operation.

"I would propose, therefore, to obtain the number required in the following manner: To select 12 of the best battalions now at home, and having selected in each battalion the captain and 3 subalterns best suited for the work, direct him to obtain 109 volunteers of all ranks to form a company. That would give a total of 1308 non-commissioned officers and men, divided into twelve companies. To divide that number into two battalions, each to consist of six companies under the command of a selected lieutenant-colonel, having one selected major to assist him.

The detail of a battalion to be as follows:—

Lieut.-Colonel,	 1	Sergeant-Major,	. . .	1
Major,	 1	Q.M.-Sergeant,	. . .	1
Captains,	 6	Orderly-room Sergeant,	. .	1
Subalterns,	 18	Colour-Sergeants,	. . .	6
Adjutant,	 1	Sergeants,	. . . . .	24
Medical Officer,	. . . 1	Corporals,	. . . . .	30
Quartermaster,	 1	Buglers,	. . . . . .	14
	—	Privates,	. . . . .	577
Total of officers,	. . . 29	Total N.C.O. and men, 654		

"In order to obtain the best men as volunteers (no man under two years' service to be accepted), I consider it would be necessary to give them extra pay at the following daily rates, to be in addition to free rations from date of embarkation to date of return to England:—

Sergeant-Major, ...	1s. 6d.
Q.M.-Sergeants, ...	1s. 4d.
Colour-Sergeants, ...	1s. 2d.
Sergeants, ...	1s. 0d.
Corporals, ...	0s. 8d.
Privates, ...	0s. 6d.

Every man to be medically inspected by the doctor, and none but the strongest to be accepted.

"I feel convinced that the small force required, if obtained in this manner, would be in every way equal to twice that number if supplied by detailing whole battalions as they exist at present; and as the men of each individual company would all belong to one regiment, serving under the immediate command of their own officers, the *esprit de corps* in the whole body would, in fact, not be weakened but intensified.

"The artillery and engineers required should in a similar manner be selected volunteers.

"The extra pay thus given would, I am sure, be the most profitable item of expenditure in the total cost of the expedition.

"The men should also be provided with a special kit at the public expense."

The cost of kit in detail was added, as also a memorandum as to the detail of staff proposed for the expedition.

These opinions and proposals were laid by Sir Garnet Wolseley before her Majesty's Government, and were taken under consideration.

It will be noticed that the memorandum contains two distinct propositions : the first, that two battalions of European infantry, with detachments of other services, should be despatched to Cape Coast in time to commence operations on the 1st December; the second, that the battalions and other detachments should be composed of specially selected officers and men.

The proposal as to the composition of the battalions and detachments was negatived. There was supposed to be no precedent for such a course. It was considered that the traditions of the British service were opposed to it, and that it would interfere with the regimental system of the army; and it was decided that if European troops were to be used, the two battalions first on the roster for foreign service, after the troops already under orders for India, should be employed.

The proposal to send out the troops so that they should arrive at the Gold Coast by the 1st December was equally negatived. The Government was evidently most powerfully influenced by the reports of the severe sickness amongst the detachment of marines landed in June. The causes, already detailed, which had operated with such exceptional severity among these men, were not appreciated at their full value, even if they were at all understood; the sufferings of the troops employed in the expedition of 1864, equally due to exceptional causes, were taken as corroborative testimony to the deadly nature of the climate; and the Government also paid great attention to certain counsel, given them with the very best of motives, but based upon that most dangerous of grounds—a short and limited personal experience of the Gold Coast, confined almost entirely to the forts on the seaboard. Her Majesty's Ministers were assured—with all the strength of that argument so hard to answer, and yet often so utterly worthless, " I have been there myself"—that the proposed march into the interior was impossible, and that every European soldier employed would have to be carried.

It was therefore decided that two battalions—the second battalion of the 23d Royal Welsh Fusiliers, and the second battalion of the Rifle Brigade—should be held in readiness for service, made up to the strength requested; but that the question of their despatch to the Gold Coast should be reserved until Sir Garnet Wolseley should, after his own arrival there, have investigated the condition of affairs, and reported fully to the Government. It would then become a Cabinet question whether the European troops should be sent out or not.

This decision of the Government made it almost impossible that the troops could arrive at Cape Coast Castle by the 1st December. Sir Garnet Wolseley was not to leave England till the 12th September. His arrival at Cape Coast might consequently be expected about the 2d October, the average length of passage being twenty days. A fortnight at least must be allowed for investigation of the conditions affecting the question; and a report despatched to England on the 16th October could not arrive before the 5th or 6th November. As this report would have to be digested, and laid before a Council of Ministers—as transport would have to be taken up, and preparations made for embarkation—it could scarcely be hoped that less than a fortnight would elapse before the troops could sail, and so the 10th December would be the earliest date at which the troops could be expected at the Gold Coast. It will be seen in subsequent chapters that the unfortunate irregularity of the mail-service added another ten days to the time thus of necessity lost by the postponement of the decision as to the despatch of the troops; but that the unexampled celerity with which H.M. Government acted, when the despatch demanding the troops was received, made up for the time lost by the delay in the mail-service.

During the days intervening between the decision of the Government and his departure, Sir Garnet drew up and sent in demands for such arms, ammunition, stores, and supplies, as seemed necessary for the conduct of an expedition, the first part of which must be entirely, or almost entirely, carried out by native allies; the second part, to a great extent, by European soldiers.

Amongst the items of these stores were included—

> 6 12-pounder mountain howitzers.
> 1000 9-pounder war-rockets, and 100 signal-rockets.
> 4000 Snider rifles.
> 4000 sets of accoutrements.
> 4000 haversacks.
> 4000 grey blankets.
> 3,200,000 rounds of Snider ammunition.
> 3000 smooth-bore percussion muskets.
> 3000 sets of old accoutrements.
> 2,400,000 rounds of smooth-bore musket ammunition.
> 30 revolvers, and 1500 rounds ammunition.
> 4000 canvas smock-frocks.
> 1500 hand-axes.
> Intrenching tools—pickaxes, shovels, spades, hammers, saws, knives, whetstones, nails, 1 forge, &c. &c.
> 30 fog-horns.
> 30 army signalling books.
> 2 steam-sappers.
> 1 surf-boat.
> 4 Fowkes' pontoons.
> 4 Blanchards' pontoons.
> 150 filters, not over 40 lb. weight.
> 20 Norton's tube-pumps.
> 10 common pumps.
> 100 railway-guard whistles.
> 20 field officers', and 50 hospital marquees.
> 2 condensers.
> 25 field-ovens.
> 100 light carts with man-harness.
> A quantity of instruments for surveying and observations.

Memoranda were also prepared and delivered to the Adjutant-General on the subject of the kits, dress, and accoutrements of officers and men. A simple grey uniform of strong serge or Canadian homespun was designed for officers and men. Officers were to have

Norfolk jackets, pantaloons, gaiters, and shooting-boots, cork helmets and puggrees. Their swords were to be left behind, and revolvers and Elcho sword-bayonets alone worn. The men were to have helmets, smock-frocks, trousers, and long sailors' boots, and to be armed with short rifles and the Elcho sword-bayonet. Every detail of kit was considered, and practical efficiency was the sole object aimed at in every item. Officers were informed that they would be allowed 50 lb. weight of kit only, to be so packed that it could be carried on the head of a native.

The absence of any demand for transport animals is conspicuous. The whole of the information received in England was to the effect that no four-footed animal capable of employment for transport would live upon the Gold Coast. Horses, mules, asses, and oxen were said to die almost immediately after landing. The country was too wet for camels. Elephants, independently of the great difficulty of landing them in the heavy surf, would with difficulty be procured in time. They would require, if obtained from India, Indian mahoûts, and there was great uncertainty as to whether Indians would live upon the Gold Coast. Sir Garnet Wolseley therefore decided upon trusting, at all events until he should have reason for changing his opinion, to the ordinary transport animals of the country, men and women, of whom there must at least be no scarcity, who do not sicken in their own native country, and who were known to be in the habit of carrying loads of from 50 to 60 lb. weight upon their heads.

The impossibility, according to all information, of employing four-footed transport animals, the great difficulties known to exist where human labour is the sole means of transport, and the often repeated statements that for many miles inland the country was flat, induced Sir Garnet Wolseley to accept the advice given him by a most distinguished officer of engineers, and to request that a railway might be prepared and sent out to be laid down along the first thirty miles of the road to the Prah. After some hesitation the Government acceded to the request; and it was understood, when the expedition left England, that the railway should be taken in hand, and a portion of it sent out without waiting for further report; but that no great quantity of railway material should be shipped till Sir Garnet should have been able to write further on the subject, after personal investigation of the actual conditions on the coast.

In these preliminary arrangements the time was fully occupied up to the date fixed for the departure of the Major-General and his staff, who, together with the special-service officers and others enumerated above, were ordered to embark at Liverpool on the 12th September.

Before leaving London, Sir Garnet Wolseley received a commission from her Majesty, as Administrator of the Government of the Gold Coast, during the absence of the Governor-in-Chief of the West African Settlements, and a warrant appointing him to the command of her Majesty's land forces in the West African Settlements; and in order to give full effect to the intention that the supreme civil and military command on the Gold Coast should be vested in Sir Garnet Wolseley, the Governor-in-Chief received instructions not to visit the Gold Coast during Sir Garnet's tenure of office; the ordinary routine, under which the Administrator reports through the Governor-in-Chief, was suspended, and the Major-General was directed to correspond direct with the Home Government.

Instructions as to his mission were conveyed to the newly appointed Administrator and Commander of the Forces by both the Secretary of State for the Colonies and the Secretary of State for War; and as all his subsequent operations had to be based upon these, they are here given *in extenso*.

The two following letters were addressed to Sir Garnet Wolseley by Lord Kimberley:—

No. 1.   "DOWNING STREET, 10*th September* 1873.

"SIR,—Her Majesty's Government having determined, in consequence of the critical state of affairs on the Gold Coast caused by the Ashanti invasion, to unite the chief civil and military command in the settlement in the hands of an officer of high reputation and experience, I have the honour to acquaint you that her Majesty has been pleased to approve of your appointment to administer the government of the Gold Coast Settlement, and I transmit to you herewith her Majesty's commission as Administrator.

"2. You will, as Administrator, correspond directly with this office, and not through the Governor-in-Chief of the West African Settlements, who will be instructed during your tenure of office to abstain from all interference in the affairs of the Gold Coast.

"3. The circumstances which have led to the present position of affairs on the Coast appear to be briefly as follows:—

"4. The King of Ashanti, as you will find on referring to the document dated 19th of August 1871, which is printed at page 34 of the correspondence presented to Parliament on Gold Coast affairs in February 1872, disclaimed the pretension put forward in his letter to Mr Ussher, No. 24, of the 24th November 1870, that Elmina was his by right; but in his letter to Colonel Harley of 20th of last March, the king again asserted that the fort of Elmina and its dependencies are his, and it seems beyond a doubt that one of the main objects of his mission was the assertion of Ashanti supremacy over Elmina.

"5. But independently of Elmina, it must be remembered that peace had never been formally re-established with the Ashanti kingdom since the war of 1864, and that a petty warfare had from time to time been carried on between the Ashantis and the border tribes.

"6. It has been asserted that Mr Plange, the messenger sent by Mr Hennessy to Coomassie, did not faithfully deliver the friendly messages with which he was intrusted from the British authorities to the king; it is, however, a remarkable fact that almost up to the time of the news arriving of the invasion, the Gold Coast Government was in apparently friendly communication both with the King of Ashanti and his ambassadors at Cape Coast, and that the Administrator was in daily expectation of hearing that the captive missionaries had been released, and that amicable relations had been permanently established with the Ashanti kingdom.

"7. No indication had been given by the King of Ashanti that he had any serious ground of quarrel with the British Government, whether as regards Elmina or any other matter; and no opportunity was afforded to the Administrator to endeavour to remove peacefully any cause of complaint which the king might allege against the British Government or against the tribes in alliance with her Majesty.

"8. The statement in a letter from Mr Salmon, then acting Administrator, to Mr Hennessy, dated 8th of November 1872, that the Ashantis were at that time and had been purchasing very large quantities of ammunition, guns, gunpowder, and lead bars, seems to show that the invasion had been deliberately planned, and that it was not the result of a sudden outbreak of savage violence, on account of any supposed affront or neglect on the part of the British authorities. It is to be observed, moreover, that in the letter to Colonel Harley to which I have referred above, the King of Ashanti by no means limits his demands to Elmina, but calls upon the Administrator to restore the Denkerahs, Akims, and Assins, to their former position as his subjects, in direct contravention of the treaty of 1831, in which it is stated that 'the King of Ashanti has renounced all right or title to any tribute or homage from the Kings of Denkera, Assin, and others formerly his subjects.'

"9. I need scarcely say that her Majesty's Government cannot for a moment listen to such preposterous demands, nor can they allow the territories of the tribes in alliance with her Majesty to be devastated, the inhabitants butchered or driven away into slavery, and all progress and commerce stopped on the Coast by hordes of barbarians.

"10. At the same time, her Majesty's Government have never had any desire to prevent the Ashantis from peaceful intercourse with the Coast; on the contrary, they have always been anxious in every way to foster and encourage such intercourse; and one of the advantages which they anticipated from the possession of the forts at Elmina was, that through the friendly connection between the Elminas and the Ashantis, increased facilities would have been afforded for trade with the latter.

"11. On your assuming the government, or as soon after as you may think advisable, you will address a communication to the King of Ashanti, summoning him to withdraw his forces from the territories of our allies within such a period as you may fix, and to make adequate reparation for the injuries and losses which he has inflicted upon our allies, and give securities for the maintenance of peace in future. I have in another despatch indicated to you generally the nature of the conditions which her Majesty's Government would consider equitable.

"12. You will intimate to him that active measures are in preparation against him, and that if he refuses to comply with our demands, or delays to withdraw his forces within the time named, he may rest assured that means will not be wanting to compel him to do so, and to inflict such a defeat upon him as will effectually deter him from repeating his aggressions.

"13. Colonel Harley has been instructed to invite the principal kings and chiefs of the friendly tribes to meet you on your arrival at Cape Coast, and you will of course lose no time in endeavouring to collect and organise any native force which you may judge to be necessary for conducting any operations which may appear to you certain, or in a high degree likely, to be undertaken.

"14. You should state to the native kings that the Queen, on learning the calamitous position in which her allies are placed by the invasion of their country by the Ashantis, and their inability, without further assistance, to repel the invaders, has sent out specially an officer of high authority and experience, uniting the chief civil and military command, for the purpose of rendering them that assistance.

"15. You should explain to them that while her Majesty's Government are prepared to take such measures as may be found expedient on your advice to aid them in carrying on the war against the Ashantis, they expect the native tribes to use their utmost efforts to defend themselves, and to place their resources unreservedly at your disposal.

"16. The native tribes undoubtedly made considerable efforts at the beginning of the war; but since their last defeat, they appear to have been unable to rouse themselves to even the most necessary exertions for their own protection. The reports received by her Majesty's Government show that at Cape Coast the natives have not even taken steps to clear away the bush which endangers the safety of the town, and that nothing has been done by them to obtain trustworthy information of the movements of the Ashantis. You will intimate plainly to the native kings that it is impossible to help those who are unwilling to help themselves; and that unless they unite together cordially in their own defence, and show themselves prepared to make every sacrifice in their power to maintain themselves against the invader, they must not look for aid to her Majesty's Government.

"17. Her Majesty's Government are unable to give

you more precise instructions as to the measures which should be taken in order to bring the war to a speedy and successful termination, without further information than they at present possess. Much will depend upon the amount of co-operation which you may be able to obtain from the friendly tribes, the position and force of the Ashantis, concerning which but imperfect intelligence has hitherto been received, and upon the opinion which you may form after examination of the state of affairs on the spot as to the practicability of an expedition into the interior, and the number and composition of the force with which you might recommend that such an expedition should be undertaken. It may be that you will find the forces at your disposal upon the Coast sufficient for the accomplishment of any object which you may think it proper to undertake. But if you should find it necessary to ask for any considerable reinforcement of European troops, I have to request that you will enter into full explanations as to the circumstances in which you propose to employ them, and the reasons which may lead you to believe that they can be employed without an unjustifiable exposure, and with a well-grounded anticipation of success.—I have, &c.,

"KIMBERLEY."

No. 2.

"DOWNING STREET, 10*th September* 1873.

"SIR,—Her Majesty's Government wish to leave you a large discretion as to the terms which you may think it advisable to require from the King of Ashanti, but I may point out to you that the treaty which was concluded with Ashanti in 1831, and of which I enclose a copy for your information,* seems to afford a reasonable basis for any fresh convention.

"2. It would certainly be desirable to include in such a convention an explicit renewal by the King of Ashanti of the renunciation contained in the treaty of 1831, of all claim to tribute or homage from the native kings who are in alliance with her Majesty,—and further, a renunciation on his part to supremacy over Elmina, or over any of the tribes formerly connected with the Dutch, and to any tribute or homage from such tribes, as well as to any payment or acknowledgment in any shape by the British Government, in respect of Elmina or any other of the British forts or possessions on the Coast.

"3. The king should also, for his own interest no less than with a view to the general benefit of the country, engage to keep the paths open through his dominions, to promote lawful commerce to and through the Ashanti country, and to protect all peaceful traders passing through his dominions to the coast; and it might be expedient that a stipulation should be made that a resident British consul or agent should be received at the Ashanti capital if her Majesty should think fit at any time to appoint one.

"4. You will of course be careful to avoid as far as possible anything which may endanger the lives of the European missionaries and their families who have so long been held in captivity at Coomassie, without any fault of their own so far as her Majesty's Government are aware, and you will use every effort to secure their safe release.

"5. You will also endeavour to procure the surrender

* For this treaty, see Appendix No. I.

of all the prisoners taken by the Ashantis from the tribes in alliance with her Majesty.

"6. It is a usual practice with the native tribes to demand hostages for the faithful performance of treaties of peace. This was done in 1831, when two hostages of high rank were delivered over to the British Government by the King of Ashanti. If you should find it advisable to make a similar demand on the present occasion, you will bear in mind that the hostages should be men of high rank and position in Ashanti.

"7. It would be reasonable to exact from the king the payment of such an indemnity as may be within his means, which are said to be considerable, for the expenses of the war, and the injuries inflicted on her Majesty's allies.

"8. Lastly, the opportunity should not be lost for putting an end if possible to the human sacrifices and the slave-hunting which, with other barbarities, prevail in the Ashanti kingdom.—I have, &c., KIMBERLEY."

We have in these despatches the political instructions distinct from the military instructions conveyed to Sir Garnet Wolseley.

Passing over the remarks as to the causes of quarrel with the King of Ashanti, already sufficiently dealt with in the earlier chapters, we find the Government in these instructions distinctly holding its protection over the tribes in our alliance, refusing to recognise the "preposterous" demands of the King of Ashanti for sovereignty over them, stating its determination not to allow their countries to be devastated, their inhabitants butchered and driven into slavery, and the trade and commerce of the Coast stopped by hordes of barbarians.

Sir Garnet Wolseley is therefore to summon the king to withdraw from the Protectorate within a given period, to make adequate reparation for the losses inflicted on our allies, and to give securities for peace in future. The menace of signal and effectual defeat in case of non-compliance is to be held out.

Meanwhile Sir Garnet is to take immediate steps to collect and organise native forces, and to inform the kings assembled in conclave that they must help themselves, or they will not be helped.

Further instructions as to the steps necessary "to bring the war to a speedy and successful termination" cannot be given till certain points are settled, amongst them Sir Garnet's opinion formed on the spot as to "the practicability of an expedition into the interior," and the force required for such an expedition.

What, in the eyes of the Government, would be a successful termination of the war, we learn from the second despatch. A lasting peace is required—and a peace on conditions such as these :—

A renewed renunciation of the king's rights over the Protectorate and Elmina.

The keeping open of paths in Ashanti, and promotion of commerce through the interior with the coast.

The safe release of the European missionaries.

The release of all prisoners taken from the protected tribes.

Hostages of distinction given to us.

An indemnity for the war expenses, and for the injuries inflicted on our allies.

If possible, the diminution or cessation of human sacrifices and slave-hunting on the part of the Ashantis.

Such terms of peace as these could evidently not be hoped for from an enemy in actual possession of the territory he claimed, stopping all passage to the interior, holding captive not only the European missionaries but hundreds of slaves taken from the Protectorate, living on the produce of the land he had invaded, and sacrificing Fanti slaves on the death of every chief—unless by giving him an idea of our power to enforce our demands, vastly different from that he must derive by seeing us hemmed in and confined to a narrow strip of seaboard by his victorious troops.

How far the necessary means for enforcing our demands were promised to the commander of the expedition must be judged from the following letter addressed to him by the Secretary of State for War:—

"WAR OFFICE, 8*th September* 1873.

"SIR,—I have the honour to inform you that the command of her Majesty's land forces on the Gold Coast has been conferred upon you during the present troubles with the Ashantis, in combination with the civil administration of the settlement.

"The objects with which this arrangement has been made have been communicated to you by the Secretary of State for the Colonies. My duty is to give you such general instructions in respect to your military command, as may be necessary to convey to you the views of her Majesty's Government in that respect.

"The difficulties with which you will have to contend are not such as are to be encountered from an enemy formidable in the field. They are the far more serious difficulties of contending with a climate peculiarly fatal, especially at particular seasons of the year, to the constitutions of European soldiers, and, in a less degree, of all soldiers recruited anywhere else than upon the Coast itself.

"In determining what reinforcements it may be necessary to send you from time to time, her Majesty's Government will be greatly influenced by the reports they will receive from you after your arrival on the Coast, when you will have had time to communicate with those whose experience on the Coast, and knowledge of the immediate circumstances of the case, will best enable you to judge what measures you ought to adopt in order to give effect to the views of her Majesty's Government, as conveyed to you by the Secretary of State for the Colonies, and what means it is necessary to employ for that purpose.

"The force at present upon the Coast appears, by the latest reports, to be fully adequate for the defence of the British settlements themselves against the attacks of the Ashantis. It will be for you to consider what military measures will be necessary to free those settlements from the continued menace of such attacks, and to accomplish the further objects of your mission. In arriving at a judgment on this subject, you will not fail to bear in mind the following considerations—viz.:

"1. That European troops ought never to be exposed to the influence of that climate, when the service required can be performed by Houssas, or by native auxiliaries, or by any other force indigenous to the country.

"2. Nor, unless the service is one of paramount importance to the main object of your mission.

"3. Nor, unless it can be accomplished with a rapidity of execution which may render the exposure to the climate very short.

"For this reason, if the employment of Europeans shall become a necessity, every preparation should be made in advance; and no European force should be landed on the Coast until the time for decisive action has arrived. The period when the risk of loss from climate is at a minimum, appears to be that comprised within the months of December, January, February, and March, and it is consequently of much importance that your decision should be arrived at as soon after your arrival on the Coast as you may be enabled to frame it with sufficient knowledge of the circumstances, and with satisfaction to yourself.

"You will be able to judge what prospect Captain Glover has of raising a local force, so as to make a decided impression upon the invaders by his movement upon the Volta, and how far it is possible to organise that not inconsiderable body of natives, of whom Colonel Harley speaks as available, when supplies of food shall have been placed at your disposal for their use. You will also be able to judge what assistance native attendants will be able to render to the European troops, if you shall eventually find that you are compelled to employ Europeans in order to effect the purposes which her Majesty's Government have in view.

"The reports just received by the Himalaya give an account of the sickness of the marines employed upon the defence of the settlement before the arrival of the West Indian troops, and of the West Indian troops themselves, which her Majesty's Government have received with great concern. It is true that the season in which your operations will be carried on will be much less exposed to the hazards of the African climate than that which has just passed; and there seems good reason to believe that those hazards are greater upon the seaboard than in some favoured parts of the interior; but it is to be remembered, on the other hand, that service on a march is exposed to trials of its own, which do not affect men living on board ship or in quarters.

"I have thought it right to state for your guidance these general considerations, because nothing but a conviction of necessity would induce her Majesty's Government to engage in any operation involving the possibility of its requiring the service of Europeans at the Gold Coast. But it is far from my intention to fetter your judgment in the responsible and arduous duties which have been intrusted to you; and no one, I am sure, will be more sensible than yourself of the cardinal importance of the considerations to which I have invited your attention, or more desirous to spare to the utmost of your power the exposure of European soldiers or marines to the climate of the Gold Coast.— I am, &c., EDWARD CARDWELL."

Remembering the actual condition of affairs on the Gold Coast at the time when these instructions were written, and the political results expected by Lord Kimberley from the new mission, the instructions of the two Ministers, read together, appear, at first sight, much like orders to make bricks without straw. No European troops are sent out, or even promised. For at least three months to come, Sir Garnet Wolseley can have no force at his disposal beyond that small body of disciplined troops, which is only considered "fully adequate to the defence of the British settlements," and "that not inconsiderable body of natives," of whom, it is true, Colonel Harley speaks as available, but whom Lord Kimberley describes as "unable to rouse themselves to even the most necessary exertions for their own protection."

Was it possible that with such material the King of Ashanti could be humbled to the extent demanded by the instructions of the Secretary of State for the Colonies? Evidently not. Sir Garnet Wolseley was therefore placed in the position that he must either attempt an impossibility with the force under his hand, abandon the idea of obtaining from the King of Ashanti such terms as were required, or incur the responsibility of advising the Government to send out an expedition of European troops to a country whose climate Mr Cardwell sums up in the few words, "peculiarly fatal to the constitutions of European soldiers." Fortunately Sir Garnet Wolseley was not afraid of responsibility.

The reader is now in a position to appreciate the conditions under which Captain Glover and Sir Garnet Wolseley were despatched from home. The one, a volunteer, is sent in command of a roving expedition, with almost *carte blanche* as to his line and method of operations, so long as he acts against the flank and rear of the Ashantis, and almost without responsibility beyond such as he might owe to the Government that his acts represented a fair return for the money spent in their accomplishment. The other is called to effect a lasting peace with an enemy in possession of territory from which he must be driven—a peace, the terms of which are laid down beforehand—a peace which cannot be obtained except at the sword's point; while the sword itself is withheld, and will only be given if the Commander accept in full the responsibility of demanding it, under conditions which render that responsibility as heavy as mortal shoulders could well bear.

CHAPTER IV.

CONDITION OF AFFAIRS ON ARRIVAL OF SIR GARNET WOLSELEY—MEASURES ADOPTED UPON ARRIVAL — THE ACTION OF ESSAMAN, 14TH OCTOBER.

THOSE who remember the gloomy prophecies which preceded the departure from home of Sir Garnet Wolseley's expedition, the warnings of a climate fatal to European life, of death lurking in every breath of air and every cup of water in the African bush, will need no convincing that the little band of officers who sailed from Liverpool on the 12th September were not men likely to be easily discouraged; yet even they were dispirited and disgusted long before blue water was reached. Sent to sea in a ship whose berths were being painted twelve hours before they had to be slept in, through whose cabin-floors bilge-water oozed, which was absurdly underhanded for all purposes of attendance, was reeking with foul smells below, and flooded above owing to the absence of bulwarks—the passengers in the West African Company's steam-ship Ambriz were as miserable as they could be made. Far from laying in a stock of vigour and energy from the three weeks' voyage, one after another they complained that they were being poisoned; and the discomforts suffered in the Bay of Biscay are looked back upon now as exceeding any that the campaign itself induced.

Not till we reached Madeira was there any relief. That delightful day on shore will not soon be forgotten. The bright, fresh, cool air; the beautiful scenery; the ride round the lovely corral; the sleigh-slide down from the church; and not least of all, the creature comforts—the baskets of ripe purple figs and golden grapes; the clean white linen at dinner; the fresh fish, cool champagne, and sunny island wine; the baths (luxuries unknown to the Ambriz), will long remain as a memory of an oasis in a desert. Here, too, we learnt the disaster of the Prah, and the news of Commodore Commerell's wound. May it be confessed that, mingled with regret, was a dim belief that Providence had specially interfered to convince the authorities at home that the matter in hand was not that easy walk-over which, climate excepted, so many judged it to be; but was, as those who had studied the facts had long known, a serious and difficult military undertaking.

On the 27th September the Ambriz arrived at Sierra Leone, and Sir Garnet Wolseley assumed command of her Majesty's land forces in the West African settlements. The General and his staff were received and most hospitably entertained by Mr Berkeley, the Governor-in-Chief. Sierra Leone, "the white man's grave," disclosed a scene of quite unexpected beauty, and the view from the terrace of Government House surprised many to whom tropical scenery was familiar. But there was no time for gazing at the blue waters and the waving palms, for there was work to be done.

Sir Garnet Wolseley's instructions made it incumbent upon him to use every possible effort to accomplish his mission by the aid of native troops, and he had determined upon raising and .disciplining two regiments of natives, under command of the two senior special-service officers, Lieut.-Colonel Wood, and Major Baker Russell, to whose respective command the other officers were told off. For these regiments he was most anxious to obtain men from places other than those in the immediate neighbourhood of Cape Coast Castle, considering that such men, being removed from their homes, would be dependent upon him, and likely to remain at their posts; and that he would be thus more independent of the Fantis, and less at their mercy as regarded the supply of men.

It had accordingly been decided before landing, that Captain Furse of the 42d Highlanders, and Lieutenant Saunders, R.A., should be sent to Bathurst, on the river Gambia, for the purpose of raising a body of native Mohammedans from the Mandingo and Jollif tribes, and that Lieut. Gordon of the 93d Highlanders should remain at Sierra Leone and endeavour to raise men there. Every possible assistance was given by Mr Berkeley. He kindly placed the colonial steamer Sherboro at the disposal of Captain Furse to convey him to the Gambia and bring back recruits, and requested the Administrator to give him every assistance. The instructions given to these officers were to enlist men for six months, promising them a free conveyance back to Bathurst or Sierra Leone at the termination of that period. Pay and rations similar to those given to the West Indian regiments were promised, and an equipment of blanket, smock-frock, arms and ammunition, on arrival at Cape Coast Castle. Captain Furse was directed to enlist Mohammedans only, their superiority as fighting men being well known; but it was hoped that Lieut. Gordon would succeed at Sierra Leone in recruiting pensioners from the West Indian regiments, who would be valuable as drill-instructors. For these men pay and rations similar to those of the West Indian regiments would be granted, in addition to their pensions. Before many hours had passed, a proclamation had been issued, and these terms had been made known by criers throughout Sierra Leone.

There was another source from which it was hoped to obtain a considerable supply of native soldiers. The Kossoo tribe was known to be more than usually warlike; it had indeed more than once come into collision with our own authorities; and application was made through Mr Berkeley to Mr Loggie, C.M.G., the collector of customs at Sherboro, whose influence with the tribe was well known, requesting him to enlist, upon terms similar to those already described, as large a force as possible of these men. He was authorised to make payments to the chiefs, to engage head-men at a higher rate of pay, and to enlist interpreters; it being at the same time pointed out, that in order to be of any real service, the men must land at Cape Coast not later than the first week in November.

Captain Strahan, the newly appointed administrator at Lagos, had been a passenger on board the Ambriz; and it was now arranged in consultation with him and Mr Berkeley, that a detachment of 150 Houssas at Lagos should be sent to the Gold Coast, being relieved by a detachment of 75 of the 2d West Indian Regiment from Cape Coast. To the great regret of all our party Captain Strahan left us at Sierra Leone, and remained as Mr Berkeley's guest for a short time, before proceeding to take up his abode at Lagos in the Government House, which has been described by some cheerful writer as a "corrugated iron coffin, that contains a dead governor once every year."

During the time thus occupied at headquarters, a certain number of men had been enlisted either to act as soldiers or as soldier-servants to the officers; while Major Home, the Commanding Royal Engineer, had succeeded in obtaining a body of 33 artificers and 20 labourers; and this motley crew was now stowed away on deck. As it was known that more artificers could be obtained at Accra, Lieutenant Bolton, 1st West India Regiment, was placed under orders to proceed there immediately on arrival at Cape Coast, and to recruit them, provided Captain Glover had no objection. He was then to proceed to Winnebah, and enlist fighting men.

All these steps to recruit men having been taken, the Ambriz continued her voyage. After waiting a few hours at Monrovia, the capital of the republic of Liberia, that abortive effort to bestow the blessings of free government upon the negro, another halt was made at Cape Palmas, where Commissary O'Connor was landed with instructions to enlist Kroomen as carriers. Though permission was given to him to enlist fighting men also, it was not anticipated that he would succeed in obtaining any; for the character of the Krooman, or Krooboy as he is more commonly called, is too well known. Physically as strong as Hercules, magnificently proportioned, full of power of work, the Krooman loathes fighting. He likes the sea; in a surf-boat or a canoe he is happy; turn him into the water, he swims like a fish: but he is not fond of hard labour on land, and he hates the smell of powder. Mr O'Connor, however, was well known on the Coast, with which a residence of many years had made him familiar; and great things were hoped as to the number of carriers he would obtain.

The passage was now somewhat enlivened by watching the games of the natives on board. But whenever it came on to rain, and a succession of tornadoes swept over us, the misery of these poor wretches was extreme. Sick to death, without any shelter, they presented a pitiable spectacle; and they must have been no less rejoiced than were the remainder of the passengers when, on the early morning of the 2d October, the Ambriz dropped anchor in Cape Coast Roads.

The first view of the town destined to be our headquarters for many months, was not calculated to make a favourable impression. Officers familiar with the aspect of bombarded towns vowed that this must be Elmina, for it showed apparent signs of the ravages of shells and fire. Yet this was only the ordinary aspect of Fanti architecture under the effects of a rainy season. Crumbling mud-houses, interspersed here and there with a more pretentious whitewashed dwelling—a yellow surf-lashed shore—a quaint castellated building, thrust out close to the sea, and presenting that dreary aspect of salt-stained stucco familiar to the visitor of an inferior watering-place—a background of rounded rolling hills, devoid of forest-trees, but covered with low scrub,—such was the capital of the Gold Coast. Yet we hailed it as the Land of Promise.

Sir Garnet Wolseley did not land till late in the day. In the mean time he had received visits from Captain Fremantle, Colonel Festing, Deputy Surgeon-General

Home, and other officers, and had learnt something of the condition of affairs. In the course of the day, Lieut.-Colonel Wood and the officers told off to serve under him were despatched in a steam-pinnace to Elmina, while some of the staff landed, and made dispositions for the accommodation of the officers to be quartered at Cape Coast. A large house on a hill to the north of the town, known as Prospect House, was hired as quarters for Major Baker Russell and the officers under his command. The headquarter staff could be temporarily housed in Government House; and the artillery, engineers, control and medical officers in the Castle. In the afternoon Sir Garnet landed under the usual salutes, and was received at Government House by Colonel Harley. The ceremony of swearing-in was gone through; and in the evening the new Governor and the staff were entertained by Colonel Harley at a dinner, whose *menu* gave hopes of happy times to come.

It is important to understand the exact position of affairs at the date of Sir Garnet Wolseley's arrival on the Gold Coast. The Major-General had counted upon finding at his command a force of some 300 trained and disciplined Houssas, armed with Snider rifles; but they had all been taken away by Captain Glover to Accra. Instructions had been sent to Colonel Harley to place the Houssa police at Captain Glover's disposal; but that "while her Majesty's Government desire that all possible assistance should be afforded to Captain Glover in order that he may be enabled to proceed up the Volta without delay, the Houssas must of course not be withdrawn from any place, if, after conferring with the officer commanding the troops, you are satisfied that their removal would, at the particular moment when Captain Glover requires them, be attended with actual danger to the settlement." If troops were available for the purpose, the commanding officer was requested to give all the aid in his power to enable the Houssas to proceed on the Volta service, by the substitution of a military detachment, where Colonel Harley might concur in thinking this course desirable.

On the strength of these instructions, Colonel Harley had considered it his duty to send the Houssas away with Captain Glover to Accra; and the result was, that the only troops available in the neighbourhood of the main camp of the Ashanti army, were some detachments from the 2d West India Regiment, which, scarcely 700 strong, was employed in garrisoning the whole of our West African settlements,* together with a very small force of Fanti police, under command of Captain Thompson of the Queen's Bays. The detachment of the 2d West India Regiment at Cape Coast Castle was now further weakened by the despatch of fifty men to Lagos; and after deducting the garrisons of Sierra Leone, Axim, Dixcove, and Secondee, the numerous sick, and the men absolutely required for garrison duties and not available for the field, the entire force of which the Major-General could dispose at Elmina, Cape Coast, and the outposts, was under 400 strong. Scarcely a hundred effective bayonets could be counted upon for the defence of Cape Coast itself; while on the 4th October, Captain Thompson reported the number of armed police available at Cape Coast for general duty

* The 2d West India Regiment on the Gold Coast was distributed as follows: Cape Coast Castle, 150; Elmina, 170; Secondee, 25; Dixcove, 50; Axim, 48; Napoleon, 50; Abbaye, 100; Accroful, 50.

to be *ten,* the rest being mere recruits, or men detailed for civil work.

While this was the position, as regards men, the situation as regards officers was almost worse. Already from Sierra Leone Sir Garnet had written home requesting that 12 additional special-service officers might be sent out; and on arrival at Cape Coast, he again urgently demanded them, pointing out that there were only 13 officers available for duty with the West India Regiment. Fortunately, at the back of the Major-General there was always the fleet; and he knew from the first that he could rely upon Captain Fremantle. This officer, however, was much fettered by the instructions left behind by Commodore Commerell. He had been distinctly ordered that unless he should receive special orders from their lordships, no officers or men were to be landed for service on the coast, nor were they to proceed up any rivers unless absolutely necessary for the protection of British life and property; and he was urgently reminded that the loss of one human life from his forces would but very inadequately compensate for any amount of injury he might do to the savage natives. Captain Fremantle's orders were positive. It was impossible for him, until these orders should be modified, to take any part in offensive operations; but he at once promised his fullest support to the Major-General within the scope of his powers; and the latter was thus enabled to report to the Home Government on the 10th October that, small as the force at his command would be, he felt confident in the issue of the event should an attack be made upon him; and that he believed that not only might her Majesty's Government and subjects at Cape Coast Castle be protected, but that he could repulse the enemy with such loss as should produce a valuable moral effect in our favour.

Nor did it appear altogether unlikely that such an attack might be made. Rumours of this nature were rife. The Ashanti army, generally estimated as 40,000 strong, was known to be encamped at Mampon and Jooquah, four or five hours' march from Cape Coast or Elmina. Large reinforcements were reported as having crossed the Prah, and it was said that the Ashantis intended to attack Cape Coast Castle. On the 8th October, Captain Glover paid the captain of the mail-steamer Soudan £250 to leave Accra without waiting to load cargo, in order to carry immediately to Sir Garnet Wolseley the following report, made on the authority of an Aquapim chief, one Ababue of Adooma. An Ashanti deserter stated—so said this chief—that he had deserted about three weeks before, from the force sent down to reinforce the army in the Fanti country. This force comprised the whole remaining fighting men of Ashanti, leaving only a body-guard of 2000 men at Coomassie for the king. There was great commotion in Coomassie when he left, and, as far as he could learn, some great undertaking was on foot. The king himself desired to take the command of the troops proceeding to reinforce the army in Fanti, but the fetish priests pronounced it unlucky if the king went in person at that precise moment. The force which left on this occasion was estimated at 12,000 men, but must not be confounded with that which had been despatched about a fortnight previous under Adoo Boffoo, and which numbered at least 20,000. In the event of the contemplated attack on Cape Coast failing, nothing would remain but for the king to proceed in person to join his armies; but there would be no force worth speaking of in Coomassie for him to take along with him. The orders given to the commander of the Ashanti armies in Fanti were to the effect that he should not return home without the remains of the late King Quaku Duah—and that unless those remains were recovered, not a single man was to return; and there was no doubt that this order would be implicitly obeyed. Captain Glover gave the more credence to the statement, as it was known that the remains of the late King Quaku Duah had been carried about with their army by the Ashantis, and had fallen in the action of 5th June into the hands of the King of Denkera, by whom they had been sent to the house of his daughter at Cape Coast.

Circumstantial as this statement was, it raised no alarm at headquarters at Cape Coast; but in spite of the confidence which was seen there, the inhabitants of the town were in a chronic state of terror. The Ashanti army was, as a matter of fact, close by. The outposts at Napoleon and Abbaye conveyed to the native and civilian mind but little idea of protection. The incident of Colonel Harley's having left Government House and taken up his residence in the Castle, was construed into a confession that the town was unsafe; and even Sir Garnet Wolseley's reoccupation of the house did not set the native mind at rest. Even white men were not always free from panic; and it was a standing joke how one gentleman had presented himself at Government House with a report of an imminent invasion, and on being laughed at for his anxieties, had replied, "Oh! it's all very well for you fellows who live in a defensible house!" In short, Cape Coast was in a state of panic.

Under these circumstances it was evidently most important that something should be done to restore confidence; and yet it was clear that no operations could be undertaken on a large scale. First of all, there were not sufficient troops; and in the next place, supplies and arms were wanting for the armament of native levies, should they be found to enlist in any numbers. Although large quantities of supplies were on their road, the actual quantities in store at Cape Coast Castle were, as reported by the Deputy-Controller on the 4th October, only equal to four days' rations for the force of regular troops on the coast; and there were only 19 Snider rifles in the imperial stores, and 400 Enfield rifles in the colonial stores, together with a few Dutch rifles for which there was no ammunition. Application was immediately made by way of Madeira, whence telegraphic communication existed to Lisbon and England, for 500,000 lb. salt beef in small packages, in addition to the quantities already demanded.* Pending the arrival of supplies at Cape Coast, salt meat and biscuit were obtained from the ships of war in port; and the Gertrude store-ship, which arrived in port on the 6th with stores for Sir Garnet Wolseley and Captain Glover, was detained till 300 Snider rifles could be taken from Captain Glover's consignment, to replace those which he had taken away with the Houssas already referred to.

The steps taken to obtain men from the Gambia, Sherboro, Sierra Leone, Winnebah, and Lagos, have

* This telegram reached London on the 21st, and the requisition was immediately complied with. The cable between Madeira and Lisbon parted shortly afterwards, and no subsequent telegram was able to be sent from Madeira. But the Government at once sent out H.M.S. Vigilant to Madeira, to carry despatches to Lisbon, to be telegraphed thence to England.

been already described. It remains now to relate the efforts made to induce the Fanti tribes to furnish men for the protection of their own country.

On the 4th October, less than forty-eight hours after landing, Sir Garnet Wolseley held a reception of the kings and chiefs who had been previously summoned to meet him,—a *durbar*, as it would be called in India. A large marquee had been pitched on the terrace in front of Government House, and towards this wended the kings, in more or less tawdry finery, each preceded by his sword-bearer and cane-bearer, and followed by a motley suite. Conspicuous among them was Amfoo Ottoo, the King of Abrah, whose stature of some inches over six feet well became his strong frame and not unhandsome face. This one with a half cocoa-nut, partly gilt or tinselled, on his head, and the bloodshot eyes, is Quasi Kaye, the King of Denkera; and the young, pleasant-looking man on whom his majesty of Denkera somewhat unsteadily leans, is Ammono, King of Annamaboe. The elderly, rather gentlemanly-looking personage is Ed-doo, King of Mankessim, said to be the first station of the Fanti tribes when they reached the coast,—the puppet put up by the movers of the Fanti Confederation, and the king who set the first example of flight at Dunquah in the preceding June. The handsome, curled and combed monarch, is Chibboo, one of the two kings of Assin. His fellow-monarch, Inkie, is not here to-day. The face under the frill of white hair, singularly reminding one of the animal known as a "ruffed lemur," belongs to King Solomon of Domonassie. The red coat covers the body of no less a person than Mr Bentil, "Field-Marshal" of Goomoah. Attah, the leading chief of Cape Coast, soon destined to obtain the unenviable reputation of being the greatest coward of all the Fantis, is here in native apparel; and other Cape Coast chiefs, Thompson, Robertson, and the rest, in the disfiguring European dress of tail-coats, waistcoats, and trousers. Other and lesser chiefs it is not necessary to particularise.

After the ceremony of presentation and hand-shaking had been gone through, the Major-General, surrounded by his staff, the officials, and officers of the garrison, addressed the assembled kings to the following effect :—

"I am very glad to meet so many kings and chiefs who are loyal allies of the English nation. Her Majesty the Queen, having been informed of the injuries that have been inflicted upon her allies in this part of the world by the Ashantis, who without any just cause have invaded your country, and having learnt that you were unable to repulse your enemies without assistance, has sent me to unite in one person the chief military and civil administration, so that as a general officer I may be able to help you. The Queen is most anxious to assist you; and I am desired to tell you that she will give orders to have carried out whatever measures I may consider necessary, after I have conferred with you all, for prosecuting the war against the Ashantis. Before I can form any opinion on the subject, it is absolutely necessary that I should learn from you what you can, and what you are prepared to do. I can assure you that if you place all your available resources at my disposal, and are loyally determined to fight your hereditary enemies now, I will guarantee to you that I, with God's assistance, shall drive them out of your territory, and that I will inflict such a terrible punishment upon them, that for all time to come you can have nothing to dread from them. My intention is to chase them out of your country, and, if necessary, to pursue them into Ashanti territory. It is for you, therefore, to consider to-day among yourselves, so as to give me information without delay of what you are prepared to do. Her Majesty cannot help those who will not help themselves, and unless you are determined to unite together cordially in your own defence, and are fully prepared to make every necessary sacrifice for the prosecution of the war, I tell you frankly that you must not look to the Queen for any assistance whatever. The only interest that her Majesty has here is to secure your happiness by spreading amongst you the blessings of peace and civilisation. This war is not her Majesty's war, but is your war. You must remember that the Ashantis declared in 1863 and 1864, when these troubles began, that their quarrel was with you, and not with the English. Since then no peace has ever been formally made with the King of Coomassie. The forts that are occupied along the coasts by her Majesty's troops are so strong that we can laugh at all attempts that may be made by any one to capture them. Her Majesty might therefore, if she consulted her own interests, without any regard to the interests of the kings and chiefs of the surrounding peoples who are allied to her, content herself by keeping her troops within the forts. But she feels that to do so would result in your destruction; and she is therefore most anxious to assist you with advice, with able and selected officers, with ammunition, and with supplies of food, to enable you to punish those who have ravaged your country. I want to know from you how many fighting men you can furnish, and the date that you will have them at Dunquah. You must yourselves accompany your men, and remain with them whilst the operations last. I propose to give to each of you kings a subsidy of £10 per month for every 1000 fighting men you furnish, to supply you with ammunition; and when the supplies of food, shortly expected here from England, arrive, I propose to issue daily at Cape Coast Castle provisions upon the following scale for all the fighting men you supply —viz., a pint of rice and ¼ lb. of salt meat daily for each fighting man. Until those provisions arrive, I propose to issue to you in lieu thereof 4½d. a-day for each fighting man; and, in order to impress upon you the earnestness of her Majesty's desire to help you, I propose to issue to each fighting man, through the chiefs recognised by the kings, a daily pay of 3d. a-day whilst their services are made use of in the field. I shall send with each king an English officer, through whom all payments and issues of stores will be made. He will be my representative with each of you, and will advise you upon all points. In telling you this, I must add that you must obey the orders I send to you, and that these will be conveyed to you through the officer I send to each of you. If my propositions are met by you in the cordial manner that I anticipate, it is necessary that you should clearly understand that although I am prepared to act in her Majesty's name most liberally to you, I shall also be prepared to enforce in the most stringent manner the terms of our agreement, punishing severely all those who may be guilty of disobedience or of unmanly conduct. When once you take the field I cannot listen to any excuses about your being unable to enforce your orders upon your own people; you must exert your authority, and I will support you in doing so. War can only be made successfully when the general's orders are strictly and promptly carried out; and I have to impress upon you most emphatically that I shall not fail to enforce the orders that I may issue. When I am in a position to issue daily rations to you, you must, without reducing your force in the field, make your own arrangements for the conveyance of the supplies from this place to the field army, wherever it may happen to be, as I cannot undertake to carry for you either ammunition or provisions. Her Majesty has been grieved to learn that you still continue to follow the barbarous practices of your enemies, and are still in the habit of killing your prisoners and mutilating your dead enemies. Brave men in civilised nations never do so, and I have to urge upon you the necessity for putting a stop to these practices. My time is so fully occupied that I have no leisure for frequent interviews with you; I have therefore to request an early reply to what I have said to you. I shall be happy to see you all when peace has been secured, and to listen to all you have to say regarding your private affairs. Until that happy time has arrived, let us all bend our thoughts upon the prosecution of this war that has been unjustly forced upon you by the Ashantis."

It will be seen that this address was strictly framed upon the instructions issued by Lord Kimberley, and quoted in the last chapter. The rates of payment were based upon the advice which the Major-General received as to the market value of labour and price of provisions.

The durbar being over, a present of gin, according to custom, was made to the kings and chiefs; and they retired to consult together, with instructions to return on the 6th. During the interval, hints were thrown out to the Governor that the pay offered was not enough, that the chiefs wanted more money, and that their men would rather act as commissariat-carriers at a shilling a-day than as soldiers at sevenpence half-penny. So far as could be judged, it was intended to view the matter as a mercantile transaction. But on the 6th, when a second reception was held, the kings and chiefs as a body expressed their willingness to comply with the terms offered, and their readiness to proceed to collect their men. Only in one or two cases the native character showed itself — the cloven foot peeped out. King Quasi Kaye wanted to send a captain to collect his men instead of going himself; and when he was told he must go himself, he said that if he must he would, and would cut off the head of any of his men who refused to turn out. Warned that he must not do this, he laughed; but months afterwards, when his men deserted, and he was severely spoken to, he complained that he could only make his men turn out like the Ashantis if the same power were allowed to him as to the Ashanti chiefs—the power of life and death over his people. In almost every case the laziness inherent in the West African showed forth. Not one king said, "I will start to-day;" scarcely one, "I will start to-morrow." Each and all they begged for delay, and the Cape Coast chiefs claimed the disgraceful privilege to be the last to turn out into the field.

In one respect the kings were unanimous. They begged for the services of English officers to assist them in collecting their men, acknowledging tacitly that which others had pronounced to be the case, that their power over their people was not otherwise sufficient for the purpose. Their wish was acceded to, and the promise was made that an officer should be attached to each king to act as the representative of the Major-General, and to aid the king in enforcing his commands. The necessity of keeping faith was impressed upon those present; and they dispersed to proceed leisurely to the appointed posts. Denkera and Assin being in the hands of the enemy, the kings of those provinces gave rendezvous at Domonassie; and the list of officers appointed special commissioners to the native kings stood as under. It will be seen that the Major-General was obliged to apply to the senior naval officer for officers for this duty, as well as to take others from the 2d West India Regiment and the Royal Marines. Each of these officers was granted the special-service allowance of a guinea a-day :—

Bt.-Major Lazenby,*	100th Regt.	to King	Eddoo	at Mankessim.
Capt. Godwin,	103d	,,	Ammono	,, Annamaboe.
,, Bromhead,	24th	,,	{ Chibboo of E. Assin }	,, Domonassie.
Sub-Lieut. Filliter,	2d W.I.	,,	Solomon	,, ,,
Lieut. Hearle,	R.M.L.T.	,,	{ Quasi Kaye of Denkera }	,, ,,
Lieut. Pollard,	R.N.	,,	{ Amfoo Ottoo of Abra }	,, Dunquah.
Sub-Lieut. Cochrane,	R.N.	,,	Quasi Ancasia	,, Assayboo.
Sub-Lieut. Lang,	R.N.	,,	Assano	,, Yamolanza.
Lieut. Graves,	{ 18th Ryl. Irish Rgt. }	,,	Akinny	,, Acoomfie.

Some of the kings on whose co-operation the Major-General counted, had not appeared. To these—viz., Kings Tando of Goomoah, Yadadoo of Insabah, Apecoon of Essecooma, Moquah of Adjumacoe, Inkie of

* This appointment of Brigade-Major held by this officer was abolished on the arrival of the Major-General and headquarter staff.

W. Assin, Queen Amoquah and King Quabina Fuah of Western Akim—letters were addressed, calling upon them to assemble their men at Dunquah, at which place all the kings present at the durbar had been ordered to assemble their troops.

Lieutenant Gordon of the 98th was informed of the intention to form a camp at Dunquah, and was ordered to retain the houses at that place for regular troops, and to tell off a camping ground for each native king and chief, on which their men could hut themselves on arrival. On the 5th, the Major-General had abolished this officer's appointment as adjutant of police, and taken him on the list of special-service officers.

Captain Thompson of the Queen's Bays, being anxious to take back to Dixcove a detachment of police to whom he had promised release from service at this date, and a free passage home, the opportunity was taken of endeavouring to obtain recruits for the native regiments about to be formed. Captain Thompson was instructed to proceed to Dixcove, and thence, at his own suggestion, into the Wassaw country, the senior naval officer having placed H.M.S. Merlin at his disposal for the purpose. He was directed to communicate with the kings of Wassaw, and urge on them the necessity of combining to strike a blow at the Ashantis. He was to tell them all the steps being taken by the Major-General, and to urge upon them to collect their forces, and march in the direction of Prahsu, sending 200 men to be trained and disciplined in a native regiment, and to form part of his Excellency's body-guard. Captain Thompson was further instructed to use every endeavour to communicate with the Gamans, that formidable tribe, containing many Mohammedans, which lies to the north-west of Ashanti, and had so often been engaged in war with that power.

Before proceeding to narrate the results of the various missions to the native kings, and to the coast tribes previously named, it will be well to mention some of the other points which had engaged the attention of the commander of the expedition.

One evident difficulty would lie in the landing and storage of supplies and stores. The ships arriving from England would have to lie nearly a mile from the shore, and everything must be landed in surf-boats, which were supplied in small numbers by a contractor, at an excessively high price. It was therefore decided to establish a boat-service, independent of contract, as soon as Kroomen should arrive. The want of storage room was great; and considerable confusion existed, chiefly amongst the warlike stores, owing to the want of accommodation, and to the fact that the control officers had been constantly moved. The officer in charge at Cape Coast had less than two years' service, and had only just arrived to replace the experienced officer sent to join Captain Glover's expedition. Huts were immediately erected by the engineers. It was reported on the 7th, that three large double huts had already been put up. Major Home's difficulties commenced early. His Sierra Leone artificers and labourers were lazy, and he had felt obliged to make an example by flogging one of them for refusing to work, on the beach, within a few hours of landing.

A corps of native carriers was found already established, consisting of 2 superintendents, 26 head-men, and 631 carriers. They were paid at the rate of a shilling a-day, and it was hoped that they would soon be augmented by a large body of Kroomen from Cape Palmas.

Another point requiring attention was postal communication with the outposts. A line of police-runners was immediately formed, and a headquarter military post-office established. Runners were posted at the different stations, and at intervals of about six miles apart on the main road. Assistant postmasters were appointed at the several outposts, with orders to report daily to headquarters. "Time-slips" were given to each runner, on which the hours of departure and arrival at each place were noted by the postmaster; and fines were instituted to insure regularity in the transit of letters.

In the face of the persistent rumours of contemplated attack, it was necessary to take steps for the immediate defence of Cape Coast Castle and the town. Lieutenant-Colonel Festing was placed in command of the troops at Cape Coast and its immediate vicinity, and was charged with the responsibility for local defence. He proposed a system of defence by the occupation and strengthening of the small hills surrounding the town, and by clearing the bush in the valleys: the plan included the landing of the Royal Marines and bluejackets, with rifled guns and rockets from the ships of the fleet. The senior naval officer gave his cordial promise of support in case of necessity; signals were arranged for day and night; and it was fervently hoped that their evil genius might tempt the Ashantis to run their head against our shelter-trenches, and the guns, rockets, and Sniders. The detachment of the 2d West India Regiment was removed from the Castle and encamped on Connor's Hill, a fine healthy spot, the highest in the neighbourhood; and a picket was established on the hill where Prospect House stands, overlooking the country to the north.

Lieut.-Colonel Evelyn Wood also prepared a scheme for the defence of Elmina.

In view of the probable large increase of European residents at Cape Coast, sanitary measures claimed a large share of attention. The sanitary committee for the town had ceased to exist, or at all events to exercise its functions. "It is impossible," wrote the Major-General on the 7th, "to describe the foul stench which arose from the exposed heaps of ordure at the edges of the town, more especially those close to the ponds from which the natives draw their supplies of water by the side of the road to Dunquah." From the ditch known as the Cape Coast river running through the town, from a foul stagnant pond in the town, also arose smells of the most nauseous description. It was scarcely possible to walk a hundred yards from Government House without being sickened. The filthy habits of the natives, whom no idea of decency restrained from making the streets the receptacle for their filth, and whom no considerations of health kept from polluting the water which they must themselves use, rendered the town, its environs, and the beach, one vast open cesspit. The ordure-heaps were now buried; an attempt at surface-drainage was introduced; a sanitary committee, consisting of the principal medical officer, a D. A. Q. M. G., and the colonial surveyor, was formed, and ordered to report. Its report was a satire. Short of turning the Sweet River, five miles distant, through the town, nothing satisfactory could be done; but a standing sanitary committee was appointed, some ordinary precautionary measures were adopted, and stringently enforced by the police. Latrines were established for the natives, and the bush immediately surrounding the town was cleared away and burnt when dry.

Perhaps no more curious illustration of the slumber in which the Gold Coast ordinarily lies buried could be found, than the fact that, although for many long years it had been garrisoned by her Majesty's troops, although a military expedition had been sent to the Prah, and encamped there for months, no one had ever surveyed a yard of the country. The only maps existing were in the old works of Bowdich, Hutton, &c., and their distances were computed solely by judging from the time taken in travelling by hammock—a most uncertain method. This had to be remedied; and the survey department was placed in the hands of Captain Huyshe, Rifle Brigade, Deputy-Assistant Quartermaster-General. On the second day after his arrival he left Cape Coast for the most advanced post on the Prah road, and made a road-sketch and military sketches of the positions of Accroful and Dunquah. Lieut. Hart, 31st Regt., was detailed to assist Captain Huyshe, and surveyed the greater portion of the country about Cape Coast. A general order was issued requesting officers commanding stations to encourage their officers to make surveys in the vicinity of their respective posts, but not to incur unnecessary exposure. A scale of 2 inches to a mile was decided on for road-sketches, and 4 inches for positions. Officers from Elmina surveyed the country between Elmina, Abbaye, and the Sweet River in the direction of Cape Coast.

When the Major-General arrived, the most advanced

post was occupied by men of the armed police, who were independent of the military authorities. The inspector-general of police was now informed that all men of the armed police, when employed in the field, were in future to be considered as a portion of the military force in the command, and that all reports relating to them were to be made to the military authorities. Captain Thompson was also instructed not to form new posts, or strengthen or diminish those already existing, without orders from headquarters. In proof of the necessity of combined military and civil command, it may be remarked that, had the Major-General not been invested with authority as civil governor, he would in his military capacity only have had no authority over the armed police, on whom, in the absence of any sufficient body of troops, he was now obliged largely to depend.

By the exertions of Lieut. Gordon a road reported as practicable for artillery had been made as far as Dunquah; and a few days after Sir Garnet's arrival that officer pushed on to Yancoomassie with a party of 50 men, of whom 15 were armed police and the remainder native volunteers from Cape Coast, in order to protect the head of the road, which the Major-General was anxious to advance as far as possible, consistently with reasonable chance of safety. At the end of the first week in October, the outposts established were as follow :—

1. At Abbaye, some 5 miles north of Elmina, a detachment of 2 officers, 100 non-commissioned officers and men of the 2d West India Regiment, and 125 volunteer natives of Cape Coast.

2. At Napoleon, about 6 miles south-east of Abbaye and about $4\frac{3}{4}$ miles from Cape Coast on the Abbaye

road, 1 officer and 48 non-commissioned officers and men of the 2d West India Regiment.

3. At Accroful, on the Dunquah road, about 15 miles north-east of Cape Coast, 1 officer and 49 non-commissioned officers and men of the 2d West India Regiment.

4. At Yancoomassie and Dunquah, Lieutenant Gordon's party as above related.

These detached posts were placed in communication with each other, and were furnished with a week's supplies. They were all intrenched posts, and the officers commanding had orders to protect themselves by patrols.

Captain Huyshe's road-report did not quite bear out that previously made as to the condition of the road to Yancoomassie. For example, one stream was reported as being fifty yards wide and hip-deep; and accordingly the Major-General directed the commanding engineer to commence work at the earliest possible date, to improve the road already constructed, and to open it up as far as possible in the direction of the Prah. Engineer officers and men were expected by the first mail from England, and in the mean time it was hoped, and the results justified the hope, that such an amount of hut accommodation might be erected at Cape Coast as would admit of the engineer artificers and labourers being removed for employment on the road.

The description above given sufficiently indicates the condition of affairs at Cape Coast, and the steps first taken. So far as defence was concerned, the cordon of posts established from Abbaye to Dunquah, and the measures taken to defend Elmina and Cape Coast, were sufficient. It was never doubted that any fortified post, held by disciplined troops armed with breech-loading rifles, could withstand for an indefinite time the attack of any body of badly-armed savages. So far as regards offence, no steps had yet been taken beyond the attempts to collect men, and the advance of our parties along the main road as far as Yancoomassie, threatening indirectly the Ashanti army's communications with Prahsu. But, as already said, a purely defensive attitude did not breed confidence; and it was vitally important to take some step which should show that the English were in earnest, and inspire some courage into the half-hearted Fanti tribes. If this movement could, at the same time, be of military as well as moral value, the gain would be great indeed. Such an operation was very soon undertaken.

Captain Buller, 60th Rifles, D.A.Q.M.G., had been placed in charge of the Intelligence Department of the expedition, and had, from the beginning, shown a skill and judgment worthy of a trained detective. The information existing as to the enemy's positions and plans was very vague. The Administrator himself could not lay his finger on the map with any certainty and say, "Here is Mampon, or here is Jooquah." The distance of Abbaye from the Ashanti camp was greatly underestimated; the numbers of the enemy were but dimly known; no machinery existed for obtaining information; in short, an intelligence department had to be created. Captain Buller at once set to work. He commenced forming a corps of interpreters for service at headquarters, and with the officers employed as commissioners to native kings. He placed himself in communication with all those persons known to have at any time afforded trustworthy information from the traders coming coastward from the interior. By bribes, by promises, and by threats gently administered, he succeeded in learning something from disaffected Elminas. He examined all the Ashanti prisoners previously in captivity or brought in from our outposts; and he set to work to obtain spies from among the Elminas, and from the Assins, the only people capable of speaking Ashanti without betraying themselves as strangers.

Early in October Captain Buller reported: "Great endeavours have been made to obtain trustworthy spies and scouts. At Elmina, two women and a boy have brought some valuable information, and one bold and apparently trustworthy Assin has been of use in the eastern district. Pressure having been put upon the Fanti chiefs, they have sent out numerous scouts in their own districts; but the information thus obtained is for the most part not to be relied upon.

"Many escaped prisoners of the Ashantis have come in, but the information to be obtained from them is most meagre; the constant fear of death under which they have lived seeming to have frightened all memory out of them. No offers, either of gold to the poor, place to the ambitious, or freedom to the prisoners, can induce any one to approach the Ashanti camp, such a step being regarded as certain death."

The general tenor of the information obtained was to this effect: 40,000 Ashantis, under command of Amonquatia, were said to be encamped at Mampon and Jooquah. Dysentery was prevailing in their camp. Reports differed as to their future intentions. They were said to be meditating retreat across the Prah, having cut a new road through the bush to the Prah road, above Mansu. It was asserted that the detachment in Apollonia had received orders to retire also. But, on the other hand, repeated reports reached headquarters of an intended attack on Cape Coast Castle; and Captain Glover's information was, as we have seen, to the same effect.

One thing, however, was quite certain in the midst of other conflicting rumours. The Ashantis were short of supplies of food, and were drawing most of that which they had from Elmina and the sea-coast villages to windward. The villages of Ampenee and Amquana on the coast supplied food, chiefly fish; and the line of communication with them lay through Essaman, through which place also and Saltpond, supplies were derived from Elmina itself.

As early as the 6th, the Major-General had written to Lieutenant-Colonel Wood that he heard Boitoo, one of the Elmina captains, was in the Ashanti camp at Mampon, and was in the habit of getting soap, cloth, tobacco, and other articles for the Ashantis from Elmina and Cape Coast. Their road lying through the villages already named as the sources of supply to the camp, Sir Garnet thought of destroying those villages, but first desired Colonel Wood to send to their chiefs, summoning them to see him, and telling them that if they did not stop the traffic with the Ashantis' camp, he should destroy their villages.

Colonel Wood had accordingly sent letters to the chiefs of these villages. They not only refused to come in, but sent insulting answers; and it leaked out that the Ashantis had promised their protection to the inhabitants, in case the white men should attack them, saying that they were more courageous than the white men, who would not dare to advance into the bush. A considerable number of Ashantis were sent to reinforce these villages, and Amonquatia himself was said to have moved nearer to Essaman. Nay, more, the Ashantis talked in their camp of attacking Elmina, by way of Saltpond, where they met in large bodies for trade every evening. English officers could not go out for any distance from Elmina without being insulted and threatened with attack.

Under these circumstances, Sir Garnet decided to attack and destroy the villages of Essaman, Amquana, and Ampenee, hoping thereby not only to check the supply of food to the camp at Mampon, but by gaining a success in the bush, to instil some courage into the Fanti tribes. Success must be assured beforehand, as any check would be fatal. The Ashantis were in such force at Mampon, and the numbers at Sir Garnet's disposal were so small, that success could not be insured, if the designed attack should reach the enemy's ears. Everything known in Cape Coast reached the enemy within a few hours; and therefore it became vitally important to keep the planned operation secret.

On the 10th, a detachment of 138 Houssa recruits arrived from Lagos in H.M.S. Bittern. They were armed at once with Sniders taken from the Gertrude; and on the 11th, Sir Garnet and his staff went on board the Bittern, and accompanied the Houssas to Elmina, a report having been allowed to spread that Colonel Wood expected to be attacked. The Snider was a new arm to the Houssas, and the two hours' voyage was passed by the staff in teaching the men how to load and fire. It was a trying task, for the ship rolled more than most of us had conceived possible; and the smell of Rangoon oil was, under the circumstances, disturbing. But the men showed remarkable aptitude. Landing at Elmina, Sir Garnet told Colonel Wood in secrecy his plan of operations, and returned in the evening to Cape Coast. The Houssas were left at Elmina.

On the 12th, the Major-General went on board H.M.S. Barracouta, under pretext of returning the senior naval officer's official visit, and confided to Captain Fremantle his intentions, inviting assistance. Captain Fremantle had on the 10th received instructions from home, which to a certain extent freed him from his previous fettering orders, and allowed him to act on his own responsibility; and now, as on every occasion when he was called upon, he promised his most hearty co-operation. On the same day, the Major-General announced that he had received bad news from the Volta, that Captain Glover, at Addah, was in danger of being surrounded, and that he should move a force to his aid. Throughout the 12th and 13th this news spread, and was firmly believed by all except the very few whom it had been absolutely necessary for Sir Garnet to take into his confidence. Many of his own staff were as completely deceived as the outside public.

On Monday the 13th, at 6 P.M., the detachment of the 2d W.I. Regiment at Cape Coast was embarked on board H.M.S. Decoy, expecting to sail for Accra. At 10 P.M. Sir Garnet and several officers of his staff embarked in the Barracouta. A naval officer and 40 blue-jackets were landed as a guard for Cape Coast Castle, and arrangements were made for an officer and 20 blue-jackets to garrison Elmina during the absence of the troops. It had been arranged that 150 of the Royal Marines should take part in the operation, together with 20 blue-jackets in charge of a 7-pounder rifled gun with 60 rounds of ammunition, and a rocket-trough with 36 rockets. At 2 P.M. Assistant-Commissary Beardmore had left for Elmina by road with 250 labourers, stores, and cots; but Lieutenant-Colonel Wood made no preparations at Elmina till after the drawbridge of the fort was raised at night, so that complete secrecy was preserved. He, too, had given out the news of Sir Garnet's intended departure to relieve Captain Glover at Addah, and his probable absence for three or four days. During the night he posted a cordon of police round Elmina, so as to prevent egress from the town after the movement of troops should become evident in the early morning.

The Barracouta and the Decoy started soon after midnight, and the embarkation from the ships into boats off Elmina commenced at 3 A.M., at which hour the Major-General and Captain Fremantle landed in the Barracouta's gig. There was, however, great delay in landing the troops. Four paddle-box boats were towed in by one steam-launch. There was only one officer to superintend the whole; and, quick and active as he was, much difficulty was experienced. He did not know the landing: high tide had been expected; it was almost low water. The result was that we all grounded on the bar, were wet through by the heavy rollers, and nearly swamped. The boat containing Captain Buller, the writer, and Mr Winwood Reade, the 'Times' correspondent, was one hour and fifty minutes in her passage from the ship to the landing-place. Thus the march was much delayed. Four o'clock had been named for departure; but the advanced-guard could not move off till 4.30, and the main body not till a quarter past five.

The actual order of march was as follows, the whole operation being under the command of Lieutenant-Colonel Wood, and the Major-General accompanying it, not to take command or interfere in the arrangements, but to make it plain to the natives that he had come out not merely to administer the government, but as a general officer to command her Majesty's troops and personally to take part in all military operations :—

126 Houssas, under Lieutenant Richmond.
16 2d W.I. Regiment, under Lieutenant Eyre.
29 Blue-jackets, under Captain Fremantle, R.N.
1 7-pounder gun and ammunition, carried first by naval Kroomen, and later in the day by carriers.
1 Rocket-tube and rockets.
30 Labourers with axes, under Capt. Buller, D.A.Q.M.G.
20 Royal Marine Artillery, under Lieutenant Allen, R.M.A.
129 Royal Marine Light Infantry, under Captain Crease, R.M.A.
60 Labourers with reserve ammunition and hammocks, under Assistant-Commissary Beardmore.
124 2d W.I. Regiment, }
210 Labourers, } Capt. Forbes, 2d W.I. Regt.
65 2d W.I. Regiment, }

The column was accompanied by chiefs Esservie and Andooa, and twenty Elminas who acted as guides.

The Houssas marched away from the column at starting, and did not occupy the small village of Embofra Akinnum, about a mile and a half from Elmina, though halting for some time in full view of it. It is therefore probable that, even if no information had previously been sent to Essaman, news of our movement was sent on from this village, which was subsequently burnt by Chief Esservie's men. After the Houssas were caught up, the column proceeded at a fair pace. The track led through a swamp, knee-deep for about eighty yards, and later through a very narrow bush path, with high thick jungle on each side.

After a halt about 2000 yards from a hill behind which Essaman was said to lie, the Houssas were met by the enemy's scouts at a point where the path runs through very dense bush. One Houssa must have been almost touched by the muzzle of the gun which wounded him mortally. The Houssas commenced immediately a violent fire. When in a few minutes the Major-General reached the front, they were firing wildly into the bush and into the air. An alarm was raised that the enemy was in the bush on our right, and a few marines were sent in to skirmish. New to the work, they showed great excitement, and fired wildly also; but a cool word from an officer seemed to exercise a calming effect on every individual almost immediately. The bush on our right was too dense for them to penetrate into it for any distance.

The Houssas were now continuing their wild firing into a mass of high grass on the left of the path from a comparatively open place on the brow of a small hill. On the top of this hill the path bent to the right, and ran in a sort of cutting to the village of Essaman, about 200 yards off. On the right front, some 300 yards off, was a high wooded hill, on which some Ashantis were visible. The guns and rockets were now up, but did not yet come into action. The Houssas began to get out of hand, but Lieutenant Richmond got them together, and brought a number of them down into the path. Even here they fired into the bush on both sides, and it was most dangerous to enter it, while the marines also became influenced by their excitement.

Captain Buller had pushed on down the path, and saw into the village. A number of armed men were there, and a war-drum was being beaten. Finding a clear space to the left of the path, Captain Fremantle brought the gun and rockets up to it; but the absence of a key to unscrew the plug in the shell caused considerable delay in opening fire with the gun. Colonel M'Neill at the same time took some men into the bush to the left, and began working round the flank of the village. A heavy fire was opened by the enemy; Captain Fremantle was shot through the arm; a slug penetrated the leather case of Captain Buller's prismatic compass, and broke the vane; Colonel M'Neill was badly wounded in the arm, and Captain Buller took his place.

The first of the rockets fired had turned round in the bush, but they were now making good practice into the village, as was also the gun with common shells. The troops were all very excited. The noise of the first rocket caused two marines standing close beside the writer to discharge their rifles simultaneously;—a remonstrance bringing the reply from one of them, "I thought it was a lot on 'em charging at me through the bush."

The slugs, and apparently bullets, were cutting the leaves from the trees beside the path, and it seemed necessary to clear the dense bush on the right. Accordingly Captain Crease took some marines into the bush; and as it was evident that in such a dense thicket one officer could not control many men, the Major-General sent the Hon. A. Charteris and the writer with them. We had to cut our way with our sword-bayonets to the edge of the clearing. Captain Crease led some men to clear the hill on the right, and protect our flank, leaving the two staff officers to enter the village with the remainder, which we did, while heavy firing was still going on from the houses on the left. We found the village deserted, got the rocket-fire stopped, pushed on to the far end, and posted a guard. Breaking open the houses, in one of them we saw a small child, whom we left, but whom Captain Crease afterwards took, and saved from being burnt, for the village was soon in flames.*

Meanwhile the usual Ashanti tactics had been employed, and a body of the enemy had tried to turn the left of the West India Regiment, still on the brow of the hill, where the Houssas had first been met. In this attack three of the carriers were hit; whereupon they all put down their loads and bolted under cover, but returned as soon as the enemy was repulsed. The West India troops themselves were to some extent demoralised for a moment, and Lieut.-Colonel Wood and Major Baker were engaged in restoring order. When this attack was repulsed, the West Indians advanced on the village by a road cut by the axemen on the left.

At half-past eight the assembly was sounded, and the troops, who had all one day's cooked rations, halted for an hour and a quarter. During the halt some uneasiness was caused by the sound of war-drums, but it proved to be only the beating of two which had been captured in the village by our troops. It was quite impossible to estimate the enemy's strength or his loss.

* This child was taken care of by Captain Crease, and subsequently restored to its mother, who claimed it some weeks later. Great care had to be taken to make her prove her ownership, for the value of a child as a slave would be quite sufficient to induce a fraudulent claim to be set up.

The bush was denser than in any subsequent action; and very few bodies were found.

At 9.45 the column marched off for Amquana, which it reached at 12.20. It was found deserted, and we set it on fire. The march was intensely fatiguing. The thick bush shut out every breath of air, and there were no forest-trees to give shade. The path was rugged, and the way seemed never-ending. Then for the first time we learnt the terrible strain of performing staff duties on foot in such a climate, yet no one would give in. Lieutenant Eyre, who had volunteered to act with his detachment as a flanking-party, struggled on till he dropped with exhaustion, but nothing would induce him to be carried.

We halted on the beach at Amquana. The wounded were sent back to Elmina under an escort of men pronounced too much exhausted to continue the march. At two o'clock a detachment of 150 West Indians, the Houssas, 12 blue-jackets with rockets, and 20 marines (volunteers under Captain Crease), marched for Akimfoo, along the beach. The rest of the marines remained halted at Amquana. Half-way we were met by the men of H.M. ships Argus and Decoy, and a short halt was allowed, during which water and biscuit, that Captain Luxmoore and Lieutenant Hext had brought on shore, were given to the men. We reached Akimfoo at 3.50, found the village deserted, and burnt it. Half a mile further on we reached Ampenee; this village also was found deserted and burnt, the rats running by hundreds from the flaming houses.

And now fire was opened from the bush beyond the village, to which the marines and blue-jackets replied from the edge of the bush. The troops were formed up on the beach; the freshly landed sailors were very anxious to attack, but it was far too late. The Major-General ordered the assembly to be sounded, embarked on board H.M.S. Decoy, and steamed for Cape Coast Castle. The troops remained to cover the embarkation of the men of the Argus and Decoy, and the West Indians opened fire on a detachment of the enemy who showed in the bush to the east of the village. At 5.20 the last troops marched off, and, picking up the marines at Amquana, reached Elmina at 8 P.M.

The distances marched were estimated by the staff officer, who traversed the road as we marched, as follows:—

Elmina to Essaman,	$3\frac{1}{2}$ miles.
Essaman to Amquana,	4 ,,
Amquana to Ampenee,	$4\frac{1}{2}$,,
Ampenee to Elmina,	9 ,,
Total,	21 ,,

The white troops, officers, sailors, and marines, had been up all night, and had marched, many of them, 21 miles under a burning sun. Yet there were only two cases of sunstroke, one dangerous, and only four men were admitted to hospital on the following day with slight complaints. On the 16th, the principal medical officer reported: "The occasion has shown that Europeans are quite equal to one very arduous day's work in the bush, and that marches of half the distance could be easily borne by them. Of course it is premature to speak of the possible as yet undeveloped effects of the day's exertion on them. Great difficulty was experienced in arranging for the presence of cots for the wounded just where they were wanted. The supply of water was insufficient." Yet every man had started with his water-bottle full, and two breakers of water had been carried by Kroomen. Unfortunately, the only water met on the march had been in pools on low ground, quite unfit for drinking. The men had been prevented from drinking it, and many were six hours without water. Alike for officers and men, the supply brought to the beach from the ships had been a great and unlooked-for relief.

This action has been described at greater length than the numbers engaged may seem to warrant; but it has a special interest. It was the first attempt made to seek out the enemy in his own position, and there attack him; and it taught many important lessons. What those lessons were may be described in the words of Sir Garnet's despatch to the Secretary of State for War :—

"But no less important is the lesson I have myself learnt from this affair. I have been shown how little reliance can be placed on even the best native troops in this bush-fighting, where it is impossible to keep them under the immediate control of European officers.

"The Houssas showed undeniable courage and spirit; but their uncontrollable wildness, the way in which they fired volley after volley in the air, or at imaginary foes in the bush, expending all their ammunition, shows how little use they are for the work we have in hand.

"I do not doubt they will improve under the teaching of the officers of my force, and I hope shortly to have them more under control, but I cannot expect ever to make of them a thoroughly disciplined body.

"The dress and equipment of the 2d West India Regiment is utterly unsuited to bush-fighting. It has an admirable appearance on parade, but for the march and in a thorny bush it is difficult to conceive anything worse; and the superintendence and leading of the men, as with most natives, require special activity and ability on the part of the officers, both on the march and before the enemy.

"One point stands forward prominently from the experience of this day,—viz., that for fighting in the African bush a very exceptionally large proportion of officers is required. Owing to the dense cover, an officer can only exercise control over the men close to him, and for this kind of work there should be at least one officer to every 20 men. I beg, therefore, most strongly to urge that such be the proportion of company officers in the small European contingent for which I have asked in my despatch of 13th instant.

"I have learnt from yesterday's action, that a small body of very highly disciplined troops, well supplied with selected officers, would be of far greater service for warfare in this country, than a much larger number detailed for service in the ordinary tour of duty.

"Owing to the dense nature of the bush and to the necessary absence of mounted officers, rendering it impossible to convey orders for any distance, it is very difficult to exercise any general control over the course of a fight. Hence officers are thrown on their own resources; and unless the officers are very numerous, the men get entirely out of hand. Under these circumstances, undisciplined troops involve the utmost danger to their own officers and to each other. They fire indiscriminately and recklessly into the bush; the great smoke and noise make it impossible to judge the enemy's strength or position; and their manner of fighting is likely to excite unduly even very good European troops in action by their side.

"These are the conditions under which we work here; and I beg to urge in the strongest terms my conviction, that the very best officers and the most highly disciplined troops are alone capable of bringing this war to a speedy and successful issue."

The moral effect of this success, independently of the actual military gain, was incalculable. At once a new tone seemed to pervade Cape Coast. Our friends were encouraged, and our enemies seriously alarmed. A new life and vigour was instilled into both officers and men. One serious loss, however, had to be placed to the other side of the account. Colonel M'Neill, V.C., C.M.G., the chief staff officer, was so seriously wounded that he had to be conveyed on board H.M.S. Simoom, our temporary hospital-ship, and was subsequently compelled to leave for England. His wrist had been torn through by a charge of slugs fired at very short range; it was feared that lockjaw might supervene, and at all events his hand would for long be useless. It would be presumptuous for the writer to speak other words of praise of this gallant officer than those used by Sir Garnet Wolseley himself. "His temporary absence from the duties for which he is so efficient, is a serious loss to the service at this time. His soldier-like qualities, his powers of mind and body, render him an invaluable assistant to any general commanding a force." But Sir Garnet's selected staff was not so

PAGE 184 VOL I.

Sketch to illustrate the
ACTION AT ESSAMAN
14th October, 1873.

From the H.Q. Staff Survey.

Scale of English Miles

composed that its work would collapse by the absence of any one of its number; and, pending the arrival of Colonel Greaves, for whose services the Major-General now applied, Major Baker, the Assistant Adjutant-General, carried on the duties of chief of the staff, in addition to his own work, "to the entire satisfaction" of the Major-General.

CHAPTER V.

EVENTS CONTINUED TO THE BREAKING UP OF THE ASHANTI CAMP AT MAMPON, 25TH OCTOBER.

BEFORE starting on the expedition against Essaman, the Major-General had taken two important steps. The first was to make a demand upon the Home Government for the European troops whom he had requested might be held in readiness. The instructions given to him by the Secretary of State for War had made it incumbent upon him, should he demand them, to make out a strong case for the absolute necessity for these troops; and the reasons given by the Major-General will be found in the following despatch, which is here given in its entirety :—

"CAPE COAST CASTLE, 13th October 1872.

"SIR,—I have the honour to request that the troops (strength as per margin) which, before my departure from England, I requested might be held in readiness for service in the Ashanti Expedition, may be despatched to this station at the earliest possible date after the receipt of this letter.

2 Battalions of Infantry, 650 each	1300
Detachment R.A.	60
Detachment R.E.	40
Administrative Services	50
	1450

The above number is ex-

"In making this request, I bear

fully in mind the instructions which I had the honour to receive from you before leaving England; and I do not make this demand hastily, or without having freely communicated with those who have experi- ence on the Coast, and knowledge of the immediate circumstances. On the other hand I remember your desire, that my decision as to the employment of European troops should be arrived at 'as soon after my arrival on the Coast, as I might be enabled to form it with sufficient knowledge of the circumstances and satisfaction to myself.' I have therefore consulted all those whose experience and knowledge was at my disposal, and I have studied the question in its various bearings.

clusive of officers. Two subalterns (but no captain) to be sent with the R.A., also a double proportion of non-commissioned officers to take charge of small-arm ammunition.

"From these consultations and this study, results my firm conviction of the necessity for the employment of European troops, and of the perfect feasibility of employing them without undue risk, for those purposes which your instructions specify—namely, 'to free these settlements from the continued menace of the attacks of the Ashantis, and to accomplish the further objects of my mission.'

"There is, Sir, but one method of freeing these settlements from the continued menace of Ashanti invasion; and this is, to defeat the Ashanti army in the field, to drive it from the protected territories, and, if necessary, to pursue it into its own land, and to march victorious on the Ashanti capital, and show not only to the king, but to those chiefs who urge him on to constant war, that the arm of her Majesty is powerful to punish, and can reach even to the very heart of their kingdom.

"By no means short of this can lasting peace be insured; one truce after another may be made, but they will again and again be broken, for the Ashantis have learned to believe that they may with impunity invade and lay waste the protected territory, and dwell there unmolested by the white man, till they arrive under the very walls of our forts.

"If the history of former wars with the Ashantis be examined, it will be found that every sign of weakness, and every unsuccessful effort of ours, has been followed by renewed hostilities on their part; and on the other hand, that the show of military strength alone has brought peace.

"It was thus that the Ashanti advance to Annamaboe in 1807 was followed by the invasion of 1811; this again by the advance to Cape Coast Castle in 1817, when the Ashantis were bought off; and this by the insult and invasion of 1823. The sad failure of Sir Charles Macarthy's expedition in 1824 brought the enemy to the walls of our forts, and again, in 1826, they renewed their attacks. Now for the first time they were not only defeated but routed; and the signal victory of Dodowah freed the country for many a long year. The King of Ashanti sent to say 'that he found it was no use fighting against white men,' and the truce was declared which ended in the peace of 1831.

"For twenty-five years—almost the time of a generation—this lesson had its effect. But in 1853 the restless chiefs again urged on the king to war, and the perpetual dread of invasion was renewed. Though happily staved off by the judicious measures of Governor Hill, and a show of strength, the invasion was kept hanging over the heads of the protected tribes; and the unmeasured threats of the king led to the expedition which was undertaken in Governor Pine's rule, when a detachment of our African troops marched to, and encamped upon, the Prah, and were left there inactive to suffer and to die, till the wreck which remained were recalled at the expiration of five months, three months of which had been passed in a severe rainy season.

"From that day to this there has been no peace between the Ashantis and England. No strength has been shown by England, except defensive strength when our forts have been actually attacked. Our Fanti allies, who fell back before the enemy, have disbanded and become demoralised. They have lost their confidence in the English power of protection; and in proportion the Ashantis have grown bold and confident. Their forces lie in security within nine miles of our forts, and for six months they have lived on the produce of the land said to be protected by us.

"Her Majesty has confided to me the task of insuring a lasting peace. Past history, the experience of those who have watched the condition of the Coast, and my own observation of the actual state of affairs, alike convince me that by no method but such signal chastisement as I have described, can such peace be insured, and that such punishment cannot be inflicted without the assistance of British troops.

"It cannot, I think, be doubted, that under the influence of civilisation and European protection, the Fanti tribes have grown less warlike and more peaceful than formerly. Yet even in their best times they were no match for the Ashantis. When left alone they were conquered and overrun; and when, later, English officers cast in their lot with them, they could not be induced to turn out their whole strength; for I am able to state that the numbers reported as having taken the field are enormously exaggerated, and that there were never 10,000 men present under arms. Sir Charles Macarthy was outnumbered by the cowardly defection of his native allies; and the success of the earlier actions of this present year, and the presence of English officers, failed to induce the natives to stand firm. On one excuse or another they retreated from before the enemy, whom they now believe to be too strong for them, and against whom they are evidently very reluctant to fight.

"I have hold interviews with the kings. I have seen the greedy mercantile spirit in which the war is viewed by them, and the excuses made to delay their departure for the field. They tell me they have little influence in raising their men; that their men prefer trading to fighting, and have gone to far countries to hide. The Cape Coast people actually claim the privilege of being the *last* to turn out to fight the invaders of their country.

"In the face of these facts, ignorant as I am as yet of the force which may be raised by the officers employed in recruiting along the coast—whether it is to be counted by thousands or by tens only—ignorant as I must also for some time be as to what force the surrounding kings will produce—and the hour having arrived when on account of the advancing season my decision as to the need for European troops must be made, it is impossible for me to say that my prospects are such that I dare undertake to carry out my mission with native forces only; nor would the Government or the country hold me excused were the valuable lives of the

THE ASHANTI WAR. 191

British officers who have volunteered for this expedition sacrificed, and the prestige of our country lowered, by the desertion of these native forces—a result which I foresee is too likely were I to rely solely upon them, and give them no nucleus of first-rate material to set them an example, and afford them a point on which to rally.

"Under no circumstances, it appears to me, could I rely on such native troops alone to pursue the war into the enemy's territory. Nor would their presence serve to show the power of her Majesty as would that of a body of English soldiers.

"I am by no means the first high official in this colony who has seen the necessity for the employment of thoroughly disciplined troops to stop these perpetual Ashanti invasions.

"In 1824, after Sir C. Macarthy's disaster, M. Dupuis wrote as follows:—

"'Government will see the necessity of now doing what ought to have been done long ago. Unless 3000 to 4000 men are sent out to beat these savages out of hand, they will keep the country agitated until they effect the total subjugation of the Coast.'

"In 1853, Governor Hill wrote:—

"'A disciplined force should be sent here, as I am perfectly satisfied that 1000 men from the West India Regiment, with their bayonets, would do more than ten times that number of natives imperfectly armed and disciplined.'

"And in 1863, Governor Pine said:—

"'That his earnest desire is that a final blow should be struck at the Ashanti power, and the question set at rest for ever as to whether an arbitrary and a sanguinary monarch shall be for ever permitted to insult the British flag and outrage the laws of civilisation.' He goes on to recommend, 'that a force of 2000 disciplined soldiers should be transported to these shores, so that, combined with a native force of upwards of 50,000 men, it might march straight on Coomassie.'

"With these forcible opinions in support of the necessity of trained and disciplined troops, and with your instructions before me, I consider it my duty to state that, in my opinion, the desired effect cannot be obtained by the employment of West Indian Regiments alone. In the first place, the moral effect of their presence upon the Ashantis is not to be compared with that which a similar number of Europeans would exert; and, in the next place, they are not physically by any means as capable of withstanding the climate, still less exertion and fatigue.

"It is a well-known fact here that Europeans suffer from the climate less than black men from other localities.

"The medical reports on the expedition of 1864 say that 'Black troops have none of the hardihood and spirited endurance of the white man. They suffer more from the effects of the climate on their arrival than white men do. They are not accustomed to very onerous duties, which they had to perform on this occasion.'

"And you will find that Captain, now Sir A. Clarke, in his Report of 1864, strongly advocates the substitution of an European force for a West Indian Regiment, owing to their suffering less from the climate, having more power of endurance, and being able to do the same work with fewer men. I might also refer you to the opinion of Colonel de Ruvignès, that 'the West

Indian troops are worse than useless, and are constantly embroiled with the natives.'

"I have no wish to deprecate the West Indian Regiments, but I could not enter upon my task with that confidence which is so necessary for success were I not supported by some of her Majesty's English troops.

"I consider therefore, Sir, that (1) the service required cannot be performed solely by any force indigenous to the country; and (2) that the service for which I require these troops is of paramount importance to the main object of my mission,—viz., the establishment of a lasting peace with the Ashanti nation.

"But, Sir, I should still not apply for these troops, and I should even prefer to tell you that the mission intrusted to me is incapable of thorough accomplishment, were it not that I am convinced that the service for which I demand the European soldiers can be performed by them without undue risk. I believe, indeed, that the evidence upon this point is irresistible.

"Two months, or nearly two months must elapse before the troops can arrive off Cape Coast Castle. In that time the road, which is now complete to Yancoomassie, will, unless the Ashantis have been more successful than hitherto in preventing its construction, be complete at least as far as the Prah; the native troops will have attained such organisation as I can give them; the transport will be prepared for an advance; and I may even hope with the aid of the Houssas and these forces to have cleared the country on this side of the Prah.

"I may therefore say, that on the arrival of the troops in these roads about the middle of December, all will be ready for their immediate advance into the enemy's country, and that they shall not be kept inactive for one single day.

"I would here again refer to the medical reports of 1864, which say—"The effects of the climate depend to a great extent on the season of the year." Now the weather at this present season is totally different from that experienced during the rains. It is now bright and fine, without excessive heat, and it may be expected to improve from week to week. The troops would arrive soon after the commencement of that season of the year, which your instructions describe as the most healthy— viz., the months of December, January, February, and March; and as I guarantee that the operations in which they would be engaged would not last more than about six weeks, or at the most two months, they might re-embark on board ship by the beginning or middle of February, and under no circumstances would they be required to remain on shore after the commencement of the unhealthy season.

"In regard to the risk to European troops of a march up country at this season of the year, there appears to me to be a very strong probability, if not a demonstration, that the country becomes more healthy as the coast is left.

"Colonel Bird, then Acting Governor of the Gold Coast, speaks thus of the expedition in 1853:—

"'Hitherto we have been led to believe the inland districts were too unhealthy for the European constitution. This expedition has proved the fallacy of the belief. During the last two and a half months the officers who have been engaged on this expedition have enjoyed better health than they have been accustomed to do on the coast, and that in spite of exposure to sun and rain, great bodily exertions and privations, which a roving camp-life such as theirs has been necessarily entails.'

" I would also refer you to the memorandum of Lieutenant-Colonel de Ruvignès, dated 25th April 1873, wherein he says : ' I have to observe that many officers, myself amongst the number, served without detriment to their health or constitution for long periods in West Africa. I can safely say that it was only during periods of utter inaction on the coast that I suffered from illness ; though when in the interior, in the thick bush of the Fanti country bordering on Ashantee, or in the forests of Akim and Ashantee, with privations and long marches, sometimes 30 miles a-day, living in mud huts at one time, at another in open forests, I felt no ill effects, neither did any of the officers who served under my command.'

" I might multiply similar evidence, but I am unwilling to increase the length of this despatch, for there are other points to be dealt with of great importance.

" The ill-health of the troops engaged in the expedition to the Prah of 1864, and the sickness of the Royal Marines who were engaged in the early part of the present year, have, I submit, produced an exaggerated alarm as to the general influence of this climate upon European health.

" If the conditions of the expedition of 1864 to the Prah be examined, they will be found so exceptional as to afford no grounds whatever for the belief that the unfortunate results of that affair would be repeated in such an expedition as I propose. The medical reports of 1863 give the strongest proof of this.

"From these reports we learn the following facts :—

"The troops composing the expedition were remarkably bad subjects; they were not only West Indians, but they were from many causes, shown in these reports, specially unfit for any severe work. They had landed at the worst season of the year; they had been attacked by fever and dysentery immediately on their arrival at Cape Coast, and had not wholly recovered when marched up country.

"They had everything against them; heavy duties to which they were not accustomed, no excitement or interest of any kind, no enemy before them; but they had worse food than usual; they were encamped on the banks of the Prah in extremely low and marshy ground. Yet even under these conditions they were reported in March 1864 as in good spirits and fair health, busily employed in erecting stockades, completing huts, and constructing a bridge.

"But the subsequent *inaction* did its work. Depression ensued and the men became ill, though not till the rains commenced, which set in early and were very severe. The camp became a swamp; and for three months longer were the troops kept inactive in this deadly spot.

"The hospital accommodation was of the worst description—men lying on the wet ground with pools of water under them.

"Under such conditions is it not to be wondered at that a single man escaped alive? and is it not clear that this expedition affords no grounds for supposing that similar sickness would attack picked European troops actively employed on the line of march during the healthy season?

"As regards the detachment of Royal Marines who came out in H.M.S. Barracouta, and were sent home in the Himalaya, I have in the first instance to observe, from personal inspection, that the accommodation provided on board that ship (the Barracouta) for their transport, was not in any respect what European soldiers should be provided with in a voyage to the tropics. There was no light and but little air. The condenser, which was constantly at work, was on the same deck, and in the same compartment with the troops. The heat and smell from the steam-engine had free access to the place where they were berthed.

" I should not consider this proper accommodation for troops going even to a cold country; and I have good reason for saying that the men landed in an exhausted condition.*

" The principal medical officer, Dr Home, C.B., V.C., has investigated the question of the sickness of these marines, and he informs me that he believes their sufferings were exceptional.

" They landed at the worst season and without preparation. They were crowded together in unhealthy dilapidated barracks at Elmina.

"It was the tornado season and tents could not be pitched, and the medical officer at that time did not consider it desirable to expose troops to the rain, though Dr Home is now of opinion it would have been better to do so than to have so crowded them together. They were exposed, immediately on landing, to the fatigue of a long night-march. They fought a very distressing

* It is necessary to state that the Admiralty deny that these marines suffered in any way from this cause. Captain Fremantle says they landed in good condition.

action at Elmina, and suffered privations of food and rest for some time after the action.

"But far more potential in producing sickness than all these causes was the fact that they were drenched with surf on landing; and that the boats containing the party which left Cape Coast to be quartered at Elmina grounded on a sand-bank, from which cause the men were detained for two hours under an excessively heavy downpour of rain, most of them, it is believed, afterwards sleeping all night in their wet clothes.

"These conditions are then, I submit, as in the case of the expedition of 1863-4, so exceptional, as to afford no grounds for the belief that similar sickness would attack picked troops actively employed on the line of march during the healthy season.

"I have no desire to underrate the risks to health caused by a prolonged stay in this climate, but not only do I find a remarkable unanimity of opinion here as to the possibility of undertaking a march of limited duration into the interior under such conditions as I propose, but I think the existing conditions of health of the troops on this station show that such an expedition does not involve great risk.

"I would here remark, that notwithstanding all the unfavourable conditions reported as regards the Royal Marines, Dr Home remarks that their entire non-effective list, all casualties included, was on the thirty-first day after landing only 17 per cent, the remaining 83 per cent being thoroughly effective.

"In my despatch No. $\frac{20}{73}$ MS., I drew your attention to the remarkable healthiness of the troops in camp at Napoleon and Abbaye, as compared with those in barracks at Elmina.

"On the 11th instant, Dr Home reports as under of the troops at Cape Coast and Elmina: 'The health of the troops in the command has improved with the partial cessation of the rains and morning mists (locally called smokes). At Elmina the sick-rate per cent of strength is 6.76; at Cape Coast Castle 11.51 (West Indians in both cases). There is less sickness amongst the European officers.'

"I have now before me the weekly return of sick of the Abbaye detachment of 100 men, from 4th to 10th October. It is blank. There was not one case of sickness. The surgeon in charge reports the detachment, in camp now from four to six weeks, as quite healthy.

"These facts prove clearly the fact that while sickness is diminishing throughout the whole coast, by reason of the improving season, it is far less in the camps inland than in the barracks on the coast.

"Since arriving here, I have received a letter, of which I enclose a copy, from Captain Thompson, Queen's Bays, in which he withdraws the opinion he had expressed to His Royal Highness the Field-Marshal Commanding in Chief, before leaving England, that Europeans could not live in the bush.

"But, Sir, still more strong is the report of Dr Home, V.C., C.B., the principal medical officer, my responsible adviser on sanitary questions.

"I beg to refer you to his despatch to the Director-General of the Medical Department, by which it will be seen that he is of opinion that European troops may be employed without extraordinary risk, under those conditions which I propose—viz., that the men be landed the day they are to march, that every recognised sanitary precaution be taken, as far as possible, and that the longest time the men will remain in the country is two months.

"It now remains for me only to repeat my request, that as soon as possible after the receipt of this despatch, the troops above specified may be embarked for this station, and to add that I attach the greatest possible importance to the men being selected for this service, and to good accommodation being provided for them on board ship, so that they may arrive here in thoroughly healthy condition.

"Should my request be complied with, and the troops be despatched, I undertake not to land them, if, in the time which must elapse before their arrival, circumstances should induce me to consider that the object of my mission can be accomplished without their aid; and further, I undertake, should it seem possible to do with any smaller number, not to land one man more than I consider absolutely necessary to the success of my expedition.—I have, &c.

"G. J. WOLSELEY,
Major-General.

"The Right Honourable
  THE SECRETARY OF STATE FOR WAR,
      War Office."

The irregularity of the mail-service at this time was most unfortunate; no steamer, homeward bound, called at Cape Coast between the 9th and the 27th of October, and the result was that the above despatch, written on the 13th, lay at Cape Coast until the 27th.

The Major-General had also, agreeably to his orders from the Secretary of State for the Colonies, sent to the King of Ashanti a summons to the following effect:—

"CAPE COAST CASTLE, *October* 1873.

"YOUR MAJESTY,—The Queen of England has heard, with profound concern, of your recent doings, by which you have directly violated the treaty concluded in 1831 between Governor Maclean and the late King of Ashanti.

"Her Majesty's representatives were engaged in peaceful negotiations with you for the deliverance of strangers whom you had wrongfully seized, and were holding captive; yet during the continuance of these negotiations, when friends of the prisoners had consented to pay the sum demanded by you for expenses incurred on their account, whilst your Majesty's envoys were still at Cape Coast Castle, suddenly, without warning given or cause alleged, you invaded the territories of her Majesty's allies, and still continue to occupy them. You have massacred or driven into slavery all upon whom you could lay hands, you have even attacked her Majesty's forts. All this you have done whilst professing to the last a desire for her Majesty's friendship.

"It were but justice, therefore, that summary punishment should be at once inflicted upon yourself and upon your people.

"But the Queen of England, as she is strong is patient. Her Most Gracious Majesty is willing to believe that evil advisers, or, it may be, unfaithful emissaries, have deceived you. She wishes only well to the great Ashanti people, as to all the peoples of Africa. She would be glad to know that peace and happiness were enjoyed by all. She is most anxious for the permanent establishment between your nation and her subjects and allies of those commercial and friendly relations, which are so essential to the wellbeing of all, and of which, in a happier moment, your Majesty once wrote that they are 'the best support of nations, and the principal care of the wisest.'

"She wishes that all misunderstanding or imaginary cause of grievance that may exist in your Majesty's mind should be removed. She has sent me, therefore, reposing in me her fullest and most gracious confidence, to arrange with you for the establishment of a lasting peace. As, however, it is not the custom of our country to discuss terms of peace with one who persists in an attitude of aggression, I have to require as preliminaries to negotiation,—

"1. That by the 12th of November you withdraw all your forces from the territories of her Majesty's allies.

"2. That you surrender up at once all men, women, and children of every tribe and people, at present in alliance with her Majesty, whom you have captured.

"3. That you give guarantees for the payment of ample compensation to all whom you have ill used.

"If you will, in good faith, consent to these conditions, I shall be ready to treat with you in a friendly spirit, and to consider any reasonable proposals you may make. But if within twenty days I have not received an assurance from you of your readiness to comply with her Majesty's wishes, or if you have not, within the date already specified, withdrawn all your forces into your own territory, beyond the Prah river, having given such guarantees as may satisfy me for the fulfilment of the above-mentioned terms, I hereby warn you to expect the full punishment your deeds have merited.

"Rest well assured that power will not be wanting to that end. I can scarcely believe that you do not know how unequal would be the struggle which you court.

"Her Majesty's dominion reaches far and wide over the earth. Against you or your forefathers she has hitherto never found it necessary to employ more than an insignificant fraction of the special forces which guard this petty corner of the vast realms which own her as Sovereign. When you recently assailed her forts they were held only by a handful of men, yet your people were repulsed with loss. How, then, when her Majesty puts forth her might against you, can you hope to resist her? Be warned in time, lest in refusing to attend to my summons you prepare misery for yourself and for your people.

"I entreat your Majesty to be careful that the exact terms of this despatch are accurately conveyed to you. I beg you to have it read to you on two different occasions by two different persons, neither of whom is present whilst the other reads. In this way I hope that you may avoid any risk of such misunderstanding as to the exact nature of the message sent to you, as I fear may have occurred on some previous occasions.— I am, your Majesty's well-wisher,

"G. J. WOLSELEY,
Administrator of the Gold Coast,
and Commander-in-Chief of her Majesty's
West African Army.

"THE KING OF ASHANTI."

The first copy of this was sent on the 13th, and other copies were forwarded on the 17th and 18th; one of these was carried by Kotiko, an Ashanti envoy, who had been at Cape Coast when hostilities broke out, and had been detained there ever since. Accompanied by two policemen, he was passed through the outposts at Abbaye, and entered without molestation the Ashanti camp of Mampon. There the letter was read by Amanquatia, the Commander-in-Chief, and the following remarkable document was sent in reply :—

"MAMPONG, 20*th October* 1873.

" To His Excellency's,
  " Governor-in-Chief of her Majesty's Fort.

"SIR,—I have received those two letters which you sent to me in order to send them to the King of Ashanti.

"For what purpose I came here is that ;—Assin, Dankra, Akyem, Wassaw. Those four nations belong to the King of Ashanti, and they refused to serve the king, and they escaped away unto you; if the king sends his servants to or to buy something at Cape Coast, they catch them and plundered their good to. And those nations ordered the King of Ashantee that he may come to fight with them. Therefore, I said, they are not a friends with the king on account of that; I shall come down here to catch those four chieves who ordered the King of Ashanti to come to fight with him. And they fought with me six times, and I drove them away, and they escapped to be under you. But the king did not send me into Cape Coast, and then, you deliver Assin, Dankra, Akyen, and Wassaw unto me, and I shall bring unto the king there is no any quarrel with you. I send my love to you. —I am yours, AMANQUATIA."

The policemen were sent safely back with this letter, after having had the Ashanti troops paraded and reviewed before them. They reported that it had taken nearly two days for the whole of the Ashanti troops to march past their Commander-in-Chief.

It will be observed that Amanquatia renews the old claim to Assin, Denkera, Akim, and Wassaw; and repeats the old story that he has got no quarrel with the white man.

The letter was received by Sir Garnet on the 21st, and the following answer was sent back on the 22d October:—

"GOVERNMENT HOUSE,
CAPE COAST, *October* 22, 1873.

"GENERAL,—My letter sent to your camp was intended for the King of Ashanti. I shall be glad therefore if you will at once send it to him.

"You write as if the Kings of Wassaw, Denkera, Assin, and Akim were of right your master's slaves. But fully forty years ago, the then King of Ashanti, in a treaty to which the English governor was a party, renounced all claim to their allegiance.

"I am extremely glad to hear of your friendly disposition towards me. But I cannot, under any circumstances, enter into any negotiations whilst you continue to occupy the territory of tribes in alliance with her Majesty.—I am, General, your friend,

"G. J. WOLSELEY,
Major-General, Commanding her Majesty's
Troops in Western Africa, and
Administrator."

In the mean time small detachments of native levies were arriving from the various points to which the

Major-General had sent officers for their collection. The first detachment arrived on the 15th in the steamship Biafra from Sierra Leone, comprising some old soldiers and others partially drilled, to the number of 1 sergeant and 65 rank and file. They were handed over to Major Baker Russell, and formed the first instalment of Russell's Regiment of Foot, being accommodated in huts or tents pitched near Prospect House. On the 16th October, 94 men who had been collected by Lieutenant Bolton arrived from Barraco, and were also sent to join Russell's regiment. Lieut. Gordon had been unable to collect any Mandingoes at Sierra Leone, but he got together a body of 120 Kossoos, who were also attached to Russell's regiment. The company of Cape Coast Volunteers embodied under their native officers previous to Sir Garnet Wolseley's arrival, and now garrisoning Abbaye Redoubt, was transferred to Wood's Regiment of Foot to form his first company; and the Houssas who had arrived from Lagos were temporarily attached to him, previous to their subsequent despatch to Abrakrampa, where they were placed under Lieutenant Gordon, and afterwards attached to Russell's regiment.

By the 16th October, Captain Rait had got 1 sergeant, 1 corporal, and 10 Houssa gunners, whom he and Lieut. Eardley Wilmot had regularly drilled with guns, Gatlings and rockets. Captain Rait said that it was very hard to get the men to lay a gun, that they did not seem to understand it at all, and that he feared it would be necessary to have Europeans to lay each gun. Their childish delight when practising with live shells and rockets was most amusing. The difficulty of teaching natives to act as gunners, when every word of command and every detail had to be explained and interpreted, can readily be imagined; and it will be easily understood that at the early date when the Major-General applied for European troops, it was quite impossible for either Captain Rait or himself to foretell that an effective Houssa battery could be raised, and that consequently it was incumbent on the Major-General to apply for a detachment of European artillery for the service of the guns and rockets which he intended to take into the field.

Captain Furse and Lieutenant Saunders were comparatively unsuccessful in their attempt to obtain men at the Gambia; and although every possible assistance was given to them by the Administrator, Mr Kortright, only 100 men were procured. Messengers had been sent to the various tribes without any satisfactory result—the Mohammedans especially having such a dislike to leave their own country, and showing so much superstition and dread of a sea journey, that none could be induced to enlist. It was, moreover, the very time of the year at which their labours in the field were most needed, the gathering of crops having arrived. Plenty of men there were, and fine men, the chiefs and the principal warriors being mounted on ponies; their appearance, as Captain Furse said, reminding one of the description of Highland clans at the commencement of the eighteenth century.

Commissary O'Connor was unsuccessful in his attempt to obtain Kroomen, and was obliged to return to Cape Coast with less than 100—the notion that war was going on being sufficient to deter this peaceful tribe from giving their services.

The mail steamer Roquelle brought out on the 10th,

from England, Captain Buckle, Lieutenants Bell and Mann of the Royal Engineers, and Captain Nicol, Adjutant of the Hampshire Infantry Militia, a volunteer for service in the expedition. The latter officer was, at his own suggestion, sent to Bonny, to endeavour to procure men, and fulfilled his mission with some success. He played with considerable cleverness King Jaja of Opobo against the King of Bonny. These rival kings had been engaged in almost continual warfare against each other, and each was jealous of the advantage which would arise to the other if his men were drilled and trained by English officers. Captain Nicol, however, succeeded in impressing them with the belief that the only way to get out of this difficulty was for each of them to send men to be thus drilled. In this manner he collected 53 Opobos and 104 Bonnys. The latter were accompanied by Prince Charles of Bonny and Mr John Jumbo, son of Chief Oko Jumbo, both, as King George of Bonny reported in sending them down, intelligent and educated young gentlemen. On the arrival of these detachments, Prince Charles was appointed a captain of militia, and Mr Jumbo a lieutenant. King George of Bonny refused to accept any remuneration for sending these men, and collected and equipped them so far as he could at his own expense. The Opobos were subsequently attached to Russell's regiment, and the Bonnys to Wood's regiment. They did not, however, arrive at Cape Coast until November.

Lieutenant Bolton, of the 1st West India Regiment, had considerable success in raising men about Winnebah and Mumford, and two entire companies of Russell's foot were subsequently formed of men raised by him.

Russell's regiment was ultimately composed of six companies: No. 1 Company, Houssas; No. 2 Company, Sierra Leones; No. 3 Company, Mumfords; No. 4 Company, Winnebahs; No. 5 Company, Opobos; No. 6 Company, Annamaboes. Wood's regiment was composed of four companies: No. 1 Company, Cape Coast Volunteers; No. 2 Company, Elminas; No. 3 Company, Kossoos; No. 4 Company, Bonnys. The whole of the efforts made to enlist men along the coast resulted only in procuring a few hundreds, and some time was of course required in order to drill and accustom them to the use of breech-loading rifles.

The following orders were issued as to the drill of these troops; it was to be as simple as possible: They were to drill in single rank, forming fours like cavalry. Only the simplest words of command were to be taught —viz., Advance—Retire—Halt—Fours Right or Left, &c. In manual and firing exercises only such words of command as might be absolutely necessary were to be taught. The men were to be trained to fire low, and not to waste their ammunition; and in order to teach the virtue of husbanding ammunition, not more than one man in four was to be allowed to fire at the same time when at drill. Each man was to repeat the word of command at the time of movement, so that the meaning of the words might be instilled into their minds. All day long Russell and his officers at Cape Coast, and Wood with his officers at Elmina, were engaged in endeavouring to teach the rudiments of military work to these quaint and unpromising pupils. To see their black faces shining out in puzzled astonishment above their white frocks, turning in bewilderment to the right when they were told to turn to the left, and grinning complacently when they thus found themselves facing each other in the ranks, was a sight which gave one but little confidence of their ability to become valuable as soldiers ; nevertheless, the work went persistently forward, and no small service was done by them at most critical periods of the war.

As regards the native allies, the days passed, and the task seemed more and more hopeless. In his instructions to the officers employed as special commissioners, Sir Garnet had written,—" It cannot be too strongly impressed upon you that you are not dealing with educated or civilised beings ; and consequently the utmost good temper, affability, and patience, mingled with fixedness of purpose and determination, are of the greatest importance." They had been told to give every assistance to the kings to whom they were commissioned in their endeavour to collect their fighting men : coercion might be resorted to if necessary ; but they were to be careful that no punishments repugnant to humanity were inflicted; and they were to leave no stone unturned with a view of collecting all the forces of the kings to whom they were commissioned, and bringing them to Dunquah by the 20th October. What the immediate result of their labours were and what were, the difficulties with which they had to contend, may be seen from the following short summary of their letters—each commissioner apparently thinking his own king the most idle and the most untrustworthy of all the kings on the Coast :—

Major Lazenby reported from Mankessim, on the 21st October, that he hoped to arrive at Dunquah in a day or two with 1000 men ; that they were not King Eddoo's men, although he claimed them; and that King

Eddoo was so apathetic that the Major almost despaired of raising from his neighbourhood 200 men, though he thought it possible to raise more further in the interior. Actually it was not till the 13th November that he arrived in camp at Dunquah with 1100 men, who had been raised chiefly in Anyan and Adjumacoe.

Lieutenant Graves, commissioner to King Akinnie of Acoomfie, reported almost immediately after his arrival that the country was a very large one, and that from all he could learn it would take from a fortnight to a month to beat up the twenty-four towns comprising the kingdom. King Akinnie, with whom he held a long palaver, positively refused to accompany him through the district, and said that he could not even furnish him with hammock-bearers. The king insisted on a white officer personally visiting all the districts, and declined to move from his "palace" until all his men were ready to start for Dunquah. "By patience and perseverance I hope," wrote this young officer, "eventually to overcome all the difficulties." How many officers wrote the same thing before their work was over, and how unfortunately did they all fail! King Akinnie may be taken as a specimen of the West African king. "I had the greatest trouble with him," wrote Mr Graves, "as he is a true type of the lazy, palm-wine-drinking, good-for-nothing African, who, like all the other native petty princes, has got the idea into his head that the European officers are to do all the real hard work of running about all over the country collecting troops, while his majesty lies all day on his back smoking and drinking. Their total apathy, indifference, and want of energy, is almost maddening to me at times, for neither princes nor people appear at all anxious to go to war."

Orders were sent to this officer that he was on no account whatever to allow such conduct on the part of King Akinnie; and he was directed to place himself in communication with Major Brownell, the Civil Commandant at Saltpond, whose knowledge and experience of the native character was likely to be of great value. Major Brownell gave him every assistance; but it was not till he had threatened to make the king a prisoner for disloyalty that he could be induced to leave his town, from which he had actually to be driven by Major Brownell, after attempting by every possible subterfuge and most barefaced lying to avoid having to exert himself in the slightest degree. In the middle of November King Akinnie had still not moved; continual lying, continued procrastination, were all that were encountered, and Lieutenant Graves had to leave the king and proceed himself without men to the camp at Dunquah. So disgraceful had this king's conduct been, that the Major-General had decided to arrest him as a worthless and disloyal subject; but as towards the end of November he did actually arrive at Dunquah with 54 men, no further steps were taken than to place the matter in Colonel Festing's hands, who was then commander of the camp, and who not only severely reprimanded him, but fined him all pay due for men to the commencement of December, threatening him with deposition, if he did not aid the English Government to the utmost of his power in future.

Perhaps the best of all the kings, certainly the one who showed the most courage in the field, was the King of Annamaboe; but even with him the difficulties were immense. Captain Godwin, the special commissioner, reported that the king had no power whatever over his people, and that it was hard work to a degree to get anything done. He visited village after village, and all sorts of promises were made, but the men, except a very few, did not appear; those who did appear, and who believed they would be compelled to turn out as fighting men, ran away to Cape Coast, where, as labourers, they could get 1s. per day instead of the $7\frac{1}{2}$d. which they would receive as fighting men. Everything seemed to be looked upon as a mere money question. The king wrote to Captain Godwin on the 17th October, requesting him to pay his men at the rate of 1s. per day. On the 15th October Captain Godwin wrote: "I find it is useless delaying here. The king is most dilatory; his power is merely nominal amongst his people; his chiefs and captains promise they will bring a certain number of men, but when the actual time for assembly comes, only one-third of the number promised are brought, and then all sorts of excuses are made that these are all they could get to come." After much difficulty 269 armed men turned out. Under these circumstances Captain Godwin started for Dunquah with the king, his "field-marshal," and some of his captains. By slow degrees a few men followed. On the 20th October, 65 Annamaboes had arrived at Dunquah. What the armament of those native levies in general was, may be gathered from Captain Godwin's report: "The flint-and-steel arms I examined yesterday were, for the most part, in a most unserviceable state, covered with rust, and looking as if they would explode on being discharged." A week later the Annamaboes numbered 287 at Dunquah; and Captain Godwin reported, "I believe they are not a bad lot as these levies go, and if disciplined they would fight well."

King Amfoo Otto of Abrah wrote to Lieutenant Pollard, R.N., at Dunquah, on the 11th, and assured him that he could produce about 4000 men, but was anxious that they should muster at Abrakrampa instead of at Dunquah, as he had heard that the Ashanti army intended to attack that place. The Abrah people were doing good work as scouts on the track of the Ashanti army; but although Lieutenant Pollard reported them as appearing willing to go into camp, and pleased with the terms offered, they did not come in with the expected rapidity. The conduct of King Amfoo Otto and the Abrahs will be more fully described later.

Sub-Lieutenant Laing, R.N., was more successful with the Inkoorsokoom tribes, to whose king Assano he was commissioned. He succeeded in raising altogether 488 men, of whom 390 were armed. He, however, reported that the king had not the slightest power over the main body of his men, but that his field-marshal, "though not at all a fighting man," was the most influential person in the kingdom. The king complained bitterly that he had not received the same present at Cape Coast as the other kings, and stipulated that although his men would proceed to Dunquah, they should not be required to fight any enemy unless the whole of the other Fanti tribes agreed to do so. The greater number of the men of this tribe were raised by the exertions of Major Brownell at Saltpond, a town in the Inkoorsokoom district.

Sub-Lieutenant Cochran, R.N., reported that King

Ancasia of Assayboo was of no account with his people. This king laid much stress on the fact that a present of 2 lb. of tobacco, which he had expected, had not been sent to him. He seemed to have no authority over the chiefs of the surrounding district, from whom, however, the officer succeeded in getting small detachments of men to assemble at Assayboo.

Sub-Lieutenant Filliter of the 2d West India Regiment, special commissioner to King Solomon of Domonassie, found the king unwilling to do anything without first consulting his chiefs, and was of opinion that he had very little command over them. After consultation with his chiefs and captains, the king expressed his opinion that he could raise some 600 armed men, and as many men without arms; but on the 20th October he moved to Dunquah with 5 chiefs and 4 captains, but only 110 armed men and 14 unarmed. The arms consisted of one Snider without ammunition, a sporting rifle, a double fowling-piece, a few percussion-cap smooth-bores, without caps, and a number of flint-lock muskets. King Solomon had remained several days at Cape Coast before proceeding to Domonassie.

Quasi Kaye, the King of Denkera, told Lieutenant Hearle of the Royal Marines that he expected to be able to raise between 2000 and 3000 men; but there is no doubt that special difficulties were experienced in his case, owing to his country being in the hands of the enemy, and his men being distributed over the length and breadth of Fanti land. The king sent messengers to Annamaboe, Mankessim, Essecoomah, and elsewhere, and even to Cape Coast, to collect the men who did not arrive. The king reported that he could not get on without his stool-bearer, "apparently," says

Lieutenant Hearle, "a most important member of the court;" and on the 21st October he marched into Dunquah with only 30 men, 15 more arriving on the following day.

A similar difficulty existed with the Assins of King Chibboo to that already related as regards the Denkeras. The Assin territory had been overrun by the enemy; King Chibboo's men were scattered throughout the country; he informed Captain Bromhead that he had commenced war with 1500 men all armed, but he was now unable to state what number he could possibly get together. •On the 21st October, Captain Bromhead moved from Domonassie to Dunquah with such men as could be collected of the tribe; but the number was not worth mentioning. A difficulty appears to have arisen between Captain Bromhead and King Chibboo owing to the existence of two villages of the name of Yancoomassie, of which Captain Bromhead was not aware. King Chibboo's capital is Yancoomassie-Assin; but Captain Bromhead was under the impression that his capital was Yancoomassie-Fanti, and urged him to concentrate all his forces at that place instead of at Dunquah. Here again the same report was made, that the king, although treated with respect by his followers, did not appear to have much power over them; he had to consult with his chiefs as to every act. The fighting men appeared to have little faith in the resources of the king, but they all seemed eager to get ammunition.

Captain Thompson's mission to Wassaw met with but little success, though he was enabled to supply some useful information. At Dixcove he enlisted some 63 men as policemen or soldiers, and he then proceeded into the Wassaw country to meet the kings of Eastern and Western Wassaw. Enemil, the King of Eastern Wassaw, who had but lately succeeded his brother, and Prince Apecoon, King of Western Wassaw, who was said to be tributary to the King of Eastern Wassaw, said that they could bring 15,000 men into the field. The Wassaws were said to have had an encounter with the Ashantis, near Amantine, the capital of Eastern Wassaw, and to have beaten them and driven them back upon Mampon.* The Wassaws appeared to have completely separated the Ashanti detachment in Apollonia from the others at Mampon. The Ahantas, a tribe in alliance with the Ashantis, were invading the Dixcove country, had occupied Boutry and other towns on the sea-coast, and in order to oppose them the people of Dixcove had established camps eastward and westward of the town. Captain Thompson was obliged to make a great detour to avoid the hostile Ahantas, and suggested that Boutry and the other towns on the seaboard held by the hostile Ahantas should be bombarded. The chiefs of Dixcove said that they could not well spare many men to send to Cape Coast, and hoped that they might themselves be assisted in their efforts to remain loyal to the British, in the teeth of the opposition and difficulties they were encountering. Starting from Dixcove on the 13th October, Captain Thompson marched by way of Geddua and Assowa Croom to Domonassie on the river Boutry, some forty miles by this road from Dixcove. The people, who seemed glad to see a white man, the first they had seen for thirty years, were engaged in pro-

---

* This was probably a detachment of Ashantis, under the command of Quamin Agyapon, who was known at Cape Coast to have recently joined the Ashanti camp at Mampon from the Wassaw territory.

tecting the road to Wassaw from the Ashantis. The chiefs all seemed anxious to join the Wassaw kings, and to march with them upon Prahsu, as the Governor required. The road was extremely bad, even for a bush-path, the track being deep under water, and so honeycombed with pits dug for gold, that it was impossible to travel over it at night. On arrival at Domonassie, whence he had intended to march to Amantine, Captain Thompson was specially urged not to go on to that place, as it had been deserted on account of the ravages caused by small-pox. He was assured that the kings would hasten to meet him, but it was again the old story. Enemil's sword-bearers arrived, promising that he would come the next day to see Captain Thompson; but he did not come, and the chiefs would not discuss any matters until he arrived. On the 21st, the chief commanding the force of Apecoon, the King of Western Wassaw, paid Captain Thompson a visit, and said that he represented King Apecoon, who was too old to come away from his own city. He promised to take the available forces of Wassaw to the Prah : but in the first place, the men could not be collected until the fourteen chiefs who commanded them had been consulted ; and in the next place, the movement could not be made at once, as the Ashantis were now endeavouring to force a passage through Wassaw to Coomassie. He promised to give a contingent of 100 fighting men, but they never were seen. Captain Thompson was informed that Enemil was fighting against the Ashantis near the Prah, and as proofs an Ashanti captive and some heads were sent in to him. He found the greatest difficulty in getting a messenger to go to Enemil, as a great "custom" for the late king's death was pending, and almost any ordinary man was liable to be detained as one of the victims to be sacrificed at the custom, at which at least 100 men must be killed. Captain Thompson wrote: "It is most annoying to be thus wasting valuable time; but without an intimate knowledge of the absurd customs of these people, a man deals with them at a disadvantage which can with difficulty be appreciated; the knowledge of the customs of other nations absolutely misleads, and all argument by reasoning or analogy is impossible." Captain Thompson considered that there could be no doubt of the loyalty of all the Wassaw chiefs and people, but every doubt as to the probability of any early movement on their part in the direction desired by the Governor.

When King Enemil did arrive at Domonassie after Captain Thompson's departure, his one idea seemed to be to get money and ammunition from the Government. He asked for £30 and 300 guns and a quantity of gunpowder and lead, with one Snider for himself, and another for his head chief.

Such is the native African mind; all great events are lost sight of in these trivial details. A couple of pounds of tobacco, a Snider rifle, a barrel of gin, or a few pigs of lead, are considered subjects of greater importance than the destinies of a nation.

In estimating the work at this time before Sir Garnet Wolseley, it must be remembered that the task which the Major-General had in hand was complicated by its double character. He had not only to use every effort to drive the Ashantis out of the Protectorate by means of native levies and these wretched native allies, but he had always to keep in mind the certainty which he had already expressed in his despatch to the Home Government, and which was being borne in upon him more forcibly every day, that a lasting peace could only be obtained by the defeat of the Ashanti army, and in all probability by a march to Coomassie with the European troops. If any such operation were to be carried out, it must be in the months of January and February; and before the arrival of the soldiers whom the Major-General had demanded, every preparation for their reception and for their march up country must be made. It was therefore necessary to combine with the operations now immediately undertaken against the Ashanti army, the formation of a road by which European troops could advance to the Prah, the establishment of depots along that road, and the completion of halting stages, suited in all respects for the reception of the European troops. It was necessary, also, that a complete scheme of transport of supplies, stores, and ammunition outwards from Cape Coast, and of sick and wounded back to Cape Coast, should be devised; and all this had to be thought out and arranged under the pressure of an enemy's army within a few miles, and under the most unfavourable conditions of climate.

Before the arrival of Sir Garnet Wolseley—in fact, on the very day on which he left England, Deputy Surgeon-General Home had sent to the Army Medical Department a most able report as to the possibility of carrying out a march to Coomassie. In it he had sketched generally a scheme for the transport of the sick and wounded, and for the arrangements of hospitals along the line of march and at the base of operations. He estimated that the probable amount of sickness in a picked European force not landed until the day it was wanted to march, and with every known sanitary precaution adopted, operating for six weeks or two months only, would be from 30 to 40 per cent of the whole at the end of the time; but that the mortality would not be in any degree in proportion to the amount of the sickness. Subsequent experience showed that these calculations were singularly correct. A detailed scheme for the transport of sick and wounded was now, as early as October, prepared and submitted to the Major-General; it contemplated provision for the carriage of 14 per cent of the entire force to reach Cape Coast in nine days from the farthest point in hammocks, with relays of bearers, hospital resting-places being provided at every ten miles along the line. A general scheme for the medical and sanitary arrangements of the campaign was at the same time submitted. The details of these arrangements will be entered into at greater length in a subsequent chapter, when the preparations for the march into Ashanti are considered.

The preparation of a road to the Prah was evidently a matter requiring so much time, and involving so many difficulties, that the Major-General was anxious to push it on with the utmost possible rapidity. For the first eight days, Major Home was the only Engineer officer present, Captain Buckle and two subalterns not arriving till the 10th; and it was not until the 13th that the work of erecting huts, and the formation of the rough works for the defence of Cape Coast and the connecting road, could be sufficiently completed to allow of Major Home proceeding to inspect the road. On the 13th he went to Accroful, and reported that four miles of the road between Yamolanza and Butteyan still required much work, though 200 men were already engaged upon it. Lieutenant Mann had accompanied Major Home, and was at once put to work upon the road. Both labourers and tools were at first wanting; but all the available tools were sent up from Cape Coast, and the chiefs of Butteyan and Assayboo were required to furnish men. Major Home then proceeded to Yancoomassie-Fanti, and on the 16th October had pushed on to Wonkorsu, a few miles south of Mansu. Hence he reported that he had given orders to advance on the following morning to Mansu, but that his men were holding a meeting and organising a strike, being afraid of the Ashantis should they proceed any further. Their alarm had been added to by the return of a corporal of police, with a messenger who had undertaken to proceed with a letter from Sir Garnet to the King of Ashanti, but who came back reporting that they could not proceed along the road. Major Home had also received instructions to report upon sites for encampments, the first and second to be at such distances as to give but short marches to the troops. Each camp was to be calculated to hold 400 Europeans, in addition to a garrison of 50 men for the post.

A small detachment of Cape Coast Volunteers, under command of Lieutenant Gordon, was still the only escort on the road; and Major Home urged that some more reliable troops should be sent to support his party as soon as possible, expressing an opinion that with a couple of hundred Houssas the road might be easily opened up for a considerable distance. But the bulk of the Houssas had to be sent to Abrakrampa under charge of Lieutenant Woodgate, in consequence of reports made by prisoners that it was the intention of the Ashanti army to attack that place or Napoleon, and the necessity for establishing another outpost between Napoleon and the main road. Napoleon was sufficiently strong; and the Houssas were therefore ordered to Abrakrampa, Lieutenant Gordon being relieved from his duties at the head of the road by Captain Huyshe, D.A.Q.M.G., and ordered to Abrakrampa to take command of the Houssas, and to intrench the post. Surgeon Atkins was also ordered to Abrakrampa for duty.

Lieutenant Pollard had been there since the 15th, and had already made preparations for defence. On the 17th he had reported himself quite ready to meet the enemy, though he had only ten West India soldiers, three policemen, and eighty Abrah natives. On the 18th the Houssas arrived. Captain Huyshe also proceeded there with some intrenching tools, and found the town deserted by all but the garrison. An alarm occurred about noon that the Ashantis were coming; but it turned out to be false, and the work of intrenchment proceeded.

Abrakrampa was a village of some 300 houses standing on the slope of a hill. At the upper or northern end of the village stood a mission church built by the Wesleyans, and in the centre of the village main street was a mission house which became headquarters. On the 19th, when Gordon arrived, the church had already been loopholed, and its thatched roof removed, a boarded ceiling remaining. Into this church, intended as a last *réduit*, Captain Huyshe conveyed food and water. The houses facing to the north, west, and south were loopholed, and connecting shelter-trenches thrown up. A strong central intrenchment was afterwards made in the centre of the village, to contain the store, magazine, &c. On this day, the 19th, the Abrah scouts reported Ashantis at Ainsa and Quacodayo, and pickets were put out on every road.

The same day, Lieutenant Bell joined Major Home at Mansu, where, on the previous day, he had commenced the erection of a fort. This fort, subsequently christened Fort Cambridge, contained a central redoubt, cut out of a large ant-hill, which, when roofed in, formed an excellent magazine. It commanded the main road, and would hold a garrison of 200 men, though capable from its peculiar shape of being defended by 60 or 70. The weather was extremely bad, tornadoes alternating with heavy rains much impeding work. As soon as the fort was finished, Major Home recommenced operations upon the road. On the 21st the road was reported fit for the march of infantry in fours as far as Mansu.

On the 20th, Colonel Festing, who had been placed on the list of special-service officers, was ordered to Dunquah to take the command of the proposed native camp there, and of the advanced posts generally; and an assistant commissary was also sent there, with a view to the formation of a depot of stores. A strong post already existed at Accroful, held by a detachment of 40 West Indians.

Hearing from Lieutenant Gordon that the Ashantis, were on the march by way of Ainsa to Dunquah, Colonel Festing took on with him this detachment from Accroful, and sent for Houssas to Abrakrampa. Huyshe and Gordon at once started with 44 Houssas, and arrived in the night at Dunquah. Colonel Festing also sent word to Mansu, desiring Major Home to fall back on Dunquah if possible; but if intercepted, to march eastward on Annamaboe. This latter order did not meet with the Major-General's approval. On receipt of Colonel Festing's report, he ordered Major Home to remain at Mansu, and to hold on to the place if attacked. He considered that its abandonment would have a very bad effect on the minds of the natives; and he desired Colonel Festing to reinforce Major Home with 100 native allies from the 250 at his disposal at Dunquah, and at once to intrench himself at Dunquah. Colonel Festing was also desired on no account to leave Abrakrampa without a sufficient force; its position rendering it even more exposed than Dunquah. At the same time a fresh detachment of 40 West Indians was sent to Accroful from Cape Coast.

Major Home had not complied with the order to fall back to Mansu, considering himself justified in remaining, as his fort was already strong enough "to hold out for ever;" and already the work of intrenchment had commenced at Dunquah, Captain Huyshe's services being here again of great value.

On the 22d, Major Home reported that the fort of Mansu was fraised and stockaded for artillery, and that he could hold it with his 50 natives. The position which he had held for the last day or two had been, like those so often previously held by Gordon, and later by Pollard at Abrakrampa, somewhat critical, as he was alone with none but natives, on whom very much dependence could not be placed. Fortunately he had found a most valuable assistant in Lieutenant Smith of the Cape Coast Volunteers, whose services had already been so well reported on by Gordon. He was now reinforced by 100 native allies (Assins); and the rumours of attack on Abrakrampa being steadily repeated, the Houssas at Dunquah and all the police were sent to that village.

The following orders were at this time issued with regard to military posts: Immediately after the establishment of any such post, the officer commanding was to strengthen it to the utmost possible extent, and to clear the bush round it for a radius of at least 60 yards. Should the water-supply be at any distance from the intrenchment, steps were to be taken to collect a quantity in barrels, or any other convenient receptacle. To meet emergency, a reserve of 100 rounds of ammunition per man of the garrison, and a week's supply of provisions, was always to be kept in each post. At Elmina and places on the seaboard, the reserve of ammunition was to be 200 rounds per man; and of provisions, one month's supply.

Between the 18th and the 20th a quantity of powder and lead was sent to Dunquah; 20 Enfields, with 2000 rounds of ammunition, to Abrakrampa; 200 Enfields, and 25,000 rounds of ammunition to Napoleon; and a quantity of powder for natives to both Napoleon and Abbaye. The officers commanding this latter station were instructed not to issue more than 30 rounds of Enfield ammunition or 5 ounces of powder at a time to each man of the native levies. 6500 rounds of ammunition were sent to Mansu as a reserve of 100 rounds per man for the 50 volunteers and 15 police there stationed.

On the 22d the Abrah scouts again reported Ashantis moving with baggage from Quacodayo to Ainsa; and as the enemy seemed to be taking the direction of

Dunquah, the panic in Abrakrampa began to subside, and the women came back to the town. Gordon had some target-practice this day with his Houssas. Out of 50 shots fired at 50 yards range, only 5 would have hit a man, the rest being wild and high.

On the 23d the number of the allies assembled at Dunquah was about 500, and arrangements were made for the despatch of rocket-troughs and rockets to Mansu, Abrakrampa, and Dunquah.

Reports received from the 20th to the 23d went to prove that there was a general feeling of dissatisfaction in the camp at Mampon, the younger chiefs desiring to return to Coomassie, and the elder to remain in the country. Amanquatia was said to be alarmed for the safety of his retreat, in consequence of our attack on Essaman and the occupation of Mansu and Dunquah; and the arrival of the Governor's letter was said to have hastened his decision to break up his camp at Mampon and to return to Coomassie, without waiting for orders from the king.

On the 23d news was again received from the scouts that Ashantis to the number of 1000 were moving from Mampon towards Dunquah. In consequence of this, Lieutenant Gordon undertook a reconnaissance with 40 Houssas and 60 native allies from Abrakrampa on Ainsa in a northerly direction. He found here the remains of an Ashanti encampment of leaf-thatched huts, evidently abandoned that morning or the previous night, and traces that the Ashantis had moved in the direction of Dunquah: a fetish finger-post, consisting of a rough drawing of a hand, traced in blood, having been left to show the direction of their line of march. This reconnaissance confirmed the belief already entertained, that our operations of the 14th October had so alarmed the Ashantis that they were endeavouring to reach the Prah road at Dunquah. Some days before, an armed party of the enemy had moved to Quacodayo; and prisoners captured had asserted that a party under the Ashanti General Quasi Doomfie had been sent to strike the Prah road at Dunquah. But the rumours that Abrakrampa was to be attacked still continued. On the same day Major Home reported from Mansu that the garrison of his post now consisted of 223 armed men, including 21 Houssas, sent there under Captain Huyshe, and that he had in addition 252 unarmed labourers. He had opened up the road to the eastward for about a mile, so as to allow non-combatants to retreat in case of attack. The fort was by this time strongly palisaded and fraised all round. It would still require more than a week to clear the ground for a large encampment, and to open up the road, for four miles to the south were yet incomplete.

The same day (23d) Captain Butler, half-pay 69th Regiment, the well-known author of 'The Great Lone Land,' arrived from England by mail-steamer on special service, together with 4 surgeons, 3 control officers, and 6 rank and file of the Royal Engineers. Captain Buller had already been seized with a severe attack of fever, and been sent on board the Simoon; and Captain Butler was temporarily attached to headquarters, and took charge of the intelligence department.

On the 24th, Lieutenant Woodgate with 40 Houssas, and Lieutenant Pollard with 100 Abrah natives, made a reconnaissance to Quacodayo, which was found empty; but traces of the recent presence of Ashantis in small numbers were seen. Prisoners captured in this reconnaissance related that in two days Amanquatia was going to leave Mampon, and march by way of Ainsa and Yancoomassie to the Prah.

On the 25th definite information was received of the break-up of the camp at Mampon; but before narrating the exact nature of this intelligence, which led to an entirely new series of movements on our part, it would be well to sum up what was the condition of affairs generally in the various departments at this time:—

First of all as regards men. All the efforts made to rouse our Fanti allies to exertion had been in vain: some 500 assembled at Dunquah, and from 300 to 400 elsewhere, at Mansu, Napoleon, and Abrakrampa, represented the whole Fanti force in the field. As yet only very small detachments had arrived for Wood's and Russell's regiments; and on the 24th, Sir Garnet had written to the Secretary of State for War applying for the services of a third battalion in addition to the two previously demanded on the 13th. "Since the date of that letter," he wrote, "eleven days have passed, pregnant with facts of vital importance in relation to the conduct of this campaign. I have seen the days pass by since I held a reception of the native kings and chiefs, and no native levies of any importance have taken the field. Apathy, if not cowardice, seems to have enveloped the people of these tribes. I had hoped to raise large native levies from every portion of the Coast; but a few scores of men from each tribe, amounting altogether to only a few hundreds, seem all that I am likely to obtain. I have seen the danger of depending on ill-disciplined levies in bush-warfare. I have learned that the 2d West Indian Regiment, on which I had relied as an effective battalion, is unable to furnish more than about 100 bayonets for the field." The despatch went on to say that each day's experience of the country was proving that it was quite possible for European troops to stand the work, and to beat the natives in bush-fighting; and that he foresaw the probability of his having, very soon after the arrival of the English contingent, to fight an action on this side of the Prah, in which the losses might be so heavy as to make his weak battalions insufficient for the advance to Coomassie. He therefore considered it most important that he should have a reserve in hand to meet the losses he was likely to experience, and again urged that the composition of this battalion might be considered, and that it might be formed of selected officers and men, according to his original proposal, in which case he begged that the command might be given to Lieut.-Colonel Colley. He also wrote requesting that two colonels might be sent out, Colonel Greaves and another to be specially selected, as employment could be found for one of them as chief of the staff, and for the other in command of the European battalions.

The Control Department, having received a small addition to its strength of officers from England, was busily employed in landing, sorting, and storing arms, ammunition, supplies, and military stores, coming in in freight-ships from England, and in sending up stores of all kinds to the front as far as Mansu. Already great difficulty was experienced in keeping the labourers at work; the Sierra Leone men were idle and refused to work, and many of the Fanti labourers deserted. Such great difficulty had been experienced in finding hammock-men, and the price demanded by them was so great, that a Board had assembled by order of the Major-General to discuss the question of hammock-allowance to officers; and in consequence of its report, the Major-General had decided that no hammock-allowance should be granted to any one, and that whenever it was necessary, hammocks should be provided at the public expense. In this way, instead of a number of hammock-men, comparatively seldom used, being kept idle in the employ of officers, all that were procured were placed in the hands of the Control, who would supply a hammock whenever it was necessary for the conveyance of an officer. A general order was issued informing officers that they must march on foot, except in very special cases, when hammocks would be sanctioned by the Quartermaster-General.

As regards the Medical Department, the principal medical officer had reported on the 23d that four of the officers who had landed on the 2d had suffered from fever. Moist weather having prevailed, the periods of accession of the illness had doubtless been determined by meteorological influences. The arrival of four surgeons on the 23d had enabled medical officers to be attached to the various outposts. The health of the West Indian troops had improved since our arrival, although the weather had not been favourable.

The Engineers had, as already related, been constantly engaged in this bad weather at work upon the roads and in the erection of huts at Cape Coast.

As to the Artillery, Captain Rait had prepared and sent to the Major-General a most admirable scheme for the transport of small-arm ammunition, artillery ammunition, and of the third reserve, which will be again noticed. He continued drilling his men and practising them with both guns and rockets, his number being gradually increased; and experiments were made in the transport of ammunition by trench-carts which arrived on the 21st from England.

Surveys of the main road as far as Mansu, and of the cross-road leading from Assayboo to Abrakrampa, had been made and forwarded to England.*

All was quiet at Elmina and Cape Coast; the outposts at Napoleon and Abbaye, and at Mansu, Dunquah, and Accroful, on the main road, were all fortified and sufficiently strongly garrisoned; and Lieutenant Gordon had reported Abrakrampa as sufficiently prepared to resist any attack; when, in the course of the morning of the 25th, a prisoner was brought in who gave us the most useful intelligence and the most interesting information which had yet been received since we had reached the Coast. The prisoner was a girl not more than 18 or 19 years of age, by name Abraba Bosuma, the daughter of a Fanti woman by an Ashanti father. She was conducted to Government House, and examined in the office by Captain Butler, through the medium of Mr Davis, the Government interpreter. Sitting on the floor, but scantily clothed, in a worn thin robe, whence from time to time she delicately removed the insects that long dwelling in the Ashanti camp had fostered, she gave her evidence in the most straightforward and intelligent way. She was not without a certain coquetry of manner, that never left her in our long subsequent acquaintance. When our march up country

* Within forty-eight hours of the arrival of these sketches in England they had been lithographed in the Intelligence Department, and a sufficient number of copies struck off for use by the regiments despatched from England, and the staff at Cape Coast.

began, Major Baker hired her as a carrier, and she grew sleek and fat almost beyond recognition before we reached Coomassie. She was always merry and good-natured, and fond of her master, though much surprised on the first day's march that she was not to play Ruth to his Boaz, and lie at her master's feet. What has become of her now? When last the writer inquired after her he heard she was "living with No. 1 company."

Her story was to this effect: She was the slave wife of one Koffee Essandoo, an Ashanti captain of note. This chief was very fond of her; but his sister and mother were very jealous of his affection for her, treated her badly, and threatened to kill her. Her life having become weary from their threats, she had left the camp at Mampon two hours before daylight this same morning, and had made her way through the bush in the direction in which she had heard the Ashantis say there were white men and Fanti soldiers. Striking the path, she had arrived at Napoleon and been brought in from that place. She had been at Mampon, she told us, for five months, and had heard and seen much of what was going on. She said that the Ashantis at Mampon had become much alarmed on finding Essaman attacked by white soldiers, and at the same time, or very soon afterwards, learning that there were soldiers at Dunquah and at Mansu; and that when the Governor's letter had reached Amanquatia in his camp three days before, the Ashantis began to pack up their baggage and to move towards Coomassie. They had marched, she said, in many parties, taking the direction of Jooquah, from whence they were to strike the main road to the Prah.

She declared that no road existed from Mampon to the Prah except the old track of Dunquah, Mansu, and Prahsu, and a cross-road from Jooquah to Dunquah. Along this she said that the Ashantis were retiring. The chiefs Amanquatia and Quamin Agyapon were to move from Mampon that very day, the 25th, for Jooquah, their horns and drums having been blowing and sounding all the previous night. She said that about twenty days ago news had come down from Coomassie by an Ashanti party which had marched to the Prah; that Amanquatia had endeavoured to communicate with this party by sending Quasi Doomfie in the direction of Dunquah, but that in the mean time the road had been closed, and Quasi Doomfie was unable to get through to the Prah, and was still remaining in the bush between Mampon and Dunquah. She said that the sick and Fanti slaves were being sent away with this party of Quasi Doomfie's, and that the Chamah people had bought the Wassaw captives from the Ashantis; and she corroborated the previous statements as to the losses from dysentery in the camp.

There was no doubting the truth of this girl's statement. Her manner, the circumstantial nature of her evidence, and the absence of any contradiction when carefully examined a second and third time, placed it practically beyond all doubt that the Ashanti camp at Mampon was broken up; that the army had the intention of retreating; that it intended to move in the direction of Dunquah, and then strike the main Prah road. On receipt of this information, tallying as it did with previous reports, the Major-General decided to take the steps which will be narrated at the commencement of the next chapter.

CHAPTER VI.

EVENTS TO THE RE-CROSSING OF THE PRAH BY THE ENEMY—THE MARCH TO ASSANCHI—ACTIONS OF ISCABIO—DEFENCE OF ABRA-KRAMPA—RECONNAISSANCES—ACTION OF FAISOWAH—FLIGHT OF THE ASHANTI ARMY ACROSS THE PRAH.

THE breaking up of the camp at Mampon being now, on the 25th October, an established fact, the Major-General at once informed the officers commanding posts on the main road and at Abrakrampa; and with a view of strengthening the force on the road, a detachment of fifty of the 2d West Indian Regiment, with two 7-pr. guns of Rait's artillery, under Captain Rait, marched the same afternoon for Assayboo, proceeding to Dunquah on the 26th. The officer commanding at Elmina was ordered to take immediate steps to reconnoitre from Abbaye, in the direction of Mampon, with a view of ascertaining the exact position of affairs. He was to move all the available force at Elmina to Abbaye, calling on the officer commanding H.M.S Druid to garrison the forts at Elmina during his absence. From Abbaye he was to push on half-way to Mampon, and then use his own discretion as to his further movements, the object being to harass any rear-guard the enemy might have left at Mampon. Should the enemy really be retreating, in this case

Colonel Wood was to use his best endeavours to start with the native levies in pursuit, with orders to hang on the enemy's rear, and attack him without ceasing. The Major-General contemplated marching a force of marines and Russell's Regiment on the 26th to Dunquah. A reconnaissance was also ordered from Napoleon in the direction of Mampon.

On the morning of the 26th October, Captain Despard, R.M.L.I., marched from Abbaye with all his available force in the direction of Mampon; and Colonel Wood marched from Elmina at daybreak with sixty of the 2d West Indians, and some rockets, and thirty-five Elminas of Wood's Regiment.

Colonel Wood reached Simeo about 11, and shortly before noon the Abbaye reconnaissance returned to that place, with some Ashanti prisoners captured near Essiam and Mampon. The reconnoitring party had passed through several empty camps, but had not entered Mampon, as it was still occupied by the Ashantis, to the number only, however, of from 700 to 2000, according to the reports of the prisoners. Colonel Wood reported from Simeo that the Aquafoos and Agoonahs, from Abbaye, positively declined to follow up the Ashantis; that they would not go half a mile without the regular troops, and were most anxious to return to Abbaye. As the evening drew on, they multiplied the 2000 men at Mampon to 8000; and finding that Colonel Wood intended to remain at Simeo, they returned to Abbaye, leaving their chiefs at Simeo. The reconnaissance from Napoleon was not pushed far, and did not find any Ashantis.

Colonel Wood proposed to attack Mampon on the following day, and invited the co-operation of Captain

Blake and the men of the Druid to march to Abbaye. Colonel Wood was, however, instructed to return to Elmina.

On the same day the Major-General marched with a force of 100 of Russell's foot and 250 marines and blue-jackets from Cape Coast to Assayboo, at the junction of the roads to Abrakrampa and Dunquah. Russell's detachment preceded the white troops, and Major Russell was ordered to select a site for their encampment. The marines and sailors started about 3 o'clock in the afternoon, but it was not till long after dark that they arrived at Assayboo. The earlier part of the march along the main road, under the blazing afternoon sun, without a particle of shade, was so fearfully fatiguing that numbers of the troops fell out. Great gaps were caused in the column by the difficulty experienced in moving two water-carts which had been sent on in the middle of the day, and also some hand-carts carrying baggage over the very steep hills on the road. On arrival at Assayboo, the only cleared space was found to be quite unequal to accommodate more than a very small number of men, and the marines bivouacked along the main road. Two tents were pitched : in one of them the Major-General and his staff huddled together on the ground; and in the other, Captain Fremantle and as many officers as possible of the Naval Brigade.

During the day scouts returned to Accroful had reported a large body of Ashantis moving past Abrakrampa in the direction of Dunquah; and in the night a report was received at Assayboo from Lieutenant Gordon at Abrakrampa, saying that a body of the enemy was encamped at Assanchi, about six miles from Abrakrampa, and that they were evidently moving along the road leading by way of Iscabio, with the probable view of collecting a sufficient force to attack one of the posts on the main road. It was evident that detached bodies of the enemy were moving in that direction; and it was equally evident that very large masses of the enemy could not already have reached the neighbourhood of Dunquah, owing to the time required for the passage of large bodies of men with baggage and sick along the narrow bush-tracks, in which the march must be in single file; and accordingly, a favourable opportunity appeared to exist for attacking a fragment of the enemy's force, any attack upon his main body being quite out of the question.

The Major-General therefore decided on moving the force to Abrakrampa rather than to Dunquah, hoping that from that place he would be able to make an attack on the flank of some one of the bodies of Ashantis moving from Mampon towards Dunquah.

Colonel Festing had received orders on the 26th that he was to do all in his power to obtain information regarding the enemy's movements, and that if possible they were not to be permitted to evade us by striking the road north of Mansu. Further orders were sent on the early morning of the 27th, which Colonel Festing received about 10 A.M., to march with his whole available force along the road in the direction of Iscabio. This road was known as "the haunted road," the Ashantis having performed fetish upon it during their eastward march in April, in order to deter the superstitious Fanti natives from using it. The fetish had probably been the slaughter of Fanti captives.

Agreeably to his orders, Colonel Festing marched

about half-past 10 with a detachment of 12 officers and 701 men, of whom 73 were of the 2d West India Regiment, and 615 were Fanti allies, and advanced about three miles in a drenching thunderstorm. At this distance Captain Godwin, who was leading the column with the Annamaboes, captured a prisoner, and in spite of the noise of the thunder the sounds of a large camp could be heard. The enemy were evidently quite unconscious of the approach of Colonel Festing's detachment, as they could be heard beating cankey, cutting trees, and building huts. Guided by this prisoner the Annamaboes approached the camp quite unperceived, and rushed in upon the camp about 2 P.M., followed by the whole force. The enemy, who were engaged in preparing their meal, were completely surprised. Their camp was on the summit of a small hill, surrounded by some groups of huts on every side, about a mile from the village of Iscabio, and the prisoner reported it to contain from 4000 to 5000 men under the chiefs Essaman Quantah and Quasi Doomfie. The Ashantis soon recovered from their surprise, and opened a heavy fire from the bush beyond the camp, to which the Annamaboes replied; while Captain Rait fired shrapnel shell, case, and rockets into the bush, and men were sent out on the flanks to prevent the enemy surrounding the force, which he was evidently endeavouring to do. For an hour and a half the enemy kept up a fire from the surrounding bush, and then the 2d West India Regiment advanced into the bush and fired volleys from their Sniders, dispersing the Ashantis in all directions. Their camp was destroyed, together with such furniture, guns, and powder as were found in it; and Colonel Festing, as it was growing late, marched the detachment back to Dunquah. The return march was quite unmolested. While Colonel Festing was advancing from Dunquah that place was held by a detachment of the 2d West Indians from Accroful, who returned the same evening.

The only natives who had fought at all well were the Annamaboes, the remainder having to be thrashed into action by the officers, whilst numbers of them disappeared altogether from the scene, or remained huddled up in small groups without fighting. Much difficulty had been experienced in taking the guns into action: the path was so narrow that the carriages had to be taken to pieces, and the guns and carriages carried by the men. Captain Rait said that his Houssas behaved well, but were rather excitable; and he reported that as the axle-trees of his 7-prs. were only an encumbrance where wheel-traffic is not required, a light rear chock naval carriage would be better suited for this kind of warfare, and that a wooden quoin would be much better than the screw arrangement, which was apt to get bent and out of order.

In this small action 5 officers, including Colonel Festing, were wounded, and 5 non-commissioned officers and men; 1 native was killed, and 42 wounded, including the King of Annamaboe. Captain Godwin, of the 103d Regiment, was hit by a slug in the groin, and was shortly afterwards invalided to England.

The same morning the Major-General, with a detachment from Cape Coast, marched to Abrakrampa. It had originally been his intention to advance the same day to Assanchi, but the fatigued condition of the men on arrival at Abrakrampa, and the rain and intense heat of the day, convinced him that it would be rash to attempt such a march, involving, as it would, the return to Abrakrampa the same night; and he decided on making a combined movement with Colonel Festing on Assanchi on the following day, the 28th.

Scouting parties of the Abrah natives under Lieutenant Pollard were however sent out in the directions of Ainsa, Assanchi, and Quacodayo, and returned, having captured a few prisoners, who were evidently stragglers seeking for food. The same day Lieutenant-Colonel Wood returned with his party to Elmina, and a reconnaissance made from Napoleon by a native officer returned, reporting no trace of the Ashantis in that neighbourhood.

On the morning of the 28th October the Major-General advanced with the whole force from Abrakrampa upon Assanchi, hoping that Colonel Festing, of whose affair of the previous day he was in ignorance, would advance from Dunquah; and that thus the Ashantis between Assanchi and Iscabio might be attacked simultaneously in front and in rear, and severely defeated. The Abrah native allies under Lieutenant Pollard headed the march, which led through the first real forest that we had as yet seen on the Coast. No enemy was found at Assanchi, but the traces of a very recent encampment were evident. The troops halted there for about two hours, and were listening anxiously for the sound of firing in the direction of Dunquah, but none was heard; neither did any report come in from the scouts advanced in that direction to lead us to suppose that Colonel Festing had made any advance. Soon after noon, it being by this time evident that Colonel Festing could not have moved, the Major-General returned to Abrakrampa. The fatigue of that return march will not be soon forgotten. The day was one of the most exhausting which we experienced on the Gold Coast; an intense heat without a breath of wind was scarcely relieved by a drenching thunderstorm, which wet us all to the skin. Our march to Assanchi and back was at least twelve miles along a road frequently nearly knee-deep in water, and impeded by many trunks of trees. As it was almost impossible for a hammock to be carried along the path, owing to the overhanging branches and creepers, Sir Garnet Wolseley had himself, in spite of his wounded leg, to walk nearly the whole distance, as did all his staff.

The Houssas had been left at Assanchi to await the return of Lieutenant Pollard with the Abrahs, who had been sent on in the direction of Dunquah along the haunted road. Moving in the direction of Iscabio, the Abrahs had encountered Ashanti scouts, when, to their everlasting disgrace, they all, with the exception of nine men, disappeared, leaving Lieutenant Pollard, who was almost completely exhausted. These nine men remained with him, and escorted him, carrying him part of the way, to Accroful, from which he returned on the following morning to Abrakrampa. The Abrahs who had deserted him returned to Assanchi, and said to Lieutenant Gordon, whom they found there, that they had been cut off from their officer. Accordingly he advanced with the Houssas in the direction of Iscabio, whence, learning that Lieutenant Pollard had gone to Accroful, he returned to Abrakrampa, arriving late in the night, almost worn out with fatigue.

Colonel Festing had been unable to comply with the Major-General's orders to move this day upon Iscabio, and a great chance had thus been lost. He had summoned the kings to turn out with their troops at daybreak; but they made various excuses, alleging that it was impossible for them to do so. Everything was in readiness; a detachment of the 2d West Indians and Rait's artillery were on parade, but none of the native allies were forthcoming. The king of Annamaboe had been badly wounded in the right side, and the other kings and chiefs asserted that they and their men were footsore and tired, and unable to move. Every effort was used by Colonel Festing, but they would not stir; and in view of the resistance which he had experienced on the previous day, he considered that he would not be justified in attempting to march upon the camp at Iscabio with the small force of sixty-two West Indians and Rait's gun, which were alone at his disposal. It was a most unfortunate occurrence; for, had only an advance been made from Dunquah, and the sound of an attack been heard at Assanchi, the Major-General would have moved from that place upon Iscabio, and the defeat and rout of the Ashantis in camp must have been complete. In the course of this day some of Colonel Wood's scouts reported Mampon deserted; but, as usual, this was found to be a false report, the scouts not having been near the place.

During the absence of the Major-General there had been an alarm at Cape Coast. On the evening of the 26th a panic had seized the people of the villages lying between Cape Coast and Assayboo, who believed the Ashantis were coming in upon the road. Reports to

this effect had reached us at Assayboo, but had been treated as they deserved. As similar reports had reached Captain Butler, who had returned to Cape Coast from carrying the orders to Napoleon and Abbaye, he very properly reported them both to the Major-General and to Major Bravo, in command of the garrison at Cape Coast. Major Bravo, on receipt of intelligence of the alarm, which reached him at half-past 3 in the early morning of the 27th, sent word to the officer commanding the detachment of Russell's Regiment at Prospect Hill, and ordered the volunteers up to Connor's Hill camp. The greatest alarm, in consequence, spread through the town; and when the news reached the Major-General, about mid-day on the 27th, he sent Captain Peile, commanding H.M. "Simoom," back to Cape Coast, to take command of the place and its environs. He found all quiet. As Captain Fowler had written expressing an opinion that he would be attacked at Napoleon, and asking for a light gun to be sent out, Major Bravo had despatched 140 Enfield rifles, and 22,000 rounds of ammunition to the native levies there, and Captain Peile sent 60 more rifles. Judge Marshall, however, on the 27th, had visited Napoleon, and found all quiet there. The Sierra Leone volunteers at Cape Coast being rather mutinous in the absence of the troops, Captain Peile took some strong measures with them, and very soon reduced them to order.

In the course of the day the Major-General had received information to the effect that the main body of the Ashantis was about Essecroom, on the Sweet River, north of Napoleon, and that it was the intention of Amanquatia to attack Abrakrampa. Had any considerable force, even a battalion of disciplined troops, been at his command, the Major-General might have taken the initiative, and attacked the Ashantis in their camp; but without any force at his disposal but a handful of white men, and a few hundred of native allies whose utter worthlessness had been proved on every occasion on which they had been called upon to act, such a course was out of the question. To keep the whole of the marines and blue-jackets waiting at Abrakrampa an indefinite time, until it pleased Amanquatia to attack us, was out of the question on grounds of health alone; and accordingly, on the 29th, they were marched back to Assayboo, from whence, on the 30th, they returned to Cape Coast, and re-embarked on board H.M. ships.

A garrison of twenty-five blue-jackets and twenty-five marines was, however, left at Abrakrampa, under the command of Lieutenant Wells, R.N., whom the senior naval officer detailed for this duty. These troops were left there to form a nucleus of reliable men in case the place should be attacked, which seemed possible if not probable; as many prisoners had asserted that Amanquatia was resolved to attack it, in consequence of the resolute hostility which the king of Abrah had always shown to him, and the manner in which the Abrahs had harassed and annoyed the Ashanti foraging parties. Major Baker Russell was left in command of the place, and his regiment was increased to a strength of nearly 200. He had also about 80 Houssas under Lieutenant Gordon, and more than 300 Abrahs, to which tribe Captain Bromhead was now accredited as special commissioner in the place of Lieutenant Pollard, who took Captain Bromhead's place with the Assins. As the post was well provisioned and strongly entrenched, with the bush well cleared round it, it was considered that the garrison would be quite able to resist an attack of any number of the enemy.

On the 29th and 30th October further reconnaissances had been made from Napoleon and Abbaye, and had come across numbers of Ashanti foragers.

In all these movements the Major-General's operations had been directed to one end. It had been his object to avoid heading the main body of the Ashantis in their retreat upon the Prah, but at the same time to prevent their striking the main Prahsu road, and to make the greatest possible display of his European force in various directions. "I desire," wrote the Major-General in a dispatch of the 31st October, "not only to hasten the enemy's retreat, which is necessary before I can advance beyond Mansu, but to appear to be driving them out of the country, in hopes that I may thus instil some spirit into the Fantis, and induce them to rise and harass the retiring enemy, as, would they do so, they might inflict very heavy losses upon him. At the same time, I have done all in my power to spare the European troops undue fatigue."

A phrase in this despatch was much taken hold of by the press at home—" My position," wrote Sir Garnet, "is somewhat humiliating: the enemy's main column of retreat is within an easy march of my head-quarters, and I have no force capable of attacking it." Had the despatch to be written again now, it is probable that another phrase, more exactly representing the true position, might be selected; but the expression was never intended to convey any impression of bad treatment by H.M. Government, into which it was construed by most of the journals. Those among the readers of this book who have any experience of war will, however, know how painful the position must have been of seeing this force of half-armed naked savages defile at its leisure within easy striking distance, while utterly unable to strike. If the writer may venture an opinion, he would say that had H.M. Government known Sir Garnet Wolseley before he started as they know him now, they would have trusted him better. The one blot in their arrangements seems to be this:—They sent out Sir Garnet Wolseley with his staff to ascertain and report whether European troops were required. His report must be made within three or four weeks, if the troops were to be sent out in time to be of any use before the ensuing rainy season. If, at the end of these three weeks, Sir Garnet were to decide that European troops could with safety and must of necessity be employed, the moment of his decision would be singularly favourable for their employment, as it would be easier to strike an effective blow at the Ashanti army within a short distance of the Coast, than to march far into the heart of Africa to its attack. Had the Government trusted Sir Garnet thoroughly, they would assuredly have sent out the white troops within a month of his arrival, trusting to him not to use them should their employment be unnecessary, or the conditions of climate be too unfavourable to give him the chance of employing them, even if they were most important for his purpose. Had this been done, the Ashanti army would probably have been destroyed; even the native tribes might have been induced to gather themselves together for the combat; and of all Amanquatia's army, none but a few broken and scattered fugitives could by any possibility have crossed the Prah. Strategically the position held by Sir Garnet at this time was magnificent. Had he been able to march a force from Dunquah, or from above Dunquah, on the main road, towards the Ashanti army at Mampon or Essecroom, a successful action would have driven it upon our posts of Napoleon and Abbaye, and on our forts on the coast, and its destruction would have been inevitable; while our own troops could always, and with ease, have kept open their communications with the Coast. One of those opportunities was lost which occur not once in a generation. "Still," continued the Major-General, "on the whole I am somewhat better placed than I had hoped to be. In two actions we have surprised and defeated our enemies; they have broken up their camp at Mampon, which was a standing menace to Cape Coast and Elmina; and they are commencing to retire to their own country. In consequence of the strong positions we have established on the main road by which they came, they are compelled to seek another way for their retreat. On the other hand, every day's bitter experience teaches me the utter worthlessness of the native allies, from whom I had expected some little help, and convinces me more and more fully that no decisive blow can be struck at the Ashantis, and that this war can never be brought to an end, except by disciplined European troops."

This bitter experience of the native levies was destined to continue. In vain did his Excellency issue a proclamation, informing the natives of his success, and urging them to attack the enemy in their retreat. "Will you not pursue them?" said the address; "now or never is the time to show that you are men; and I, for my part, shall hold no man as the friend of her Majesty, or as the friend of this country, who delays for one moment. If you now act quickly and with vigour, the fall of your enemy and the peace of your country will be secure." The answer was as before. The same apathy and the same cowardice continued to be displayed in the retreat of the enemy which had been shown during his advance.

Towards the end of October the first signs of sickness began to show themselves among the officers who had landed with the Major-General. On the 2d four cases of fever occurred, and in every case the patient was immediately sent on board H.M.S. "Simoom" by orders of the principal medical officer. The marines engaged in these last operations had been present at the action at Essaman on the 14th October, and had made the very severe march entailed by that day's work. All but ten of those present at Essaman were able to march on the second occasion; and this led to hopes that, as the season improved, the severe work of marching and fighting would not be found to involve very great sickness. On this second occasion, however, the marines suffered more than they had done on the 14th, and four days after their re-embarkation, on the 31st, twenty-nine men of them were on the sick list, mostly, however, from foot-sores and from weakness due to exposure to the sun, though there were some cases of malarial fever.

The movements of the enemy determined the nature of operations now to be undertaken. To harass him by means of constant raids from Dunquah and Abrakrampa, both of which places must be strengthened by an increased garrison, and to press, so far as possible, upon his rear, with native allies from Napoleon and Abbaye, was the course presenting itself as the most suitable under the unfortunate condition of our inability to attack boldly his main body, caused by the paucity of troops at our disposal. Abrakrampa was strengthened by the addition of a detachment of eighty-five of the 2d West India Regiment; and a number of Kossoos and Sierra Leone men, who arrived by the mail steamer on the 2d November, together with a freshly arrived detachment of men from Mumford and Winnebah, to the number in all of 182, were sent to join Russell's regiment there. The detachment of the West Indian Regiment at Dunquah was also strengthened, and Captain Sarbah's Gold Coast company of volunteers was sent there and attached to the 2d West Indian Regiment. At the same time all the Abrahs at Dunquah were ordered to march to Abrakrampa under Captain Bromhead. The bulk of their tribe had, at the end of October, dispersed in a state of great discontent, owing to some disagreement as to their employment as carriers, and partly also from an unfortunate difference between Lieutenant Pollard and King Amfoo Ottoo. In the first days of November they were, however, re-assembled.

In order to induce the native allies at Napoleon to act against the rear of the enemy, the chief magistrate, who was well known to all the chiefs at Cape Coast, and who possessed considerable influence with them, proceeded to Napoleon and read the Governor's proclamation. He also volunteered to lead the men, and they consented to accompany him to Beulah, which was now ordered to be made their head-quarters instead of Napoleon, with a view to their reconnoitring as far to the north-east as possible, in the direction of Aboo and Abrakrampa, so as to keep in contact with the enemy, and harass him in his retreat. The garrison of Napoleon itself was made up of 70 of the West India Regiment, and one field gun was sent there; while the Cape Coast and Commendah native allies, to the number of about 900, marched to Beulah. They arrived there on the 1st of November, and on the following day commenced to clear the bush and form an encampment, to which Lieutenant-Colonel Wood proceeded to take the command, with all the troops that could be spared from Elmina, and a 7-pr. gun. A fresh detachment of Kossoos, which arrived on the 2d November, was ordered to Beulah; but their head man having been sent with the rest to Russell's Regiment at Abrakrampa, they altogether declined to remain away from him, and were subsequently sent to join the remainder of their tribe. Great difficulty was experienced by Colonel Wood in inducing the native allies to reconnoitre in any direction where it was possible that the enemy might be found.

By the end of October Colonel Festing reported that the number of natives assembled under their chiefs at Dunquah amounted to nearly 1400; and instructions were sent to him on the 1st November to the effect that the bulk of the enemy's force was supposed to be now between the Sweet River and Dunquah, and that he was to make a reconnaissance in force each day, attacking the enemy whenever he had an opportunity, hanging on to him and harassing him as much as possible.

It was considered that the force at his disposal—100 of the 2d West India Regiment, with two guns and 1400 native allies—was sufficient to allow him to send out large reconnoitring parties every day with the object of finding and attacking the enemy. He was informed of the occupation of Beulah, and of the orders given to Lieutenant-Colonel Wood to press upon the rear of the Ashantis, and was desired to do all in his power to induce the Abrah allies to attack the enemy, who was now within a very short distance of Abrakrampa, and was, so far as could be judged, concentrating in force.

On the 1st November the garrison of Abrakrampa was as under:—

	Officers.	Men.
Naval Brigade	1	59
2d W. I. Regiment	0	10
Houssas	1	99
Russell's Regiment	2	213
Kossoos	1	78
Native Allies	1	430
Staff	2	—
	8	889

and in the morning a strong reconnaissance was made from Abrakrampa towards Anasmadie, which was found occupied by the enemy in great force. They were cutting paths on each side of the road towards Abrakrampa, and had arrived within half-a-mile of the place. The officer commanding at Abrakrampa reported that he expected to be immediately attacked. On receipt of this report, orders were sent for the blue-jackets and marines, whom it had been intended to remove and re-embark, to remain a couple of days longer. Major Russell, who had expressed himself anxious to attack the enemy, was recommended rather to wait to be attacked, so far as his disciplined troops were concerned, but to do all he could to induce the Abrah people to hang on to and annoy the Ashantis; he was told of the orders which had been sent to Colonel Festing, and of the intention to move against the rear of the enemy from Beulah. On the 2d foraging parties of the Ashantis approached quite close to the village of Abrakrampa, and three prisoners were captured, who, being separately examined, all agreed in asserting that Amanquatia was encamped at Anasmadie with at least 8000 fighting men. Major Russell reported that the attempted reconnaissance with the native allies on the previous afternoon in the direction of Anasmadie had failed, as the native allies refused to proceed, although pricked on.

On receipt of Major Russell's letter, a light brass $1\frac{1}{2}$-pounder naval gun, with some langridge made up by Captain Rait, was sent out to Abrakrampa under charge of Lieutenant Saunders, R.A., who had that morning arrived from the Gambia and Sierra Leone. Lieutenant Saunders started at 6 P.M., and arrived at Abrakrampa just before midnight, proceeding by Butteyan, as the direct road from Assayboo was considered unsafe. Major Russell was urged to keep the Abrah people out in the bush as a screen round the village, and should he be attacked to reserve the fire of his regular troops until the Ashantis advanced into the open. On the 3d the Assayboo road was patrolled from Abrakrampa and reported open and safe, and a picquet was left at a village about one mile from Assayboo and another half-way between that and Abrakrampa. The Abrah people worked willingly under Captain Bromhead, scouting in the direction of Anasmadie.

In the course of the day a reconnaissance was sent out in the direction of Anasmadie, consisting of the Houssas under Lieutenant Gordon, and the Winnebahs under Lord Gifford. Coming suddenly upon some Ashantis, who opened fire, the Winnebahs took to their heels and ran, knocking down in their "backward rush" Lord Gifford and Mr. Winwood Reade, the *Times* special correspondent, who had accompanied the party. Captain Buckle of the Royal Engineers had by this time put the village of Abrakrampa into a complete state of defence, supplementing the previous labours of Captain Huyshe and Houssa Gordon.

On this same day Colonel Festing made a reconnaissance in force along the haunted road in the direction of Iscabio. His force consisted of 9 officers and 1111 men, of whom 1011 were native allies, 80 2d West India Regiment, 8 Houssas of Rait's Artillery with rockets under Lieutenant Eardley Wilmot, and 12 Fanti police. He soon fell in with the enemy's scouts, who fired upon the advance guard and retreated. Pushing on, he arrived at a large camp of the enemy, who made a stout resistance. As soon as the enemy was found to be in force, Lieutenant Wilmot went to the front with his rockets, and was almost immediately, while in action, very severely wounded in the left arm, yet in spite of this, he continued in action with the utmost gallantry, until about an hour later he was shot through the heart. Colonel Festing brought in his body from where it was lying among the wounded troops in the extreme front of the action, and in so doing was wounded by a slug in the hip.

The Annamaboes, who were leading, did not behave so well on this occasion as they had previously done. Out of about 200 all but 60 or 70 deserted at the beginning of the action. The other natives behaved still worse; whole tribes deserted, and rushed pell-mell into Dunquah, and some even beyond it. The Denkeras and the Assins showed the greatest cowardice. The detachment of the 2d West Indians stood their ground well, and engaged the Ashantis for a couple of hours, driving them about in all directions with their Sniders. The enemy's fire having been put down, and a great amount of ammunition expended on our side, Colonel Festing returned to camp with his men, who were very tired. The prisoners captured next day said that the enemy had suffered considerably, and that he was breaking up his camp, and retreating through the bush to the Prah. One rocket was reported to have fallen into a group of chiefs and captains, and killed or wounded six among their number. But the success was very dearly purchased. Of the nine officers who went into action, one was killed and five were wounded. Poor Eardley Wilmot's body was sent by Colonel Festing into Cape Coast, and on the following day was buried by the side of the body of Governor Keate in the cemetery. He was the first to die of our little "Ambriz" band, and we all sincerely mourned his loss. Beneath his quiet unassuming manner had lain the staunch loyal heart of a true English gentleman. From the day of landing he had gone steadily on with the toilsome work of teaching his Houssa recruits; and now, the first time that he went out to see the fruits of his labours, the gallant heart that knew no fear was pierced and stricken to death. When the surgeons examined his body after death, they found the wound in the arm so severe that, had he lived, amputation would have been required; yet for an hour after receiving it he had fought manfully on. When the sad news reached us, we asked each other if all the vile blood of all the Fanti tribes was worth the smallest drop in the veins of so brave and faithful a soldier.

Captain Rait had proceeded to Beulah on this day, and taken charge of the 7-pounder gun and rocket-trough there; but on hearing of Lieutenant Wilmot's death, he returned to Cape Coast Castle to attend his funeral, and remained there till the 6th. The same day, Ashanti foragers, to the number of fifty or sixty, struck the main road between Accroful and Dunquah, and a skirmish ensued between them and some Accroful scouts. An Ashanti head was brought into Accroful, and one of our allies was wounded. Lieutenant-Colonel Wood had also sent out reconnaissances from Beulah eastward and towards Essecroom; and our allies who accompanied Lieutenant Eyre in the direction of Siroof positively refused to advance when they saw some Ashanti dead bodies at the place. Lieutenant Eyre, however, by placing his pistol at the head of the leading man, succeeded in getting them as far as Essecroom. Here a very large deserted camp was found, and four coffins which appeared to have been lately disinterred, besides very many dead bodies. There were a good many sick Ashantis, who were not interfered with, but eight prisoners fit to march were made. In this reconnaissance Eyre had to cross the Sweet River, where it was nearly up to the necks of his party.

The same day the head-quarters of the 2d West India Regiment, and all available men, left Cape Coast and marched for Accroful, *en route* for Mansu, the men marching in fighting order, carrying sixty rounds of ammunition, their blankets, greatcoats, and waterproof sheets, with a field kit in their knapsacks. The duties of the garrison at Cape Coast were taken up by the armed police. Lieutenant-Colonel Webber having arrived from England, now took command of the regiment and proceeded to Mansu.

Throughout the 4th the position of affairs at Abrakrampa remained unchanged. Reconnaissances were sent out, and some prisoners were captured. Some female slaves also, who had deserted from the Ashanti camp, sought refuge at Abrakrampa. They all agreed in stating that Amanquatia was a little in rear of Anasmadie, determined on attacking Abrakrampa, and that ammunition had been issued to the men for that purpose. The enemy was said to be on the alert, employing outlying picquets. The 2d West India Regiment reached Dunquah on this day, and a detachment of fifty marines was landed in the evening, and marched to Assayboo to form a post there. Captain Buckle proceeded to Assayboo to place it in a state of defence.

Colonel Wood at the same time reported from Beulah that he could not get the native allies to move. Chief Attah had promised, for £10, to send fifty men to Anasmadie to scout, but declined point-blank to go there with his men. Colonel Wood was ordered to occupy Essecroom; but both he and the officers with him were so exhausted that he reported them unable to move that day, even if ordered.

The attack upon Abrakrampa had been so long threatened, and so often postponed,—in short " Wolf!" had been cried so many times, that the impression had become general at head-quarters that the Ashantis would never attack. Even should they do so, it was considered that the native troops at the place, including, as they did, a strong force of the 2d West India Regiment and of Houssas, would be amply sufficient to hold the post against any number of the enemy; and it had been decided to withdraw the detachment of Houssas and marines on the 4th, as the Major-General was most anxious to avoid exposing the Europeans longer than absolutely necessary to the risk of malarial fever. Through a misunderstanding, however, Major Russell supposed that they were not to be withdrawn till the 5th, and arrangements were made for their march to Assayboo at 4 P.M. on that day. Major Russell, however, on the same morning, wrote, expressing his great regret at their intended departure, and begging that other white troops might be sent in their place, as the presence of white soldiers gave the natives great confidence, and he feared that if they were withdrawn just now a good many of the Abrah men would decamp. That morning also a serious disturbance occurred amongst the Houssas. When ordered out to cut bush one man had positively refused to go, and when confined had been followed into the guard by twenty-four others, who said that they also would not work. Major Russell had marched down the Naval Brigade with loaded rifles, as the Houssas were making a great noise, and they had then submitted. He retained as a prisoner the man who had first disobeyed, disarmed the other twenty-four, and marched them off to cut bush, telling them that in case of an attack they should not be employed to fight, as they were a disgrace to the name of soldiers. It was for this reason also desirable to retain the white troops. Moreover, that morning news was received that Essaman Quanta had moved from his camp near Dunquah, and had reinforced Amanquatia before Abrakrampa. A considerable body of troops had been seen by the Kossoo scouts arriving in the enemy's camp the preceding night, and this very morning they had driven in the Fanti picquets, though they did not attempt to march through the bush into the clearing round the village.

Still, in the full spirit of discipline, Major Russell paraded his small detachment of white men at 4 P.M., and they were about to march off, when the Ashantis commenced to attack the village on the west front of the position, driving in the picquets rapidly, and opening a heavy fire on the advanced skirmishers. They repeatedly endeavoured with shouts and cheers to break out of the bush, but recoiled on reaching its edge, though Major Russell restrained the fire of his men to tempt them to advance into the open. The marines and sailors, who had actually fallen in on parade to march to Assayboo, were detained; and at about 5 P.M., the enemy's fire having slackened, a few scouts were sent out down the Assayboo road towards the right flank of the enemy, whom they found advancing in strong bodies along paths newly cut by them. Shortly afterwards a most furious attack was made on the west and south-west side of the village, the Ashantis suddenly rushing out into the open, but being repulsed by the fire of the 2d West India Regiment, Houssas, and Russell's Regiment, who lined the shelter trenches on that side. The attack was kept up with great violence for nearly two hours, then slackened, and was again repeated, and continued till midnight; after which a few shots only were fired by the enemy, and returned by picked shots from our side. A large part of the garrison bivouacked on their posts the whole night, and all the officers remained at their posts. At 4 A.M. on the 6th firing ceased, and the enemy, who up to that hour had been very noisy, became silent.

As soon as the attack commenced at 4 P.M., Major Russell sent a report of it to head-quarters, which arrived at Government House about 9 P.M., travelling by way of Butteyan, the Assayboo road being cut. At 11 o'clock at night, in reporting the further course of events to the officer commanding at Accroful, he reported the road to Assayboo cut off, and asked for a supply of rockets, which were sent to him in the course of the night. Captain Brett, commanding at Accroful, as requested, forwarded on this report, and had previously at 8 P.M. reported to Cape Coast that he had heard firing at Abrakrampa since 5 P.M., and that the usual post from Abrakrampa had not arrived at Accroful. This report reached Cape Coast at 2.15 on the morning of the 6th. On the receipt at headquarters of Major Russell's morning letter, describing the outbreak among the Houssas and the immediate probability of attack, permission had been immediately sent to him to retain the fifty blue-jackets and marines. But still very little faith was placed, at head-quarters, in the probability of the Ashantis attempting to attack; in fact, it was considered too good to be true; and at the mess table that evening, even such wise officers as Major Home and Captain Huyshe had laid wagers of

50 and 20 to 1 that Abrakrampa would not be attacked, which the writer had the pleasure of taking. Scarcely an hour had passed from the bets being made, when Major Russell's short report, dated 4 P.M., was received, saying that the place was attacked, and that he had retained the sailors and marines. No immediate steps, however, were taken, as it was assumed he would repulse the enemy; but when at a quarter past two in the morning of the 6th the report from Accroful was received, to the effect that heavy firing had been going on up to 8 P.M., and that the post from Abrakrampa had not arrived, immediate measures were taken for marching to the relief of the place. The Major-General decided on marching early in the morning with all the available blue-jackets and marines, if in the meantime information should not arrive rendering such a movement unnecessary. Accordingly at 3 A.M. orders were sent to the principal medical officer and controller at the Castle of the intended movement, and a staff officer was sent to convey on board the fleet a letter requesting the co-operation of the senior naval officer, and inviting him to make immediate arrangements to land the men at the shortest notice. Before 4 A.M. Captain Fremantle had been aroused, and had promised that everything should be in readiness to land the men on the Major-General's summons. Orders were at the same time sent by special runners to Assayboo, Accroful, and Dunquah. Should the officers at Assayboo and Accroful not have heard on receipt of these orders that the garrison of Abrakrampa had repulsed the enemy, and had no need of reinforcements, they were to do their utmost to keep in communication with the place,

and to relieve it after making all the necessary arrangements for the defence of their own posts; and they were to send on to Dunquah for the detachment of sixty of the 2d West India Regiment to be marched to Accroful. The officer commanding at Beulah was also informed, and was desired to do everything in his power to attack the flank and rear of the Ashantis at Abrakrampa.

At 7 A.M. a further report was received through Accroful, dated 11 o'clock the previous night, to the effect that an attack was still being carried on with vigour, and was expected to last all night, and probably throughout the following day. On receipt of this report, the senior naval officer was requested to land the troops who had been held in readiness, and the officers commanding posts were informed. Major Russell was also informed of all the steps which were being taken, the communication being sent to him by way of Accroful, and being received by him about noon, when he was again in the midst of action, having been attacked at half-past 11. At daybreak he had sent out picquets into the bush, who had seen only one Ashanti scout, but had brought in the head of a dead Ashanti, and a number of articles dropped by the enemy; and reported much blood in many parts of the bush. Scouts were sent on a little later towards Anasmadie, and returned reporting the enemy advancing. As long as daylight lasted on the previous day, the enemy had been seen removing their dead and wounded; and although Major Russell expressed himself quite unable to estimate the numbers or the losses of the enemy, there was no doubt, from the number of horns and drums which were heard, and from the volume of sound produced by their shouting and cheering, that they were in very great numbers, many thousands at all events.

On this second day the enemy did not show the same spirit as on the previous afternoon, never emerging in any numbers beyond the edge of the bush, but keeping up a continuous fusillade from its edge.

The light naval gun "Nelly" and a rocket-trough had been mounted on the boarded roof of the church, whence, on this day, and on the previous evening, Lieutenant Saunders had opened fire, expending in all twenty-eight rockets, and thirty rounds of langridge. The only white man wounded—except such slight touches by slugs as the officers took no notice of—was a sailor, who was hit in the eye while looking out from this church roof; but the slugs flew about the village, and everybody, including Mr. Boyle, the special correspondent of the *Daily Telegraph*, had the honour of being hit on the helmet or the gaiters. The Ashanti chiefs could be heard urging on their men, and the peculiar singing cheer of the enemy told by its force how large their numbers were.

A little before 9 A.M. the following officers and men had been landed at Cape Coast, and commenced their march from the beach :—H.M.S. "Encounter," 7 officers and 100 men; H.M.S. "Simoom," 4 officers and 87 men; H.M.S. "Bittern," 4 officers and 35 men; H.M.S. "Beacon," 3 officers and 21 men; H.M.S. "Barracouta," 4 officers and 60 men: making in all 22 officers and 303 men. Captain Rait accompanied the column, taking with him 50 9-pr. rockets. On no other occasion, either before or since, did the troops suffer to the same extent as they apparently did upon this march. The road from Cape Coast to Assayboo is entirely destitute of shade, except in one or two places, and the heat appeared to affect the men most seriously. The greater part of them had no head-dress suited for the climate. Most of the marines had no helmets, and the sailors wore low caps with white covers. The blue-jackets bore the heat and exertion very much better than the marines; yet they fell out in large numbers. The road the whole way to Assayboo, which was reached soon after noon, was literally strewn with men unable to march in the ranks. On this occasion we saw again, as we had before seen at Essaman, and on our march to Assanchi, the unflagging self-devotion of our principal medical officer, Dr. Home. When all were nearly fainting with exhaustion, his apparently frail frame was borne up by the gallant spirit within, and he never ceased his personal attentions to the men. Not a man who fell out but was at once treated—drawn into the shade—loosened at the neck and chest—fanned—and given water and stimulants—with such results, that of more than 100 men, more or less affected by solar insolation, not one was dangerously ill a week later. The men from H.M.S. "Encounter," who were the last to arrive from England, appeared to suffer the most, only about 50 out of 100 who started marching in with the column to Assayboo. A large number of men who had fallen out on the march were, however, able to join again at Assayboo, though 32, or more than 10 per cent of the whole force, could not reach that point.

On the road to Assayboo, the Major-General received Major Russell's despatch of the morning, reporting that the enemy was said to be advancing; and on arrival at Assayboo we found firing had been heard from the direction of Abrakrampa, showing that the attack had been renewed. The troops were, however, so exhausted, that it was impossible to continue the march without some hours' rest, and they were halted for some time. Warm chocolate having been given to the men, which greatly refreshed them, towards 4 o'clock in the afternoon the march was continued by way of Butteyan. The 50 marines that had formed the garrison of Assayboo headed the column; but only 141 out of the detachment of 303 who had landed in the morning, were able to continue the march. Nothing could more forcibly show the exhausting nature of the climate to men out of training and not properly clothed. From Cape Coast Castle to Assayboo is only ten miles, yet ten per cent of the men failed to accomplish it; and after four hours' rest scarcely half the remainder were able to march four miles farther.

Whilst resting at Assayboo, Major Russell's despatch, dated 12.15 P.M., arrived from Accroful, stating that the enemy had again attacked, but not advanced beyond the outskirts of the wood. Orders were at once sent from Assayboo to the deputy-controller at Cape Coast to send 50,000 rounds of ammunition to Assayboo.

Colonel Wood had early sent Judge Marshall, and Lieutenant Allen of the Royal Marine Artillery, to Essecroom, to urge the Cape Coast people now encamped there to move on to Aboo, and he moved on with his own detachment to Essecroom, whence he endeavoured to induce them to march direct upon Abrakrampa; but while vowing that they were marching there, the scoundrels took another road, leading them to the south, quite clear of the Ashantis, and debouched into the main road at Assayboo, while the head-quarters were there. Colonel Wood, who, with his officers, was very much fatigued from the exertions of the last few days, was ordered to proceed to Butteyan immediately, and establish himself there with his levies until further orders. In the course of the evening he mustered the bulk of them together at that point.

Towards 4 P.M. the head-quarters and marines and sailors left Assayboo, and marched, by way of Butteyan, for Abrakrampa. At the village where the roads from Butteyan and Accroful meet, we joined a detachment of the 2d West India Regiment, which had marched from Accroful, and we were also met by King Amfoo Ottoo of Abrah, who had marched out with some of his men to meet the party and guide us into Abrakrampa. As we neared Abrakrampa a good deal of firing was heard; but there was no opposition to our advance along the road, and a little before sunset we marched into the village. The marines and sailors were at once told off to the same quarters which they had occupied on the previous visit to Abrakrampa, and allowed to rest for the night, with the exception of a picquet, which was placed at the most exposed south-west corner of the village, in rear of the angle where the flanks of the Abrahs and Kossoos met. Desultory firing continued from the bush against the village throughout the evening, and even on into the night, but no further attack was made.

The officers of the garrison being much fatigued by having been now so long on the alert, several officers of the head-quarter staff volunteered to take the outlying picquets; and from the south-west angle of the village, where the writer was on duty, the Ashantis could be heard in considerable number, during the night, talking loudly, and apparently cutting the bush close to the Assayboo road, which they evidently crossed and re-crossed more than once during the night. The Houssas and Kossoos performed their night duties admirably. The Kossoos had always their sentries regularly on the alert, but the Abrah native allies who lined the space between the Assayboo and Accroful roads, slept so soundly that it was almost impossible to wake them; and they were found over and over again, when visited during the night, to have not a single man on the alert. Most certainly the Ashantis showed great want of enterprise. The bush came up to within forty yards of the lines at this point, and with a bold rush they might have penetrated into the village with the greatest ease. Equally did they show want of skill in the method of their attack. It was not merely that they did not boldly attack the entrenchments, but that they left out of their circle of attack the one most important point, namely our line of communication with Accroful and the water supply which lies besides this road. Had they extended round the village, completely surrounding it, and seized the water supply, it would have been necessary to drive them away from it, and considerable loss would have been incurred. As it was, the losses were most trifling:—1 officer and 1 private of the 2d West India Regiment were very slightly wounded; 1 seaman of the "Barracouta" was severely wounded in the right eye; and about 18 natives were hit. This fortunately slight return of casualties is doubtless to be attributed to the fact that our men were acting purely on the defensive, and were lying down under cover of shelter-trenches.

It was fully expected that the Ashantis would renew the attack on the morning of the 7th; and as the noise made by them during the night and in the early morning on the Assayboo road led to the belief that they would probably attack from that side, all the necessary arrangements were made for meeting such a movement; but the morning wore on, and beyond a few desultory shots from the bush nothing was seen of the enemy. Colonel Wood with his Cape Coast allies marched in from Butteyan, and the Major-General decided upon sending out the native allies to reconnoitre and ascertain the enemy's intentions and position. Accordingly, towards 2 P.M. the Cape Coast people, to the number of nearly 1000, were marched out of the village and ordered to enter the bush between the roads leading to Assayboo and Anasmadie. When they moved out into the clearing it was a curious spectacle to watch each company endeavouring to draw off to the left, and gain a position between the roads leading to Assayboo and Accroful, where it was known that there was no enemy. It was with the utmost difficulty that the men could be induced to enter the bush, their chiefs, Attah in particular, setting an example of most signal cowardice. The Major-General had expressed to them his great displeasure at their conduct of the previous day, and told them that he would give them this last chance of showing themselves fit to be trusted with arms. Most certainly they did not take advantage of the chance; hundreds of the men lay down at the edge of the bush, and positively refused to enter it, until they were forced in by the Kossoos, who took a malicious pleasure in driving them in with the flat of their swords, and occasionally pricking them on. Officers made free use of sticks and umbrellas on the backs of the natives; but the most that could be done with the Cape Coast people was to get them to enter the bush for a few yards, when they all, without exception, lay down. The Kossoos, however, went on in this direction, and brought in a few heads, probably of men who had been wounded in the attacks of the two preceding days, and had crawled away into the bush to die.

While this miserable exhibition was going on to the south-west of the village, the Abrahs, under Captain Bromhead, followed by Gordon and his Houssas, moved out along the road in the direction of the Anasmadie camp, and came upon it, taking its inhabitants by surprise. All the signs of a flight already commenced were apparent, and it was only, apparently, a small body left as a rear-guard that was still remaining. Shots were exchanged, and a few prisoners were captured and brought into Abrakrampa. From them we learned that a council had been held the previous night, and that in the early morning the army had commenced to move off in the direction of Ainsa. Amanquatia himself was said to have been carried away, too drunk to walk. The precipitate nature of the flight was apparent from the condition of the camp, into which Captain Bromhead penetrated: great quantities of baggage had been left behind, several chiefs' chairs and stools were captured, among them one chair made to be carried by bearers, and said to have belonged to Amanquatia himself. A number of war drums were also taken.*

The rear-guard had been completely surprised. One incident which came within the writer's observation will suffice to show how complete the surprise was. A young woman, carrying her child on her back, was brought into Abrakrampa as a prisoner. On her neck was a slight cut, broad, and quite freshly made, from which blood was trickling. Her alarm was so great that it was with difficulty she could be got to speak coherently, but as soon as she had calmed down, and was assured that she was in the hands of those who would treat her kindly and well, she related her story. She was a Commendah woman who had been captured some months before by the Ashantis, and had been kept as a slave by one of the chiefs. This man had grown fond of her; and when the first shots of our approaching skirmishers were heard, a few minutes before, he had ordered her to seize her child and some household goods, and to rush away with him. Before she had time to obey him, shots came nearer, and because she was slow—so she said—in his fear that he would not be able to carry her away, he had taken his knife and actually commenced to cut her throat, when he was shot down by one of our people. The mark on her throat, and the terribly frightened look in the eyes that had so recently looked death close in the face, were the best witnesses to the truth of her tale. Many other prisoners were captured, some of them in a most terrible state of disease and starvation. The common

* Two of these may now be seen in the Museum of the United Service Institution in London.

expression, "a living skeleton," had never conveyed such meaning to our minds as it did on this occasion. One slave was brought in on whom actually the skin barely covered the bones, which were starting through it. Measures were taken to prevent disease being brought into our camp, and the dead bodies in the bush outside the clearing were at once buried.

A great number of Fanti slaves were freed on this occasion, and some of the cruelties of slavery were disclosed to us. A number of the slaves were "in log." The slave who is "in log" has his wrist fettered down to a large log or block of wood by an iron staple; and in more than one instance this staple had been driven in so far as to cut into the flesh, which was festering under its pressure. A slave "in log" can only walk when he carries his log upon his head, and it is so heavy that he can never raise it to his head himself, nor lower it again to the ground. This is of course a great safeguard against his escape. Another curious method of holding slaves was seen by us on this occasion: one man who was brought in having a triangle of wood and iron round his neck, to which was attached a pole some ten feet long and of considerable weight. Unfortunately we could not release all the slaves, and amongst the numerous dead bodies found in the camp were many which we knew, from the decapitated trunks, to be the bodies of murdered slaves.

The Houssas pushed on some distance through the Ashanti camp, far beyond the village of Anasmadie; but, like Captain Bromhead's Abrah levies, the temptation to plunder overcame them, and they dispersed throughout the camp. Gordon was anxious to push on and reconnoitre, in spite of some opposition which he met with at intervals along the path; but the evening was drawing on, and all his men had left him except about half-a-dozen. He therefore considered it right to return to Abrakrampa.

The garrison of Abrakrampa could now enjoy rest and a quiet night, for there was no more fear of attack by the Ashanti army. Despatches were written to England the same night in which the Major-General reported that the evidence of the demoralisation of the enemy was complete; and orders were issued for the whole of the natives to start in pursuit at daybreak on the following morning.

At daybreak Captain Bromhead endeavoured to collect his Abrahs, but could not get together more than the king and fifty men, the rest being away plundering the deserted camp. It was not till 20 minutes past 8 that Captain Bromhead was able to march with even this small number. He then advanced along the Ainsa road, about three miles, when he came upon a few Ashantis, two of whom were killed and two captured. One of these captives reported that Amanquatia was at Ainsa with 2000 men; and Captain Bromhead applied for a support of Houssas, and halted, waiting for them. In the meantime he was joined by Lieutenant Gordon of the 93d. This officer had left Abrakrampa about half-past 7, with 96 Kossoos under Woodgate, 220 Assayboos under Cochran, and 300 or 400 Cape Coast allies, and had moved along the road running due west through Anasmadie to Papagay, his march being much delayed by the amount of débris along the road. On reaching Papagay he captured some stray Ashantis, who reported their army routed, and in full retreat.

The Cape Coast allies and the Assayboos now absolutely refused to obey the orders of their officers, or to advance farther in any direction, except towards Beulah, and nearly 300 of them disappeared. Lieutenant Gordon was unable to get more than 290, out of the 500 or 600 with whom he had started, to advance, and this only by employing the Kossoos to drive them on, as had been done on the previous day at Abrakrampa. About a quarter of a mile beyond Papagay, Gordon reached a fork in the road, and took some twelve or fifteen prisoners, all of whom declared that about 2000 Ashantis under Amanquatia were about half-a-mile to the front. The Kossoos were now sent to the front, with the exception of a few left in rear to whip on the Cape Coast men; and about half-a-mile farther along the road fires were found still burning, and traces of a recent Ashanti encampment. Shortly afterwards Gordon struck the road from Abrakrampa to Ainsa, and, as above related, fell in with Captain Bromhead, who ordered him to push on towards Ainsa, proposing himself to follow as soon as the Houssas, for whom he had applied, should have arrived. About a mile farther on, the road again branched off in two directions towards the north-east and north-west, and it was evident that the Ashantis had made use of both roads. Gordon took the road to the north-east, and sent to inform Captain Bromhead, who had followed, having been reinforced by Gordon of the 93d, with fifty Houssas. Captain Bromhead now pushed on the Abrah men, somewhat strengthened by fresh detachments from Abrakrampa, with twenty-five Houssas, along the north-west road, and sent to recall Gordon from the north-east road. A little farther on an Ashanti was captured, who said that Amanquatia, reinforced by Essaman Quanta from Iscabio, held a strong position at Ainsa, with about 2000 men. Shortly afterwards some shots were fired in front, the Houssas and Abrahs advanced, and an action ensued. The Kossoos and allies from the other road almost immediately appeared, and the action became heavier, the Ashantis having evidently made a stand.

For some little time all proceeded favourably; but a few shots fired by the enemy upon the left flank immediately drew a most terrific fusillade from the Cape Coast allies, which the officers vainly endeavoured to stop, and in which the Abrahs soon joined. Fire of this nature, once commenced, spreads rapidly, and both Houssas and Kossoos, as well as the others, had soon expended nearly all their ammunition. About 4 P.M., the fire of the enemy being nearly silenced, though they were still in the bush close at hand, as evidenced by their reopening fire whenever our men ceased fire, Captain Bromhead ordered the return to Abrakrampa. The Kossoos were to lead the way, followed by the Houssas, and lastly by the native allies, who continued firing and shouting as they retired. Fearing that the Ashantis were following and surrounding them, their cowardice soon got the better of them, and they were seized with panic, rushing on over the Houssas, who had the greatest difficulty in stopping them. At one place, crossing a stream, Houssa Gordon and several of his men were knocked down into the water by the rush of these miserable cowards. In this rush one Houssa disappeared; he was probably either drowned or trampled to death by the Fantis, and his body was never recovered, having fallen into the hands of the enemy, who were by this pursuing. This wretched condition of retreat continued to within about a quarter of a mile of Abrakrampa, where Captain Bromhead halted some Abrah men, hoping thereby to allay the panic; but they opened fire, and created a worse panic than before, which ended in a general rush of the whole body of allies over the Houssas and Kossoos and their officers. The king of Abrah remained with a few men, and assisted to carry Lieutenant Woodgate and Sub-Lieutenant Cochran, who were absolutely exhausted. Captain Bromhead reported that the fatigue of beating forward the allies had alone been excessive. In this action the casualties were as follows:—One Houssa killed, one missing, and two wounded; one Kossoo killed, and two wounded.

Seventeen wounded Fantis appeared to have their wounds dressed, but the actual number wounded or killed could never be discovered, as the bulk of the men disbanded and went to their homes. We subsequently heard that as many as fifty of the Cape Coast allies were missing after this action. If so, it is probable that a large number of the casualties among them were due to their own fire. The Abrah people said they were fired into by the Cape Coast men, who were reported as being "infinitely worse than useless."

An order issued from head-quarters had directed that the native allies should remain in the bush on the track of the Ashantis for three days. It will be seen that it was quite impossible for Captain Bromhead to obey this order. In the first place, in a two hours' action, his men had fired away all their ammunition; and, in the next place, in their wretchedly demoralised condition it would have been impossible to keep them close upon the trail of the enemy. The attempt to hang on the enemy's rear was a wretched failure, although there is little doubt that the mere fact of engaging the enemy at all, so soon after his recent repulse at Abrakrampa, had the effect of increasing his demoralisation, and of hastening his effort to retreat. Writing to the Secretary of State for War, Sir Garnet Wolseley now thus summed up the situation :—" You will thus see that even the enemy's retreat cannot instil courage into these faint-hearted natives, and that they can neither be counted on to insure a victory nor to complete a defeat. They were ordered to pursue the enemy, remain in the field, and harass him in his retreat. The road was strewn with the débris of the retreating army; bodies of murdered slaves lay along the route; many prisoners were captured; the enemy's fire was silenced; and yet, such is the cowardice of these people, that they had to be driven into action, and after a success they became a panic-stricken and disorderly rabble. Still, hopeless as the task appears of stirring these tribes to any exertions, I shall not give up my efforts. Orders have been issued for the renewal of the offensive movement, and for the use of every possible method to keep the men at the front."

As soon as this reconnaissance had been well started from Abrakrampa, on the morning of the 8th, the Major-General, who was suffering much from a severe attack of ardent fever, induced by exposure to the sun, returned to Cape Coast. Fifty blue-jackets and marines were left at Abrakrampa, and the remainder marched to Assayboo, where 50 were left, 50 others being sent to Dunquah, and the rest to Cape Coast, where they re-embarked.

Before leaving Abrakrampa, orders had been sent to Colonel Festing at Dunquah, informing him of the condition of affairs, and desiring him to do all in his power to make the native allies go out in strong reconnoitring parties at once, with a view of getting into contact with the enemy and harassing him. On arrival at Cape Coast, after receipt of the report of Captain Bromhead's affair, instructions were sent to Major Russell at Abrakrampa, to carry out, so far as lay in his power, the spirit of the instructions previously communicated to him, namely that the native allies should remain in the field, following up and harassing the enemy whenever an opportunity offered. If it was necessary for the allies to be accompanied by European officers, each officer was to have a body-guard of at least ten disciplined soldiers of the 2d West India Regiment.

Instructions were also sent to Mansu, and Colonel Webber was directed to harass the enemy as much as possible with the small force at his disposal, by operating against his flank, should he endeavour to strike the main road north of Mansu, or to reach the Prah by any path parallel to the road; but he was on no account to head the enemy in any northward movement of retreat which he might make, except by resisting him at the fortified post of Mansu, should he move upon it. That post was never to be left without a sufficient garrison for its defence. Colonel Wood was placed in command at Accroful, and urged to gain all information possible by means of scouts, and to do everything in his power to aid in forwarding supplies of ammunition and provisions to the advanced posts. The post at Abbaye was broken up, and its garrison removed to Napoleon; and the detachment at Napoleon was sent to Beulah. The redoubt at Abbaye was destroyed.

To sum up the condition of affairs at this moment: the advanced posts of Beulah, Napoleon, Abrakrampa, Assayboo, Accroful, Dunquah, and Mansu, are all fortified, and sufficiently strongly garrisoned to resist any attack. It is not probable that any such attack will be made, for the enemy is in retreat, demoralised by his repulse at Abrakrampa. Orders have been issued for the native allies to press upon the rear of the Ashantis from Beulah and Abrakrampa, and upon their flank from Dunquah and Mansu. The enemy is supposed to be moving so as to strike the Prah road to the north of Mansu, and orders have been given that he is not to be headed in the movement.

The chief object now becomes to increase the rapidity of the enemy's movements across the Prah, so as to admit of our road being advanced as quickly as possible. To make this road, to push forward depôts of supplies and ammunition, and to prepare the halting-places for the European troops, are now the points requiring the greatest attention. As regards actual fighting, a lull may be expected. If judicious measures are taken, it is probable that the officer commanding at Mansu will succeed in striking the enemy a few blows before he can slip past the post; but no grave or serious operations can be undertaken, as the Major-General has resolved not to send detachments of white men up the country, both on the ground of the risk to health, and of the expenditure of labour involved in supplying them. It was fortunate that this lull occurred just at this moment; for on the arrival of the Major-General at Cape Coast, his illness took a more serious turn; high fever set in, for two or three days he was quite unable to attend to any work, and at the expiration of twenty-four hours he was removed to the hospital hut on Connor's Hill. So great, however, was the heat here, the hut having only a single roof, and the thermometer inside seldom marking less than 85°, that it was decided to send the Major-General on board the "Simoom." Captain Peile kindly gave up his cabin to him, and he was removed there, remaining on board ship for some days. He returned to Government House on the 20th. During the Major-General's illness he was nursed with indefatigable care by his private secretary, Lieutenant Maurice, of the Royal Artillery.

Sickness began now to tell heavily among the officers who had accompanied the Major-General to the Gold Coast. On the 15th November the principal medical officer reported that the staff, consisting of ten persons, had already had seven of their number ineffective from sickness, five of the cases being climatic. The officers in question had now been only six weeks in the country, and the rate of sickness among them had been 70 per cent; but they had all been exposed to very great fatigue in the most unhealthy parts of the country, and before any preparations for diminishing the evils inseparable from the work could be made. On the 21st November, out of 64 officers who had arrived on the 2d October, or a fortnight later, 29 had suffered from sickness, almost all climatic, the percentage being 45 of the strength. Returns from the various stations showed the following percentages of sickness to strength actually existing :—

Officers	$21\frac{1}{4}$ per cent.
European non-commissioned officers and men . .	$18\frac{3}{4}$,,
West Indian troops . .	12 ,,

Of the marines serving on shore at the same date, at Abrakrampa and at Dunquah, 18 per cent were in hospital, the proportions being nearly the same at both places, though the Abrakrampa detachment had been on shore a month, and the Dunquah detachment only a fortnight. By the same date, however, 16 out of the 29 officers attacked by illness had recovered, and were at their duty, the average period of ineffectiveness having been ten days. Seven officers had been invalided, —three to St. Helena, and four to England; and two had died,—one killed in action, and one, Commissary Harrymount, of climatic sickness (dysentery). The diseases from which both Europeans and West Indians had suffered were chiefly the same—malarious fever and dysentery, which latter disease began to show itself about the beginning of November, when the "little rains"—occasional showers, preceded by close, sultry weather—had come on. The Europeans had suffered in addition from ardent fever, due to exposure in the sun.

H.M.S. "Simoom," employed as an hospital ship, had by this time, in spite of all the care and skill lavished on his patients by Dr. Irwin, the Staff-Surgeon of the Royal Navy in charge, become a plague ship. At the best of times entirely unsuited for hospital purposes, already on a previous occasion, it is believed, condemned for that purpose, she had been unduly overcrowded with patients suffering from malarious fever. The exhalations from the bodies of patients suffering from this fever are singularly offensive; and it is no exaggeration to say that the main deck of the "Simoom" reeked with the smell of the swamps, given out in the perspiration of the many patients on board. Officers who had been sent on board, not suffering from fever, were taken ill with that disease on board the ship, and it was decided that no more patients should be sent to her, but that she should be despatched to St. Helena. She sailed on the morning of the 21st, having eight officers on board, who were granted leave for the recovery of their health. Colonel M'Neill was to remain at Madeira, and return if the state of his wounds should permit. Lieutenant the Hon. A. Charteris, A.D.C., who had suffered from exhaustion and a slight attack of dysentery, almost immediately after our return from the first march to Abrakrampa, and had now been attacked with fever; Captain Godwin of the 103d Regiment, severely wounded in the first action at Iscabio; and Surgeon Connellan, suffering from fever, were ordered to England. Surgeon-Major Jackson, Surgeon Bennett, Lieutenant Graves of the 18th Regiment, and Lieutenant Jones of the 2d West India Regiment, all suffering from climatic sickness, were ordered to cruise to St. Helena and return with the ship. Those for Madeira and England were to be transferred at St. Helena to the first mail steamer homeward bound from the Cape of Good Hope.

On the 10th the strength of the various garrisons was reported to be as follows :—

MANSU: 3 officers and 75 men, 2d West India Regiment; 22 Houssas, 17 police, 158 Cape Coast Volunteers, 463 native allies, besides an officer of Royal Engineers and numerous labourers.

DUNQUAH: 7 officers, 137 men, 2d West India Regiment; native allies, 1711 armed, and 116 unarmed.

ACCROFUL: 9 officers, 171 men, 2d West India Regiment, and 263 native allies.

NAPOLEON : 2 officers, 43 men, 2d West India Regiment.
BEULAH : 2 officers, 56 men, 2d West India Regiment, and 549 armed native allies.
ELMINA : 7 officers, 37 men, 2d West India Regiment.
CAPE COAST : 5 officers, 31 men, 2d West India Regiment.

At the same date there were twenty-six officers of the control department, and sixteen medical officers present, exclusive of those at the out stations along the coast. Rait's Artillery by this time had reached the strength of thirty-five men.

Colonel Wood was ordered to send the Aquafoos and Agoonas from Accroful to Simeo, and the Cape Coast natives had been ordered to Beulah, in order to carry out the following arrangements made to watch the roads leading north-east from Chamah, and those between Jooquah and the Prah. The king of Tchuful Mampon having brought an armed party of 150 men to Cape Coast, was sent back to his own country to aid in those duties, and was given some money, arms, and ammunition. A reconnaissance sent out from Abrakrampa reported the enemy as having cleared out from Ainsa and Assanchi and moved north.

Touch of the Ashantis was now completely lost. In any other country in the world a repulsed and beaten enemy would have been closely pursued, at all events by small parties. Here this could not be done. There was no cavalry, and no road for cavalry to move upon. It would have been utterly unsafe to send Europeans into the bush in small scouting parties, who would have risked being cut off and inhumanly mutilated and murdered. There were no troops available for the despatch of large parties. To send European officers singly with bodies of native troops, was to risk their capture, which would have enhanced the difficulties of the position; so there remained only our Fanti allies, who were such hopeless cowards that they simply would not remain in the proximity of the enemy. Moreover, at this time, these native allies had commenced to desert in very large numbers. As early as the 6th the Assins, Abrahs, Inkoorsokooms, and Denkeras, had run away in great numbers, and the Annamaboes to a rather less extent. However, large detachments of men came in from the direction of Mumford and Winnebah, in charge of Lieutenant Bolton, whose exertions cannot be too highly praised, and on the 13th Colonel Festing reported nearly 3000 native allies present at Dunquah. Orders were sent to him, impressing upon him in the very strongest terms that not only were his scouts to be constantly on the track of the Ashantis, but that he must take steps to annoy and harass the enemy in his retreat. A large native force was at his disposal, all of whom were available for the field, and he had an ample force of regular troops for the defence of his post. He was therefore urged not to let the natives remain idle in the camp at Dunquah, but to make them take the field and remain in the proximity of the enemy, of whom touch was for the moment lost; as it was of the utmost importance that the touch should be regained, and that the enemy, who was now badly supplied with powder, and could not obtain more from the windward ports, on account of the closing of the roads by the Commendahs, Wassaws, and others, should, while in this condition, be compelled to expend such little ammunition as he might still retain. Already, before the attack on Abrakrampa, Captain Butler had been sent to the king and queen of Western Akim to endeavour to collect the fighting men of the tribe, and bring them towards Prahsu, so as to cut off the retreat of the Ashantis in that direction; and it was hoped that the promises which had been made by the kings of Wassaw and Mampon would be fulfilled, and that they would march from the westward, so as to enclose the Ashantis in a network of enemies.

Similar instructions to those sent to Colonel Festing were given to Major Russell at Abrakrampa, and also to Colonel Webber at Mansu, who was desired to compel the Denkeras to go into the field and remain there, harassing the enemy whenever an opportunity should offer. Colonel Webber was begged to redouble his energies in the way of pushing out parties, with imperative orders that they must get into contact with the enemy, and once having done so, not lose the touch.

The only information as to the enemy's movements that could be obtained up to the 15th November, was to the effect that detachments of unarmed foraging parties had touched upon the main road at Wonkorsu on the 14th, and that Amanquatia's head-quarters had reached a place called Yanibobo, supposed to be about ten miles west of Dunquah.

The king of Abrah, when ordered to follow in this direction with his men, positively refused to go. He said that the enemy was now in the Dunquah district, and that his men did not know the country. Major Russell then took the strong step of making him a prisoner, and confining him to his house, pending further instructions. Desertion had occurred to a large extent among the Cape Coast allies, and Cape Coast itself began to fill with men not employed as control labourers, who were evidently absent from their duties in the field. Accordingly, on the 14th, the chief magistrate proceeded to Beulah, accompanied by Captain Huyshe, and there held a judicial Assessor's Court, at which the chiefs and head men of the Cape Coast companies unanimously agreed that it was the duty, in the present emergency, of every able-bodied man to assist in the defence of his country; that therefore every able-bodied man not already engaged was at once to present himself for service; and that every one refusing to do so, without a proper excuse, was to be arrested, and compelled to work without pay. This law enabled strong measures to be taken with the deserters. Cape Coast was searched by the police, and every able-bodied man found was sent to work.

On the 16th a detachment of the Gold Coast Corps and armed police was sent to Wonkorsu to protect the postal station there. On the 17th the detachments of blue-jackets and marines at Assayboo and Dunquah, with the exception of men of the detachment of Royal Marines sent out for land service, were recalled to Cape Coast, as sickness had suddenly broken out among them. The healthy only were to be embarked, and the sick men, in consequence of the experience of H.M.S. "Simoom," were to be retained for treatment on shore. Assayboo was now occupied only by a small detachment of police.

On this day Assin scouts from Mansu met parties of Ashantis at Emanfossoo, about eight miles west of

Wonkorsu ; and one scout, Agay by name, having been separated from his party, was caught and decapitated. About the same time Surgeon-Major Gore, the sanitary officer, who had been sent up to Mansu to report on the various camping stations on the road, on returning to Dunquah was fired upon from the bush, not however until his escort, consisting of police, had fired upon some Ashantis seen upon the road. One of his escort was killed, and he and four others were wounded ; but this was no very strong party of Ashantis, indeed nothing more than a mere foraging party, as was proved by the fact, that within an hour or two of Dr. Gore's return to Mansu, a very large convoy of provisions and ammunition arrived at that station from Dunquah without having experienced the slightest opposition, and without having so much as seen any sign of the enemy. On the 18th, however, Colonel Festing, fearing for the safety of the road, asked for reinforcements, and received the whole of the Houssa detachment from Abrakrampa, and the Kossoos, and a detachment of the 2d West Indians from Accroful.

As soon as Colonel Webber at Mansu had received the news of the Ashantis being in force at Emanfossoo, he despatched, at 6 P.M. on the 14th, a party of thirty-five of the Gold Coast Corps to Adda Warra, a mile and a half north of Mansu, with instructions to patrol towards the enemy's flank, along the road branching off at this point in a south-westerly direction ; and he reinforced this detachment on the morning of the 15th by a party of twenty-five of the 2d West Indians, thinking the enemy might endeavour to debouch at that point on to the main road. Two hundred armed Denkeras were to be sent on to Dadiasu, but the king of Denkera simply refused to let them go, although Major Home and Dr. Gore had gone as far as Sutah on the 14th. On the 16th a scout from Mansu having been caught by the Ashantis near Darman, Colonel Webber established a post of the Gold Coast Corps and 2d West Indians, and fifty Denkeras, at that point, with orders to patrol and keep the road clear, and to scout to the westward. On the 17th the Denkeras, at their post north of Mansu, reported that they heard the enemy cutting tracks in the bush about three miles to the west of Adda Warra. Mansu was now strengthened by about 250 Essecoomas, and the same number of Adjumacoes; but all the information given by the native scouts was vague and uncertain, though invariably tending to the conclusion that the enemy was marching northwards past Mansu.

On the morning of the 19th, some doubts existing in Colonel Festing's mind as to the safety of the road to Mansu, in consequence of alarming reports from Colonel Webber, he sent Captain Huyshe (who was at Dunquah, on a mission to the native kings, which will be subsequently described), to conduct a reconnaissance of West Indians, Kossoos, Houssas, and native allies, along the main road to Mansu. The road was found clear of Ashantis. The head-quarters and about 140 of Wood's Regiment arrived on the same day at Dunquah from Accroful.

The native allies at Mansu were now echeloned along the road for some miles north and south of that post. These troops were accompanied by the officers commissioned to their kings, each of whom was provided with a personal body-guard of twelve West Indians. The kings were ordered to encamp at the several places named, and to protect themselves by sending out scouts, placing outposts, and patrolling; and were informed that unless they obeyed these orders they would get no pay. The Denkeras at Adda Warra had their scouting parties fired on and a good many wounded; and there appeared to be every indication that the enemy was slipping past Mansu through the thick bush on the west. Straggling parties of slaves seeking plantains appeared on the road north of Mansu, from whom prisoners were captured. Nearly all of these were extremely emaciated, and agreed in saying that the Ashantis had very little powder, and had nothing to live on but wild yams and plantains.

On the 17th Major Home had conducted a reconnaisance westward from Quaman Attah, and had found all the signs of a large Ashanti encampment before him. On the paths leading to it from the main road he had heard the Ashantis, and seen the smoke of many fires. On the 18th some prisoners had been brought in by the scouts from near Quaman Attah, and firing had been heard that night, in consequence of which Colonel Webber roused his garrison, kept them under arms for an hour, from 11 to 12 P.M., and had them again under arms at 5 o'clock.

On the morning of the 19th there was a complete scare at Mansu. Reports arrived that Amanquatia intended to break into the main road at Wonkorsu; Colonel Webber drew in his parties from Darman, and reported to Dunquah; and it was in consequence of these alarms that Captain Huyshe's reconnaissance was conducted northward along the road from Dunquah. Although the reconnaissance had neither seen nor heard any signs of the enemy, although no traces of Ashantis had been found south of Mansu since the 18th, and though, on the other hand, there was every reason to believe them to be in force to the north-west of Mansu, Colonel Webber, on the 20th, conducted a strong reconnaissance, by way of Quaman Attah, in the direction where Major Home had discovered the Ashanti camp on the 17th. The reconnaissance was conducted in the following manner:—Lieutenant Bell, R.E., with only 30 men, of whom 10 were West Indians, was directed to strike due west from Quaman Attah, and to attack the Ashanti camp; while Colonel Webber, with a force of upwards of 350, of whom 150 were West Indians, marched a mile and a half farther down the main road, and thence turned in the direction of the camp. As Colonel Webber had at least two and a half miles farther to march than Lieutenant Bell, it would naturally result that the latter officer would arrive with his 30 men at the Ashanti camp long before Colonel Webber with the main body, unless very exact arrangements for the time of meeting were made. Colonel Webber's intention was to attack the camp simultaneously on the two sides, the two detachments meeting where the roads joined in the middle of the camp. The programme was carried out; and, perhaps fortunately for Lieutenant Bell and his party, the camp, which had evidently held some hundreds of men, was found deserted, the Ashantis having left it some two days earlier. The reconnaissance returned to Mansu.

On the 21st another reconnaissance was projected in a north-westerly direction from Mansu, by way of Adda Warra. Captain Huyshe took command of this party, consisting of 40 West Indians, 30 Houssas, and 60 Kossoos, with 50 Adjumacoe native allies, taking with them two days' rations, in order that they might remain out and thoroughly clear the bush to the westward of the road. But this reconnaissance, like the one carried out on the previous day by Colonel Webber, was a day too late. Captain Huyshe's party found many Ashanti camps, large enough to hold altogether 2000 or 3000 men, captured a few stragglers, and returned to camp on the 22d, not having succeeded in coming up with any portion of the enemy's force.

On the morning of the 21st, a force of 50 Houssas and 70 Cape Coast volunteers and police, and 300 armed Denkeras, marched to Acroofoomu, seven miles north of Mansu, and established itself there for the protection of the working parties; and at 5 o'clock in the evening, Colonel Webber, with a detachment of West Indians and rockets, marched out to Dadiasu, and thence on to Acroofoomu, where he arrived at 9 o'clock that night. His detachment was "to catch the enemy between himself and Captain Huyshe," but nothing was done beyond considerably fatiguing the detachment. Leaving a small party of West Indians with Major Home, Colonel Webber returned to Mansu early on the morning of the 22d, without waiting for the return of Captain Huyshe's detachment, or for further report from that officer.

Orders had been issued on the 21st to Lieutenant-Colonel Wood to construct a post in advance of Mansu at such a point as he might decide upon, in conjunction with the commanding Royal Engineer. This force was to consist of his own regiment, the Kossoos at Mansu, Captain Smith's company of Cape Coast volunteers, and the Houssas, under command of Lieutenant Gordon of the 93d Highlanders. The post was to be placed in a state of defence at once, and the 7-pounder gun from Mansu taken on to it. Colonel Wood therefore marched on the 22d from Dunquah to Mansu, and on the 23d pushed on to Acroofoomu. From this time forward he took command of the advanced guard in the operations south of the Prah.

On the afternoon of the 23d, Major Home made a reconnaissance in the direction of a camp a short distance to the west of Acroofoomu, where he was aware that a force of Ashantis was posted. The camp was on the right bank of the river Okee, and could not be approached closer than 150 yards; but Major Home determined to make a reconnaissance in force the following morning. Accordingly, at daybreak on the 24th, he moved out with a force of 20 Denkeras, 90 Kossoos, 64 Houssas, 110 2d West India Regiment, and a rocket-trough. He crossed the Okee by a fallen tree, and came on a small encampment where the fires were still red, and after a march of four miles came on the trail of the enemy, and took a few prisoners. The Denkeras had, however, led Major Home to the north of the main Ashanti camp, which, on his homeward march, he came upon—already, however, deserted. It is more than probable that the Denkeras had deliberately avoided marching through the main camp, which, according to Major Home's report, could have held 12,000 to 14,000 men. The reports of prisoners confirmed this opinion.

The information now generally gathered was to the effect that Amanquatia, with the mass of the Ashantis, was at Sutah. The enemy appeared to have retired through the thick bush west of the road and of the Okee river in three columns, marching at the rate of four to five miles a day. The strength of the advanced post at Acroofoomu had now reached the following numbers, viz.—2 officers Royal Engineers and 400 labourers; 1 officer, with 620 armed levies (Denkeras and others); 2 officers and 132 2d West India Regiment; 1 officer and 87 Houssas; 1 officer and 110 Kossoos; 3 officers and 204 Wood's Regiment; 3 officers and 50 Gold Coast Corps; 11 police; one 7-pounder gun and 1 rocket-trough.

On the 25th Captain Furse, of Wood's regiment, proceeded with a party to Sutah, and the road was cut within a mile of that place. On the 26th Colonel Wood moved on his whole party to Sutah, arriving there at 7 A.M., and capturing on the road some unarmed Ashantis. By these the statement was confirmed that the Ashantis had moved through the bush in three columns, cutting tracks, and that Amanquatia himself marched with the column nearest to the main road, and had debouched upon the road at Sutah on the night of the 24th, or daybreak of the 25th, the centre column tapping into the main road at Faysowah. The fires were found still burning in one of the many Ashanti camps about Sutah. In the course of the day Colonel Wood sent an advanced guard to Ahtoh Insu, which returned reporting the camps a mile to the north of Sutah as being very large, and the track having been much used on the previous day. Later in the day Colonel Wood sent Captain Smith of the Cape Coast Volunteers to reconnoitre as far as Faysowah. It was dark before Captain Smith got within half-a-mile of the place : he saw some fires just lighted on the road, and heard persons running from them in the bush. Colonel Wood agreed with Captain Smith in thinking that these were probably only stragglers. The road was very bad, nearly all under water, and Colonel Wood decided not to subject his officers to the risk of illness consequent upon so severe a march as would be involved by an attempt to attack the enemy at Faysowah, and return to Sutah in one day. At this time nearly all the officers with Colonel Wood were more or less suffering from climatic disease. Colonel Wood himself and Lieutenants Woodgate, Richmond, Eyre, and Bell, were all ill with fever or other sickness.

On the morning of the 27th Colonel Wood received letters from head-quarters desiring him to harass the enemy in his retreat, and authorising him to proceed beyond Sutah if he should think it desirable. He accordingly resolved to march to either Ahtoh Insu or Faysowah, according as circumstances should permit; and at 10 o'clock he marched with the following troops :—3 Royal Marine Artillery with rocket-trough, 23 2d West India Regiment, 93 Houssas, 53 Elminas, 104 Kossoos, and 6 scouts. The rocket, its ammunition, and one hammock, were carried by Assins; and Colonel Wood directed Lieutenant Eyre to wait with No. 1 Company of Wood's Regiment till 1 P.M., and then to advance with or without the carriers whom Colonel Wood hoped to obtain from the Assins of King Chibboo. Having reached Adubiassie about half-past 12, Colonel Wood was advised by an Ashanti prisoner not to continue his march, as the following chiefs, among others, were at Faysowah, and it being an Adai day, they would not retire :—Amanquatia, Essaman Quanta, Cobbina Obbin of Adansi. Colonel Wood now left all his soldiers' bundles at Adubiassie, with two men per company to guard them, and left orders for Lieutenant Eyre to follow on in the evening if no firing was heard. Captain Furse then proceeded in charge of the advance to feel the enemy. South of Faysowah the Ashantis opened fire; the Houssas and Kossoos were then extended into the bush, and drove the enemy for about three-quarters of a mile across the open ground at the village of Faysowah, and into the bush beyond, when the rocket-trough was brought into action, and several rockets fired. The Houssas were now formed up in support in the clearing, and the Elmina company of Wood's Regiment and the Kossoos were thrown into the bush, which was, however, so thick as to prevent the possibility of advancing except along the track. After half-an-hour had been passed in this position, the enemy, whose fire had not diminished in front, was enveloping the little force on both flanks; whereupon the Houssas were extended and the Elminas and Kossoos ordered to retire through them. The hammock men had run away, and there was some difficulty in removing the wounded, as the enemy had pressed on very closely in pursuit. The one hammock in which the worst wounded case was being carried broke down, and had to be abandoned; but the wounded man was supported, and not left behind.

In the meanwhile Lieutenant Eyre had arrived at Adubiassie, and proceeded to a neighbouring encampment of Assins for carriers for the soldiers' bundles, leaving a positive order with his company that they were not to advance. On his return to the village he found that the greater part of his company had pushed on, followed by Assins carrying the bundles. The retreat of Wood's force was carried on in a sufficiently orderly manner till a panic seized the Houssas, who ran in on the Kossoos, who in their turn ran into Eyre's company, which had now come up, each man carrying a great bundle on his head. In vain did Colonel Wood order these latter men to the head of the column. Some of them became jammed up in the narrow path, and with the Kossoos became an unruly mob. Strong measures had to be resorted to, to prevent the Kossoos from trampling on the Europeans with the rockets; and although Lieutenants Gordon (93d Regiment), Woodgate, and Pollard, kept some few Houssas and Kossoos together, only the Elminas, under Lieutenant Richmond, preserved real order. The column now overtook the Assins, who were carrying the soldiers' bundles; and the Ashantis, who were evidently pressing on in the flanks of the column, fired a few shots, when the carriers dropped their bundles and ran away. A number of blankets and kits were lost, as well as one cartouche-box containing thirty-two six-ounce charges. At Adubiassie Colonel Wood was joined by seventy-seven men of the 2d West India Regiment, with ammunition and supplies; but he decided on returning to Sutah, which he reached at half-past 9 at night. Neither officers nor men had eaten anything since half-past 7 in the morning, and they had made a march of more than twenty miles, four of which were through water. Colonel Wood said it was difficult to overpraise the conduct of the officers; "they all thought the enemy greatly outnumbered us, but in advancing and retiring they were always nearest to the Ashantis." One Houssa was killed while retiring, and eight men of different detachments wounded.

A great deal was said after this action about "Colonel Wood's defeat," and the disaster at Faysowah, and we shall see presently that it was reported in this light to the king of Ashanti; but, as a matter of fact, there was neither defeat nor disaster. Colonel Wood had received definite orders from the Major-General that he was to endeavour to harass the rear of the enemy as they retired along the main road to the Prah, the great object being to hasten the retreat, so as to enable the road to be pushed on as fast as possible. Although Colonel Wood was not of opinion that there was any considerable force at Faysowah, he had taken all the necessary precautions. He did not take the baggage with him, but marched to Faysowah in fighting order, and left the baggage in rear, to be brought on in case he should occupy Faysowah without opposition. He made his reconnaissance with every military precaution. He found himself in the presence of a very superior force of the enemy, engaged them for a couple of hours, and, had his troops been better, would have retired without being in any way compromised; but the untrustworthy character of the natives doubly deceived him. Brave in advance, the Houssas showed themselves liable to panic in retreat; and although the retreat became disorderly, the disorder might have been checked but for the disobedience of orders of No. 1 Company, which had marched on with bundles. Two days afterwards we learnt that, so far from the affair being a failure, it had had exactly the desired effect; for that as soon as the Ashantis gave up the pursuit, they broke up their camp, and retired precipitately through the night with torches, scarcely stopping till they reached the banks of the Prah.

The story of this retreat was told to us afterwards by an Ashanti scout, whom we captured on the other side of the Adansi hills. He told us how he was one of the party sent down from Ashanti with ammunition and reinforcements for the army south of the Prah, and how he met the retiring army hurrying along at night, without pausing, and in the utmost alarm, because the white man was on their track. It is quite true that they met with an unusual success in capturing a broken hammock and a box belonging to Lieutenant Woodgate, at whose capture they gave a yell of delight; but we could very well afford to exchange the box and the hammock against the increased rapidity of their retreat. It afterwards appeared, when our scouts went beyond Faysowah, that it was very fortunate Colonel Wood had not advanced along the path beyond the village, as the fighting men were ambushed there, and prepared to attack the force on both flanks. The worst of it was that the affair had alarmed our scouts, and they could not be got to advance; and even Colonel Wood, on the 30th, still writing from Sutah, reported—" As we are now near the enemy, and a repetition of Thursday's work would leave us without native soldiers, more caution is necessary;" adding, " I think our advance with a small force is now hazardous, and I should be inclined to bring more Europeans up, as you cannot depend on the natives."

In reality the whole Ashanti army had reached and recrossed the Prah before Colonel Wood's scouts brought him news which admitted of his advancing beyond Sutah. It was not till the 4th December that Colonel Wood made that advance. In the meantime we had scarcely had any information as to the enemy. Stragglers captured asserted that the Ashantis had received large supplies of food and powder before the action of the 27th, and reinforcements were said to have been sent down to them. On the 2d some Assins sent on from Ahtoh Insu found Yancoomassie deserted, and returning met at Faysowah scouts who had arrived there from Tchuful-Mampon, and who reported the whole country to the west clear of Ashantis. On the 5th some prisoners captured beyond Yancoomassie reported the enemy as having crossed the Prah during three consecutive days at and above Prahsu.

When at last our scouts did reach the Prah the Ashantis were all across, with the exception of a few stragglers. They crossed at three places—Prahsu, Attassi about one mile to the east of Prahsu, and Cohea, a few miles to the west. They must have retired in a miserable condition; for the main Prahsu road and the bush to each side were found strewn with their dead and dying. The first English officer to reach the river was Captain Butler, whose efforts to conduct a force of Western Akims on the flank of the retiring Ashanti army had failed; but he had with about twenty men marched upon Prahsu, arriving there on the 10th. He reported the neighbourhood of the Prah as one large deserted camp, and a few canoes visible on the shore. Lieutenant Grant of the 6th Regiment, one of a batch of special service officers who arrived on the 30th November, and who had been placed temporarily in charge of the scouts, arrived on the following day; as also did Major Home and Captain Buller. Captain Buller reported that from one position on the south bank of the Prah sixteen dead bodies could be seen—nine on the south, and seven on the north bank. As the river went down other bodies were found caught in the trees which had fallen across the river. The Ashantis had crossed in canoes, thirteen of which were secured by our scouts; and at one point opposite to where the Major-General subsequently had his head-quarters, a rope had been stretched across the river to facilitate the crossing. The scouts reported that forty Ashantis had been drowned by the upsetting of one canoe.

Thus then our last brush with the Ashantis on the south side of the Prah was the affair of Faysowah on the 27th of November. A week afterwards they had all crossed the river, and not a man was to be seen upon the north bank. The first phase of the war was ended without the assistance of European troops, and the British Protectorate was freed from the foot of the invader.

While these movements had been going on at the head of the road, other changes had taken place in the disposition of the troops nearer to the Coast, which it will not be necessary to describe in minute detail. On the 22d the redoubt at Napoleon, which was no longer required, was levelled and destroyed, and the garrison marched into Cape Coast. On the 25th the detachment of marines stationed at Abrakrampa marched thence for Cape Coast, arriving on the 26th; and on the 27th the remaining detachment from Dunquah was also called in. On the 26th Captain Rait and the headquarters of Rait's Artillery marched from Cape Coast Castle with two Gatling guns, one 7-pounder gun, one $4\frac{2}{5}$ in. howitzer, 13 Houssas, and 102 carriers. The howitzer was drawn by two bullocks, which had been brought from Ascension for food, and had been trained by Captain Rait in the few preceding days. The bullocks were taken out of draught at Dunquah, the howitzer remaining there. The two 7-pounder guns at that place went on as well as the Gatlings and the 7-pounder taken from Cape Coast.

Captain Rait marched into Mansu on the 29th with the following detail:—Two officers Royal Artillery, two non-commissioned officers Royal Marine Artillery, thirty-four Houssas, and three 7-pounder guns. On the same day orders were issued for the removal of all military stores at Abrakrampa to Accroful, with a view to abolishing the former post, now no longer of any value.

On the 28th, in consequence of Colonel Wood's report of the affair at Faysowah, his force at Sutah was strengthened by a detachment of West Indians and fifty of the Gold Coast Rifle Corps, together with a rocket-trough from Mansu. A detachment of three officers, and fifty blue-jackets and marines, with a medical officer of the Royal Navy, were also landed, and marched to reinforce the advanced post on the road. This detachment formed the first instalment of the Naval Brigade. A detachment of seventy West Indians also left Cape Coast for the front; and the headquarters of Russell's foot, and the whole garrison of Abrakrampa, marched thence to Dunquah to proceed to the head of the road. The Houssas were this day, by order, incorporated in Russell's regiment.

On the 30th the under-mentioned officers for special service arrived in the s.s. "Volta" from England, in compliance with the Major-General's demand made at the commencement of October, and were posted to regiments as follow :—

Russell's Regiment.

Captain Burnett, 15th Regt. Lieutenant Grant, 6th Regt.
Lieutenant Hare, 22d „ „ Wauchope, 42d „
„ Wynter, 33d „

WOOD'S REGIMENT.

Lieutenant Clowes, 30th Regt. Lieutenant Douglas, 7th Regt.
„   Irwin, 1st   „   „   Pollock, 21st „
„   Aylmer, 103d „

Lieutenant the Hon. H. Wood, 10th Hussars, also arrived, and was appointed acting aide-de-camp to the Major-General, during the absence of the Hon. A. Charteris, invalided. Some other officers of the 2d West India Regiment and non-combatants arrived, amongst them the Rev. R. J. Paterson, Chaplain to the Forces, who had filled a similar office in the Red River Expedition.

These officers proceeded to join their regiments on the 1st and 2d of December.

The retreat of the enemy had not, it must be admitted, been unskilfully conducted. His force cannot have numbered less than 20,000 men. Captain Huyshe, who visited the abandoned camp at Mampon to survey it, detailed it as follows :—" The great camp at Mampon is quite a sight; nearly a mile square, cleared and covered with huts; plenty of graves to be seen, and lots of skeletons, skulls, and human bones. They must have lost a great number of men by disease, besides those who died from wounds, whilst they were here. Their camps extend at intervals all along the road from near Effootoo to Mampon, and again here and between this and Quacodayo." This force had marched through the bush from Abrakrampa to the Prah, cutting its own paths for a great part of the way. Flanking detachments appear to have been regularly employed, and were felt by our scouts both north and south of Mansu ; and it is difficult to regard the detachment under Essaman Quanta, which Colonel Festing twice attacked, as other than a flanking party to protect Amanquatia's army before Abrakrampa against attack from the direction of Dunquah. The army of a civilised nation need not have been ashamed of a retreat conducted with such skill and such success.

No breathing time was even now available, though the first part of the task confided to the Major-General had been accomplished, and he had no longer to deal with an enemy in the Protectorate. All his future efforts, however, could now be brought to the great object of invading the enemy in his own territory, and teaching him the lesson which he must be taught. But the task which had thus far been accomplished had been performed at a cost of physical and mental exertion of the officers engaged which can not be over-rated. It may unhesitatingly be said that all the subsequent exertions undergone by the European troops were as child's play to what had already been gone through by the special service officers, and that the march from the Prah to Coomassie and back was but as a pleasant picnic in comparison with the arduous toil which had been gone through on the southern bank. The climate had been terribly against us, and the operations conducted near the Coast under the burning sun without shade, in the intensely hot moist weather of October and November, were incomparably more exhausting than those subsequently carried out in the shade of the forest, and in a cooler and drier season. Those who, like the writer, were engaged from the first to the last day of the campaign, know well that the Major-General never spoke more truly than when he said, in his despatch from Coomassie, that the officers who had arrived in the first fortnight in October were those upon whom the brunt of the war had fallen.

These operations in the Protectorate did indeed form of themselves a distinct campaign. On the 15th December, the Major-General, recognising this fact, wrote to the Secretary of State for War the following despatch :—

"Head-Quarters, Cape Coast Castle,
15th December 1873.

"Sir—In my despatch which accompanies this I have had the great satisfaction to report that the Ashanti army has crossed the river Prah into its own territory, and that my advanced parties are in occupation of Prahsu, on the south bank.

"The first phase of this war has thus been brought to a most satisfactory conclusion, without the assistance of any English troops, except the few marines and the available blue-jackets whom I found here on my arrival, on the 2d October last.

"At that date the position of affairs was as follows: —An invading army of Ashantis, numbering between 20,000 and 30,000 men, having overrun the Fanti territory, occupied threatening positions within an easy march of her Majesty's forts at Elmina and Cape Coast Castle. The country was filled with alarms of intended attacks upon our settlements; public confidence in us was at a very low ebb; every movement on our part was known to the enemy, regarding whose intentions, movements, numbers, or even exact position, little information was possessed by our authorities.

"I submit that the happy change which has been since that time effected has been accomplished by the untiring exertions of the few carefully-selected staff and special service officers, who landed with me here at the beginning of October.

"In the second phase of this war, when the campaign is opened in Ashanti territory, beyond the Prah, by a brigade of English troops, the operations may be more brilliant than those which have resulted in forcing the enemy to retreat into their own country; but I feel assured that they cannot entail upon those engaged in them the hard work, exposure, and privations that have been so cheerfully endured for the last two months and a half by the small band of officers of whom I speak. Of them one has been killed in action, two very severely wounded, and several slightly wounded.

"The material used in the late operations (the sailors and marines, the detachment 2d West India Regiment, and the natives) was here before their arrival; but the raising and disciplining the natives, their organisation for the field, and the directions given to the various forces, has been the work of these officers, with whom I would wish to couple the names of Lieut.-Colonel Festing, R.M.A., and Lieutenant Gordon, 98th Regiment, whose zeal and energy deserve all praise. The former officer has been twice wounded, but never prevented from remaining at his work.

"In my despatch of 15th October, wherein I reported that Colonel M'Neill, V.C., C.M.G., my chief staff officer, had been very severely wounded, I stated my high opinion of his abilities, and how deeply I felt being deprived of his valuable services.

"Since then his very arduous work has been carried on to my entire satisfaction by Major Baker, Assistant Adjutant-General, to whose untiring exertions much of our success is owing.

THE ASHANTI WAR. 305

"The amount of work performed by him can only be realised by those who have witnessed it, as the staff duties with a regular army afford no data upon which an opinion can be formed of the labour that devolves upon the chief staff officer of a force such as that under my command. As Major Baker is about to be superseded in his position as chief staff officer by a senior officer now on his way here, I take this opportunity of bringing his name to your favourable notice.

"Major Baker has been ably assisted by the Deputy-Assistant Adjutants-General, Captain Huyshe and Captain Buller, who have performed their work most efficiently. The former has had charge of the survey, and the latter of the intelligence, department.

"Of the special-service officers, where all have worked so hard and so earnestly, it is no easy matter to particularise individuals. The two seniors, Lieutenant-Colonel Wood, V.C., and Major Russell, have each raised a regiment of the strength named in the margin. Lieutenant-Colonel Wood commanded at the engagement at Essaman, as mentioned in my despatch of 15th October, in which I stated my appreciation of the manner in which he carried out the orders he had received. He is now commanding the advanced posts from Mansu to the river Prah, and displays both zeal and ability in the discharge of his duties. Major Russell had the good fortune to command at Abrakrampa when that place was attacked for two days and nights by the main body of the enemy under their Commander-in-Chief. The attacks of the first day and night are well described in Major Russell's modest report, which I had the

Margin: Wood's Regiment, 413. Russell's Regiment, 540.

VOL. I.   U

honour to enclose in my despatch of 7th ultimo. The defence, resulting in the hurried retreat of the enemy, was conducted by him in the most spirited and able manner. I have great pleasure in bringing the names of Lieutenant-Colonel Wood, V.C., and Major Russell, to your special notice.

" Captain Rait, commanding Royal Artillery, has raised and drilled a battery composed of Houssas. He has worked indefatigably under great disadvantages. He is a soldier eminently qualified for warfare of this nature, as he seems to regard difficulties as necessary evils, to be made light of and overcome. I am anxious to bring his name to your notice, as he, like Major Baker, is about to be superseded by a senior officer of Royal Artillery sent from England.

" Major Home, commanding Royal Engineers, has worked untiringly since we landed; and few that have not inspected the results of his labour could believe it possible that so much could have been performed in two and a half months with the small assistance at his disposal.

" The officers of the control and medical departments have worked with the greatest zeal and energy; but as the end of the first phase of the war does not mark any distinct epoch in their duties, I shall reserve bringing them individually before you till the termination of hostilities.—I have, &c.

" G. J. WOLSELEY,
Major-General."

In England this first campaign has not been properly recognised. No regiments with well-known names were employed; no troops had been sent ou

PAGE 306, VOL I.

Paths Surveyed by Europeans ----------

- Akossiquah
- Ainsa
- Quacoayo
- Jooquah
- Sweet R.
- Agimeroom
- Pap...
- Berassie
- Essiam
- Mampon
- Siroff
- Essecroom
- Effootoo
- Ahonton
- Sirowee R.
- Beulah
- Simeo
- Aboo
- Napoleon
- Abbaye
- Sanka
- Connors
- Essaman
- Sweet R.
- LAGOON
- CA...
- R. Beyrah
- ELMINA

Scale o...

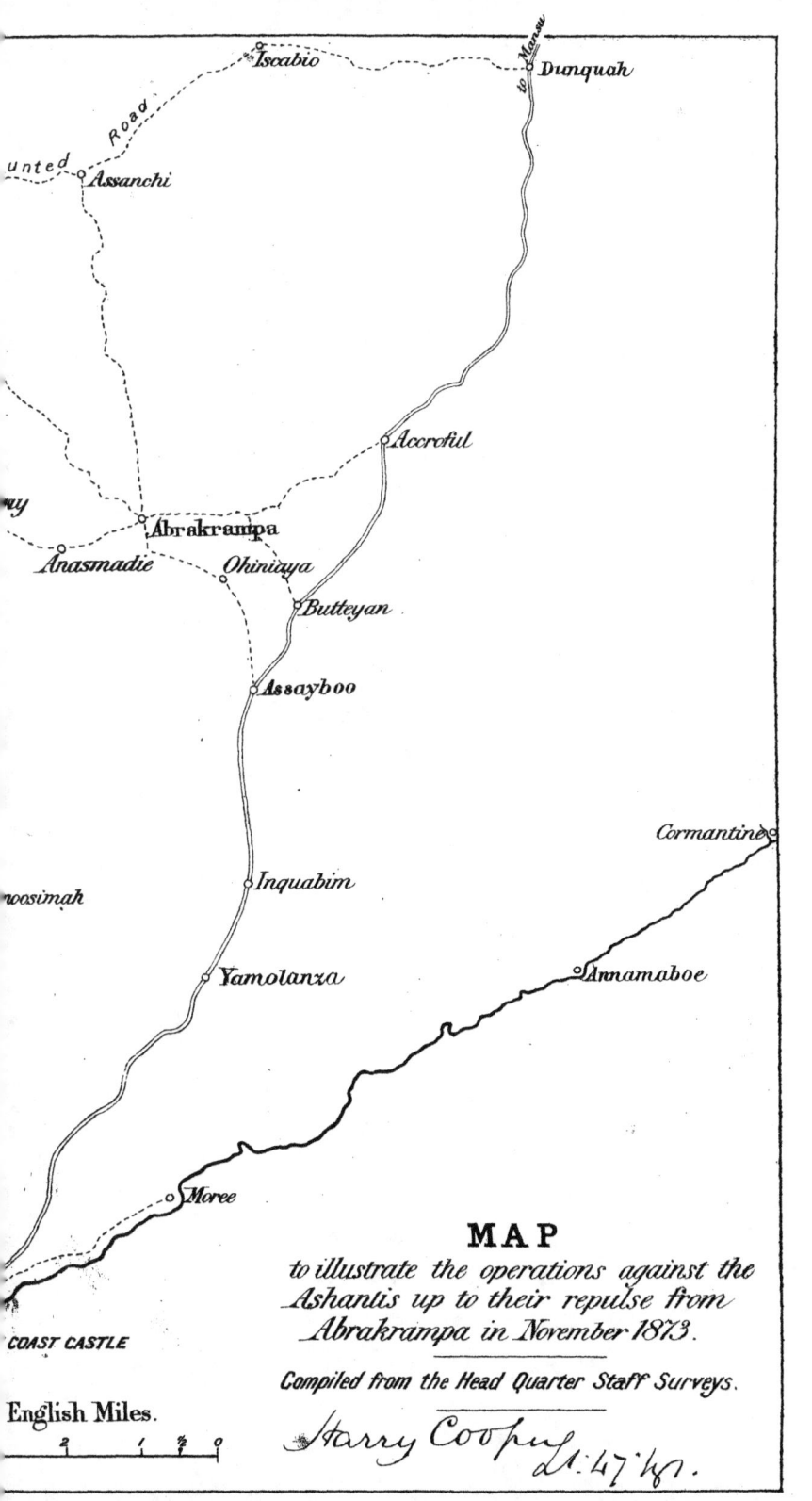

among the cheers of the people. Only a West India regiment, and a few detachments of marines and sailors had been used, and a little band of officers, who had been looked upon almost as lunatics when they volunteered for such a task, and who had been sent out in a filthy steamer, and not even allowed to take soldier servants, that the experiment might be made upon the bodies of officers only, whether white men could stand a campaign in the West African bush.

CHAPTER VII.

PREPARATIONS FOR THE INVASION OF ASHANTI—THE ROAD TO THE PRAH—CAMPING-GROUNDS FOR EUROPEAN TROOPS—SANITARY PRECAUTIONS—HOSPITALS AND TRANSPORT FOR SICK AND WOUNDED—THE TRANSPORT QUESTION GENERALLY—ARRIVAL AND DESPATCH TO SEA OF THE EUROPEAN TROOPS—ORDERS FOR THE MARCH AND FOR THE FIGHT—THE MAJOR-GENERAL'S PLAN OF INVASION.

It has already been pointed out that in the earlier stages of his operations on the Gold Coast, the Major-General had a double aim in view—to drive the enemy out of the Protectorate, and to make the necessary preparations for the subsequent invasion of Ashanti by a force of European troops. The steps taken towards the first of these ends have been described in the preceding chapters; the object of the present chapter will be to state briefly what were the most important measures adopted for the attainment of the second. The points specially requiring attention may be classed under the following heads :—

1st, The formation of the road to the Prah.

2d, The establishment of camps at proper intervals along this road.

3d, The sanitary arrangements for the troops on the march.

4th, The establishment of hospitals, and provision for the care and removal of sick and wounded.

5th, The transport of supplies and ammunition to the front.

We will deal with these subjects in order; and in doing so, will risk some repetition of what may have already been said at different points of our narrative, in order to present each subject as nearly as possible in a complete and unbroken form.

All hope of constructing a railway was given up immediately after our arrival on the Coast. On the 7th October, the Major-General reported that no railway, except one on Mr Fell's principle, could be laid and worked in the time at his disposal, as the country, so far from being flat, as he had been led to expect, was covered with rounded hills and deep intervening ravines. Before the receipt of this despatch, the War Office had already despatched six miles and a quarter of tramway, a traction-engine, and some trucks, in the transports Lilian and Joseph Dodds; but the order for further portions was countermanded; no more sleepers and rails were shipped, and the portion sent to Cape Coast was not landed. The railway scheme being thus immediately abandoned, the completion of a road became of the utmost importance.

Before the Major-General's arrival, Lieutenant Gordon had already made a road as far as Yancoomassie Fanti; but it was not made so as to be fit for the march of troops and guns; indeed, the road-making up to this time consisted only of clearing the path to a considerable width. It was necessary for much more than this to be done; it was considered very important that the troops should march dry-shod and with the least possible fatigue to the Prah, and it was therefore intended to make a road as nearly as possible twelve feet wide and clear of stubs and roots. Swamps must either be drained or avoided, or causeways must be made through them; culverts must be made, and all the streams bridged. This was the task to which Major Home and the Royal Engineers under his command devoted themselves at an early period after our arrival. Immediately after the landing of a detachment of three officers, one sergeant, and five sappers on the 10th October, Major Home proceeded up the road, having, before his departure, appointed Lieutenant Bell, R.E. adjutant and park-keeper. He arrived at Accroful on the 13th October, and reported that there were four miles of the road between Yamolanza and Butteyan still requiring a great deal to be done to them; but he thought that within a week a fairly good road could be made from Accroful to Cape Coast Castle. He at once put 200 labourers on this part of the road under Lieutenant Mann, and urgently applied for more. On the 15th he reached Yancoomassie, and reported the road to that place, with the exception of the short distance between Yamolanza and Assayboo, all fairly passable for infantry in fours. This was due to Lieutenant Gordon's work, so that the Royal Engineers, on arrival, found the rough clearing of the road done for the first 25 miles. Of course one of the greatest difficulties to be contended with was the absence of skilled labour; and Major Home reported at this date that it had taken him twelve hours to bridge a stream six feet wide at Accroful, although he had the finest material in the world.

Major Home at the outset divided his men into four parties: the first party was to clear the bush-path to 12 feet wide; the second to grub up the roots, make culverts, drains, and bridges, and clear sites for encamping-grounds; the third to erect huts and make water-supply arrangements; and the fourth, remaining at the depot in rear, to forward supplies and repair tools for the parties in advance.

The enemy's movements made it impossible to push the road far beyond Mansu, until after their retreat from Abrakrampa at the end of the first week of November: thus, for the first month, the labours of Lieutenant Mann, with the first party, were devoted to making and improving the road up to that point. The work progressed but slowly, the question of labour being always most difficult. While the Ashantis were still in their camps at Mampon and Jooquah, or feeling their way towards the main road in the direction of Dunquah, the labourers were subject to panics, in addition to the constitutional laziness which made them so difficult to deal with. On occasions they even struck work; and Major Home soon reported on the absolute necessity of more disciplined troops being sent as a covering-party to the head of the road, in order to keep the labourers in hand. On the 27th October the road from Cape Coast to Mansu was reported practicable for all arms of the service; but there were still many streams unbridged, and many wet spots and swampy places which must be put to rights before the advance of the European troops. At the end of the month there were 220 Engineer labourers engaged on the road, besides 300 more at work on the fort at Mansu and the defences of Abrakrampa, or engaged in hutting and other works at Cape Coast; but the commanding Royal Engineer earnestly requested that this number might be increased up to 1200. Everything was done for him that could be done, but road-making and fort-making were not the only matters which had now to be attended to. It was necessary to keep a large force of armed natives in the field in the presence of the Ashanti force, and the tribes were already beginning to desert. The question of obtaining 1200 labourers was, however, immediately referred to Colonel Festing, in command of the camp of native allies at Dunquah. He requested the kings to furnish him with a number of unarmed men for this purpose, but he was unable to succeed in getting them to move. Numbers of Assins, Assayboos, Inkoorsokooms, Annamaboes, and Denkeras had run away; the control department at Cape Coast was taking all the unarmed men it could get as carriers; the native armed allies at Dunquah required a certain number of unarmed men as carriers of supplies to and from their own districts; and the difficulty of obtaining men was extreme. On the 10th November Major Home, had still only 250 men employed on the road, and his number of 1200 was no nearer completion than before. Nature, too, was at this time working against the Engineers. On the 12th November, Major Home having returned to Mansu after visiting Cape Coast, and accompanying the Major-General on the march to Abrakrampa, wrote—" The road has got overgrown in a surprising way. I could hardly believe my eyes."

At this time a detachment of 130 Denkeras were sent to the head of the road, and they proved, on the whole, the best labourers of any that were handed over to the Engineers. On the 12th November, the road was open as far as Ingelasu, two miles north of Mansu; and the Okee River, 60 feet wide and 7 feet deep, with a sharp current, had been bridged. The rains were still very heavy. On the 14th, the Okee rose $3\frac{1}{2}$ feet, making a total rise of $5\frac{1}{2}$ feet in forty-eight hours; and, of course, this liability of the streams to sudden rise and fall was a considerable additional difficulty. In the third and fourth weeks of November there was great difficulty in inducing the labourers to advance. The Ashantis were known to be close to Mansu; they had, as we have seen, tapped the road with their foraging-parties, both north and south of that place; and no reconnaissance made against them from that post had ever met with even the slightest success. The unfortunate failure to strike upon the Ashantis from Mansu had its effect upon the labourers; and on the 18th November Major Home wrote: " It is not for me to offer any remarks on this subject, besides that the main body of the Ashantis are established not three miles from this place, that with native levies numbering nearly 1000 men, no information of their movements can be obtained, and that the whole of the morning has been spent in paying men who will neither scout, fight, nor labour, and who, so far as I can judge, appear to be totally out of hand, and willing to do nothing but what they choose. Viewing this matter in connection with the special duties with which I am charged, I am filled with feelings of alarm. The road from this place is cut for six miles to the northward. I cannot advance, as the men I have as labourers will not go, on account of the Ashantis; and there appear to be no means of inducing the latter to leave their present position, and thus day by day is lost. This is the 18th of November: supposing the white troops land on the 1st January, a period of six weeks is available—a period far too short to enable me, with the labour at my disposal, to make the requisite arrangements." This was a hard time for Major Home. Naturally, viewing the matter from the purely Engineer point of view, he could not realise that there was any advantage in keeping the native allies under arms. "As a simple matter of fact," he wrote, "the native allies are a gigantic swindle, who do nothing but draw pay and get in the way." And speaking of the various feeble efforts which had been made from Mansu to get upon the enemy's track, he wrote: "This may be harassing the enemy; for my part, if the enemy is only as much harassed as we are, I think it will be happy for the public service." He at this time made repeated applications for the road-party to be increased between Dunquah and Accroful; that part of the road being still, in the middle of November, incomplete. To his great delight, in the third week of November, Colonel Wood was sent to the head of the road, and the road-party there strongly reinforced. On the 20th, he wrote that he "had got as many men as he wanted at the head of the road; and that Captain Buckle, having obtained some Morees who were good workmen, had been able to reinforce Lieutenant Mann's party at Dunquah."

Still time was the great enemy, and it seemed very doubtful whether the necessary works could be accomplished in time. When once, however, Colonel Wood got to the head of the road, matters proceeded with much greater rapidity. The reconnaissance of the 27th November, although perhaps at first creating a certain amount of alarm amongst our labourers, had its effect upon the Ashantis, as we have seen; and it was soon learnt that the road in front was clear. Colonel Wood's regiment worked manfully; and not only did they clear the sites for their own encamping-grounds and build their own huts, but they assisted in road-making and clearing sites for European encampments. Still there were always difficulties. "I find," wrote Major Home on the 24th November, "that much injury is done to the road, bridges, and fascines over swamps by the native allies, who tear up the bridges for firewood to save the trouble of cutting the firewood, and pull out the fascines for the same purpose; they also invariably use the road as a latrine, and as a convenient place of deposit for all rubbish, cutting down trees and throwing them across it in the most reckless manner." The falling of trees across the road was also a constant difficulty; not one of the least obstacles to progress being the need for cutting through their enormous trunks which lay across the road and barred the path. Some of these trees had trunks of hard wood, mahogany and iron-wood, 4 or 5 feet in diameter; and of course the appliances for cutting them through were limited. The worst part of the road was that between Yancoomassie Assin and Faysowah. On either side of Sutah there was a region of clay-swamps; and the road between Sutah and Faysowah had still to be improved when all the rest was finished. With the exception of this portion, Major Home was able to report from Prahsu on Christmas-day that the road was in capital order. This section from Sutah to Faysowah was, however, put to rights by Lieutenant Bell. This officer worked with the most untiring energy. Constantly employed all day long in the noxious swamps, he suffered at times severely from fever; but went on with his work with a dauntless vigour and determination that are beyond all praise. In spite of all obstacles, owing to the exertions of Major Home and his officers and men, the whole road from Cape Coast Castle to Prahsu was in fair order before the march of the European troops commenced. On the 29th December, Major Home reported from Prahsu that no less than 237 bridges of various sorts had been made, and that the fourth layer of 9-inch fascines was then being laid on the bad section of the road between Sutah and Faysowah.

The question of selection of sites for encampments was early entered upon. Captain Huyshe, D.A.Q.M.G., was ordered to place himself in communication with Major Home, with a view to selecting camping-grounds between Cape Coast and Mansu; and Surgeon-Major Gore was appointed sanitary officer, and instructed to report upon the sites thus selected. Each camping-ground was to be large enough to hold 400 Europeans, besides the ordinary garrison of a post, say 50 men; and it was of course desirable that all the ordinary requirements of a camp should be fulfilled, that the site should be dry and healthy, and the water-supply plentiful and good. The sites ultimately decided upon for camps were as follow:—

	Distance from Cape Coast.	
	Miles.	Yards.
Inquabim,	6	1490
Accroful,	13	1160
Yancoomassie Fanti,	24	424
Mansu,	35	1056
Sutah,	46	157
Yancoomassie Assin,	58	358
Barraco,	67	602
Prahsu,	73	1402

The first two marches, it will be observed, were very short. There were several reasons for this: there is little or no shade on the first 15 miles of the road, and it was therefore most desirable that the troops should not have to march after the sun was well up; the fatigue of the first march would be increased by the fact of the troops having to disembark from the ships ; and it could not be expected that the men would be in good training for marching after a confinement of some weeks on board ship. These two short marches would therefore serve the purpose of breaking them in for the longer ones that were to follow.

The work that had to be done at these camping-grounds was immense. In the first place, the ground had to be cleared of bush, then more or less levelled ; huts to contain at least 400 European soldiers and a corresponding number of officers, had to be built, as well as control stores and hospital huts. At Mansu, the intermediate depot between Cape Coast and the Prah, everything had to be done on a very much larger scale.

The work in connection with these camps was seriously interfered with at first by the necessity of employing Engineer officers and labourers on other work ; as, for instance, the construction of huts and the defences of Cape Coast, Accroful, Dunquah, and Abrakrampa. Moreover, the difficulties were increased by the fact, that wherever any large number of natives had been encamped, the material for construction of huts in the neighbourhood of the camp had been cut down and used by them. Accordingly, at a very early stage of the operations, arrangements were made that natives should never be encamped on what was destined to be a European camping-ground. Wherever by any accident this was deviated from, there were sure to be the most unhappy results. When Colonel Festing sent the natives out from Dunquah to advance in the direction of the enemy, they deliberately sat down, to the number of some 3000, at Yancoomassie Fanti, and cut all the bamboos in the neighbourhood, to the unspeakable horror of the commanding Royal Engineer. Nor were other vexations absent. The natives being terribly wanting in respect, used the huts for purposes rather different from those for which they had been designed. At the end of November, Major Home reported that in one hospital hut at Mansu a sheep had been killed; that another had been turned into a regular harem; that the hospital huts generally were full of negroes, the European huts full of West Indian troops, and the officers' huts occupied by anybody. Still, before they were required for the European troops, all the camping-grounds up to Barraco were complete. Of Prahsu we shall speak separately later.

Some little description of these camping-grounds may here not be out of place.

The camp at Inquabim was constructed on a rising ground to the left of the road, the soil, as on the greater part of the road, consisting of disintegrated granite. Water could be derived either from the wells dug by the natives, or from a pool near the village; and though this water, as at all the stations, was reported upon by the sanitary officer, and pronounced fit to be drunk without injury to health, an additional well was sunk from which good and wholesome water was procured, and one of Crease's large filters was put up. The huts here may be taken as an example of those at all the stations. Each of the eight huts at each station was designed to hold 50 men, and was built with wattled sides and thatched with palm-leaves. Its size was 60 feet by 17 feet, and height 5 feet to the eaves. On each side of the hut a raised guard-bed was put up, made either of split bamboos or palm-stalks, long enough for the men to sleep comfortably upon, and forming a really comfortable bed, elastic, dry, and clean, 2 feet from the ground. A passage was left down the middle of the hut, 3 or 4 feet in width. Small huts were erected to hold four officers each; a separate hut was built for the commanding officer, with huts for staff officers on either side, and a large open mess-shed. A large Control store was built of planks, and a hut was erected for a hospital. An ablution shed was also put up, containing convenient troughs divided into compartments. The road through the camp was widened to a considerable distance, and the bush was cleared for some hundred yards round the station.

At Accroful similar huts were built for the men; some old native houses were utilised as quarters for officers, and the old mission-house and church converted into hospitals. Here, too, a Crease's filter was erected, although the water was good and from a running stream. The filters for Inquabim and Accroful were taken up in a steam sapper.

At the third station, Yancoomassie Fanti, the water was also obtained from a clear running stream, and a Crease's filter was erected. The Yancoomassie camp was built on the site of an old village, every vestige of which was cleared away.

Mansu was a large station. A large central parade-ground was left, and huts were built on either side. As this was to be our first advanced depot, considerable stores were built in the fort, which has already been described, and a hospital was constructed for six officers and sixty men. Water was obtained at Mansu from the Okee River, which also afforded an admirable opportunity for bathing. More rain seemed to fall at Mansu than at any other station on the road, and connecting surface-drains were laid throughout the camp, conducting the water into two deeper drains on either side of the roadway running through the centre of the encampment.

The next station was Sutah; the soil here was not so good as at other camping-grounds, consisting of a red clay, which became sticky and objectionable when wet. Both north and south of Sutah lay considerable swamps, but good water was obtained from a small clear stream running over a sandy bed some 200 paces north of the village. Close to Yancoomassie Assin also, ran through the forest a stream of deliciously pure water, with a bottom of clear white sand, affording not only first-rate drinking-water, but most delicious bathing. At Barraco it was the same. At the camping-grounds after Sutah, to which Crease's filters were not taken, sheds were erected, and a large number of basket-filters placed together, by means of which a constant supply of good filtered water was kept up for drinking.

It may reasonably be doubted whether troops ever commenced a march with more comforts provided for them. So far as it was possible to neutralise the evil effects of the detestable climate, every precaution had been taken for that end.

Towards the end of November, Surgeon-Major Gore, who had been appointed sanitary officer, sent in a very able report on the measures which should be taken to preserve the health of the troops on the march; and the greater number of his recommendations were adopted. The preparation of the road had insured that the men should march to the Prah with dry feet; shelter from the sun and rain was insured by the huts; by means of the guard-beds they were raised from the ground from 2 to 3 feet, a most necessary precaution in this country, where the surface soil almost invariably reeks with the odour of decaying vegetation; a supply of pure drinking-water was insured by the selection of the camps and the abundance of filters; and lastly, an ample supply of good food was insured by the ration which had been fixed on the recommendation of Dr Home. The European soldier's ration was as follows :—

$1\frac{1}{2}$ lb. bread, or
$1\frac{1}{2}$ lb. biscuit.
$1\frac{1}{2}$ lb. salt or fresh meat, or
1 lb. preserved meat without bone.
2 oz. rice, or peas, or
4 oz. preserved potatoes, or other vegetables.
$\frac{1}{2}$ oz. salt.
$\frac{1}{36}$ oz. pepper.
$\frac{3}{4}$ oz. tea.
3 oz. sugar.

Fresh meat was to be issued at Inquabim, Accroful, Mansu, Yancoomassie Assin, and the Prah; and bakeries were established at Cape Coast, Mansu, Yancoomassie Assin, and the Prah. Lime-juice with sugar was to be issued to the troops four times a-week on the march. Good opportunities for ablution were afforded at all the stations; supplies of dried wood were collected for the purpose of fires for cooking, and also to enable fires to be lighted at night in the huts or at the doors, as might be desirable, to dry the air and keep away miasma. A good arrangement of surface drainage was established at each camp; and a small body of sanitary police and scavengers was formed for the sole purpose of camp conservancy. Sentries were of course always placed on the water. Every morning, before starting on the march, cocoa, biscuit, and quinine, were to be given to the men. A moderate pace was enjoined for the march, which was always to be commenced at daybreak, and frequent halts were ordered. Surgeon-Major Gore, having been wounded, as already described, was invalided to Cape Coast; and Surgeon-Major Turton was appointed sanitary officer before the march commenced.

Such were the measures adopted to insure, so far as possible, the arrival of the European officers and men in sound health at Prahsu. It was, however, evident that the treacherous climate would sooner or later cause a great amount of sickness; and in addition we must expect that a certain number would suffer by the hand of the enemy. Therefore one of the most important questions of the whole campaign was the arrangement for the treatment of the sick up country, and for the removal to the coast, and thence on board ship, and to England, of those sick and wounded whose recovery could not be counted upon if they remained at the front. At the very outset careful memoranda upon these subjects had been prepared by the principal medical officer, Dr Home, and were submitted to Sir Garnet Wolseley within a fortnight of his arrival. In regard to hospitals, the original proposition, eventually only fully carried out at Mansu and at Accroful, was to have temporary hospitals at each station, independent of the barrack accommodation. The pressure of time, however, at the last entailed a modification of this; and at the other stations, except Prahsu, the arrangement eventually made was, that the best of the barracks should be improved, and be set apart for the sick after the troops had marched up. At each station the hospital provision entailed a hut for infectious cases, which might be available in case of small-pox, and a hospital hut for officers. At Prahsu a large hospital for 100 men was built; at Mansu there was a hospital for 60 men; and at the base of operations at Cape Coast there was provision on shore of 66 beds for the white troops alone, in the Colonial Church (which had been taken as a hospital) in the garrison hospital, a hut on Connor's Hill, and in hospital huts sent out from England. Had it been necessary, double this number of patients could have been accommodated by cutting down the allowance of air from 2000 to 1000 feet per man; or without this, by taking the Wesleyan Church as a hospital. There was a hospital for officers in a hut on Connor's Hill, and in a house on the beach next the garrison hospital. In all, there was accommodation at Cape Coast for 18 sick officers.

But it was not intended to keep the sick on shore at Cape Coast. H.M.S. Victor Emmanuel was sent out from England, fitted with every conceivable convenience for 240 patients. H.M.S. Himalaya, and H.M.S. Tamar, lying in the roads, could hold 100 each; besides which, in case of need, the other transports in the roads could take convalescents, and provide properly for men not requiring active medical treatment.

Every arrangement was also made for the removal of the sick to England. H.M.S. Simoom was sent to St Vincent to lie at anchor there as a receiving ship. Every ten days after the arrival of the European troops, a well-appointed steamer left Cape Coast with invalids, who were transferred to the Simoom, and remained in her until the arrival of the mail steamers from the Cape of Good Hope and elsewhere, which had been suitably and specially fitted for invalids; these transferred the sick to Southampton. The invalids were accompanied by trained orderlies of the Army Hospital Corps. Had it been necessary, invalids might also have been sent to England by one of the lines of steamers trading to the coast. Arrangements were made at Gibraltar to receive certain cases which it was not desirable to send to England in winter; and steamers were sent at intervals direct from Cape Coast to Portsmouth with invalids. In addition, every steamer chartered by Government had, in proportion to her available space, a certain number of sick cots for use as a reserve. In short, the means for removing invalids from Cape Coast to England were superabundant.

These arrangements for removal of sick from Cape Coast were made at home, and the responsibility for them did not fall upon the shoulders of the Major-General. That for which he had to provide was the transport of the sick and wounded from the front to Cape Coast. This was arranged as follows: The nature of transport was the ordinary travelling hammock of the country, or ship's cot, slung from a bamboo pole, and provided with a light movable frame as a roof for protection from the sun, and partially from the rain. This frame was made of wood, with a cover and side-curtains of canvas. Each cot had a pillow, and was conspicuously numbered. For each cot six bearers were told off, of whom four at a time carried the cot upon their heads. In the memoranda first submitted, provision was made for carriage at the rate of 14 per cent of the regular troops; but this was afterwards increased to 18 per cent when the experience of the second march to Abrakrampa had shown the necessity of the change.

The scheme for the removal of the sick and wounded was this. The transport was to be divided into two portions: 1st, Station transport at the stations; and, 2d, Transport moving with the force.

At each station 35 hammocks or cots were to be placed, an average of 13 miles being eventually fixed on as a day's journey; with power, however, to exact 16 or even 20 in very great emergency, by abolishing 2 stations in 6, and thus increasing proportionately the transport at each of the remaining stations. The 35 hammocks at each station would permit 15 sick to be sent down to the base every morning, and would leave 5 spare, giving an off-day to 30 men daily, or 1 a-week to all the men in turn. The bearers sent off one day were to return to their station next day, carrying a light load, 30 lb., for the Control, if required; thus 90 bearers would carry all the way up to the column 2700 lb. weight daily, and the loads of 4 of them might be increased to 50 lb., 2 men with the hammock carrying a light load in the hammock. To march with the column, and to be kept empty when not required for men, there were to be 85 cots and hammocks, the bearers of which were never to be employed on any other than their special duty, or in connection with hospitals.

The following memorandum was submitted by Dr Home, the principal medical officer, before leaving Cape Coast. In it will be seen, not the early draft propositions, but those really carried out; and it will be noticed that, if worked at high pressure, the material for moving 1425 sick every month was provided :

Removal of Sick and Wounded.

The calculations made suppose that 15 men will require transport to the base from the field column every morning (at 5 A M.).

At each of the 6 stations named below (and at similar stations on the further side of the Prah), should be placed 35 of the transport cots sent out from England (numbered and provided with pillows); these will suffice to take off the daily increment of sick looked for, leaving the coolies 1 off-day in 6.

1st day, Prahsu to Yancoomassie Assin,	.	18 miles.
2d ,, Yancoomassie Assin to Sutah,	.	12 ,,
3d ,, Sutah to Mansu, . .	.	11 ,,
4th ,, Mansu to Yancoomassie Fanti,	.	10½ ,,
5th ,, Yancoomassie Fanti to Accroful,	.	10½ ,,
6th ,, Accroful to Cape Coast, .	.	13 ,,
In one month, sick removed,* . .	.	450

How to increase Carriage for Sick and Wounded.

1st. Give no off-day. This will allow 2.50 men to be removed every day, equal in one month to	. 75
2d. Lengthen the journeys of the sick from an average 13 to an average 16 miles daily; this, in one month, will secure removal of	. 90
3d. In very great need, lengthen the journeys to 19 miles (about), this will give . .	. 90

Note.—The cots and hammocks now in use will at least keep up the loss from waste, perhaps add a little to resources.

* It must be noted that very trifling cases of fever, 2-4 days' illness, were not to be sent away (and these were numerous), nor men too dangerously ill to be removed.

Carriage for Wounded after Action.

The real provision here must be *special* and *emergent*; with the column it was settled to have 85 cots, but these were never contemplated as the sole resource after an action.

150 hammocks, with 15 feet pine-poles, have been sent out from England with the cots; they should be sent up to Prahsu (as they can be taken up full, they need not cost much labour). As the enemy is neared, they should be brought up (carrying stores).

If the action causes many casualties, the cots and hammocks together might remove 200 wounded, and still leave a small balance of the former (35) to march on with the column. The sick of the column meanwhile are being regularly removed every morning by means of the trans-Prah station transport (35 at each, equal to 15 sick per diem).

Note.—Only the sick and wounded of the regular troops has ever been estimated for. Natives of all sorts should be provided with the same carriage their chiefs use on emergencies — namely, rude cradles of palm-leaf stalks, carried on the heads of two men (who might be their comrades).

Further available Transport.

I applied for cots, to use instead of beds in the hospital at Prahsu (100). They are being sent out, I believe, in the Victor Emmanuel. Poles and covers might be prepared for them; and, should unexpected sickness arise, they would be available—were stated to be so, when asked for—as a large reserve of sick transport. Rush beds are on their way up to Prahsu, so that the sick there would still have something to lie on. At three journeys in one month these hospital cots could secure the removal of 300.

Note.—I have not taken similar cots at other stations into account (100).

Recapitulation.

The ordinary sick daily transport will secure the removal of, every month, ...	450
Worked under extraordinary pressure, it will give additional	225
150 hammocks, if constantly needed, will give, at three journeys a-month, . . .	450
Prahsu hospital cots will give, additional . .	300
Total, . . .	1425

Note.—A temporary choking up of the transport (say after a severe action) can be met by diverting 60 sick to the hospital at Mansu; farther, by using the huts at every station as a hospital for a day or two.

Hospital Provision on Shore at Cape Coast for Europeans.

Garrison Hospital, . . .	10 beds.
Church, ...	22 ,,
Hut on Connor's Hill, . . .	10 ,,
Hospital huts now being erected (sent out from England), ...	24 ,,
Total, . . .	66 beds.

Officers :—

One hospital hut sent out from England, now being erected, ...	8 beds.

For West Indians :—

Garrison hospital, ...	16 beds.
Huts, ...	20 ,,

Hospital marquees capable of indefinite extension.

(Signed) A. D. HOME.

In the middle of December, Dr Home, who had been on the coast since June, and to whose thoughtful care and able brain the entire organisation of these arrangements for hospitals and removal of sick and wounded was due, was seized with a most severe attack of the terrible coast fever. During all the early operations he had been present in the field, and his personal exertions had been conspicuous. On that desperately trying march to Abrakrampa, and in all our marches, he had worked on foot like a private soldier, striving amongst men suffering from the effects of the sun and exhaustion. At the beginning of December he had accompanied the Major-General as far as Sutah, to inspect the progress of the camps on the road; and now, on his return, the malarious fever laid hold of him, and he became bodily, and to a great extent mentally, prostrated. A medical Board invalided him to England, and his services were lost to the force. Only a brain specially gifted with organising power, and of remarkably clear judgment, could have arranged with such singular effectiveness for the probable contingencies of a campaign in this climate. All Dr Home's calculations were subsequently found to have been most wonderfully correct; and his successors found organised and ready to their hand a complete system. For a short time after Dr Home's being invalided, the duties of Principal Medical Officer were carried on by Surgeon-Major Woolfreys, M.D.; but before any collision had taken place with the enemy, Surgeon-Major Mackinnon, C.B., arrived, and acted as Principal Medical Officer throughout the remainder of the campaign. This officer had been sent to Madeira to endeavour to arrange for the reception there of sick men from the Gold Coast, but his mission had failed owing to the obstinacy of the Portuguese Government; and he had left Madeira and started for the Gold Coast without orders, anticipating by this act a demand which Sir Garnet Wolseley had sent to Madeira for his immediate departure for Cape Coast. The moment it was known that Dr Home would be unable to continue at his work, the Major-General had sent off for Dr Mackinnon, knowing well his physical and mental vigour, and judging rightly the immense importance of having at this crisis of operations the duties of principal medical officer performed by a man in whom he could thoroughly trust, on whose strength of character he could rely, and whose surgical skill was well established. The difficulties which Dr Mackinnon had to encounter were great; but he carried out his duties with an unceasing cheerfulness and determination, both invaluable qualities under such conditions.

While dealing with the medical preparations of the campaign, there is another point which demands special notice. Perhaps the most anxious medical trial was the keeping out of yellow fever from the Expedition. A bad epidemic of yellow fever had prevailed at Sierra Leone from December 1872 to February 1873, and, according to medical authority, a recrudescence of this disease after the rains is quite normal, and to be expected. In May 1873 a fearful epidemic of yellow fever affected all the settlements of the Oil rivers; that at the Bonny River lost two-thirds of its white residents: and here also it was to be expected that yellow fever, dormant in the rains, would spring up in the dry weather, and it did so. Sir Garnet Wolseley and the local Government had, shortly after arrival, passed a quarantine ordinance with a view of warding off this disease; but the machinery of inspection had been scarcely elaborated when, on the 31st October, the mail steamer Ethiopia arrived, and had pratique given her. The surgeon of the ship, however, considerately sent a message to Dr Home, informing him that he had cases of a bad kind of fever on board. Dr Home went to the ship, and found that four persons, including the captain of the steamer, had died of yellow fever, three of them within twelve hours, and that five others were then ill on board with the same disease. The ship was at once put in quarantine; invalided officers were prevented from embarking in her, and the persons already landed from the steamer were sent up to an isolated house outside the town, around which a sanitary cordon was drawn. A detachment of Houssas who disembarked from the Ethiopia was similarly isolated; and from that time forward the quarantine law was most admirably worked by Dr Reid of the Royal Navy, to whom Dr Home gives the credit of keeping the European force free of yellow fever. Ships subsequently arriving at Cape Coast had many cases of yellow fever on board; the Ambriz alone, on her return voyage, lost thirteen persons; and the Biafra, in which, unhappily, Lieutenant Wells of the Royal Navy, who had done such gallant service, sailed for England, had lost five before reaching Cape Coast. Lieutenant Wells died on his passage home shortly after leaving Sierra Leone, and one of the finest, handsomest, and bravest officers that ever lived was thus lost to Her Majesty's navy. It may be said that yellow fever was never known at Cape Coast. In reply, as Dr Home has pointed out to the writer, it may be answered, neither was it ever known at Buenos Ayres until the other day, when it swept out the place. The fact is, that there never was a European population at Cape Coast until the expedition arrived, and yellow fever only attacks Europeans. The combination of circumstances required to produce yellow fever there would simply have been these : A European suffering from yellow fever to land in Cape Coast, and a population in which to spread it on his arrival. The population was there, but by the strict enforcement of quarantine law the disease was never allowed to land upon the Coast.

The immunity of the Expedition from small-pox was also a point of remarkable interest, for the disease ravaged the native community. In the course of the month of December, our friend Amfoo Ottoo, the King of Abrah, amongst many others, fell a victim to this terrible scourge.

The details for the medical arrangements for this campaign, and the many questions of immense interest to the medical profession, would scarcely find their proper place in this volume ; medically and sanitarily the campaign is of the greatest interest ; and it is sincerely to be hoped that the many points of value may be elaborated by those who are competent to do so, for future medical guidance.

There remains now to be spoken of the means taken for the provision of transport. It has already been said that, upon our arrival at the Coast, a corps of native carriers was found established, to the number of about 650 ; but before the Expedition to Coomassie could be satisfactorily accomplished, this body would have to be increased to more than ten times that number. From the very first, this question enraged the most serious attention of the Major-General. Naturally, at the first out-set, while the Ashantis were in the Protectorate, and operations were constantly being undertaken against them, the great bulk of the native allies were required for service in the field; but the moment that this pressure was taken off, and that the Major-General was able, after Abrakrampa, to turn his attention more exclusively to the future expedition, all possible means were resorted to to employ the native allies as labourers and carriers.

On the 16th November, Captain Huyshe, D.A.Q.M.G., and Assistant-Commissary Elliot, were sent on a mission to the different kings at Assayboo, Abrakrampa, Dunquah, and Mansu. The following instructions were given to Captain Huyshe :—

"You, accompanied by Assistant-Commissary Elliot, will be pleased to proceed to Assayboo, Abrakrampa, Dunquah, and Mansu, where the various kings are assembled; and, at a meeting to be held at each place, give them distinctly to understand that the orders of his Excellency the Governor are, that each king should produce, by a particular date to be named, and at a certain place, the number of men and women as stated below as carriers and labourers.

"As regards the Assayboo tribes, as they have shown themselves to be such arrant cowards in the field, and have, since the attack of Abrakrampa, deserted the officer in command of them, there only remaining 30 out of 250, and as moreover they are able to give 100 labourers in excess of 300 armed men, you will be pleased to call on the king, under penalty of a fine of £20, and, if necessary, of arrest and imprisonment as a disloyal subject, on non-compliance with your order, to furnish as carriers 300 men and 200 women at Assayboo by 12 mid-day, on a day to be fixed by you.

"As regards the other tribes, you will call on them to furnish the number of carriers and labourers as follows: There being required in all 1660, viz.—1000 for the Control, to be assembled at Dunquah, with 1 chief to every 100 men, and 660 for the Royal Engineers.

"The Royal Engineers require 260 at Mansu, and 200 at Dunquah; as also 200 at Cape Coast. It would be as well, therefore, if the latter 200 were furnished by the Assayboos, they being wanted for the encampment to be formed at Inquabim. This will therefore be notified by you to the commanding Royal Engineer, with a view to arrangements being made for an officer to take them over,—similar steps being taken as regards the other details.

"The men engaged for this service will receive 1s. a-day, and the head-man or chief to each company of 100 men, 2s. 6d. a-day.

"It will be clearly explained to each king, that if he fails to produce the number required at the time and place intimated, a heavy fine will be exacted from him; and moreover, the men will be taken from those at present returned and paid for as fighting men.

"The number given as carriers and labourers, if it reaches that demanded, will be allowed to count in the number furnished by the king, as regards the allowance of £10 every 1000 men."

Then followed a list of the numbers which it was supposed could be given as carriers in excess of armed men by each tribe as under :—

Assins, Annamaboes, Abrahs, Denkeras, Inkoorsokrooms, Mankessims, Assayboos, Goomoahs, Acoomfies, &c.

It was hoped by these instructions that the number of carriers immediately required might be provided, without touching the armed natives; and that these latter could thus be left for the present, remaining available to be taken and employed as carriers at any subsequent date.

On the 18th November, Captain Lanyon, of the 2d West India Regiment, who had been appointed aide-de-camp to the Major-General in succession to Captain M'Calmont, invalided to England, and had been relieved from his duties as Colonial Secretary by Captain Lees, the Colonial Secretary at Lagos, was sent to Beulah to witness the disarming of 300 of the Cape Coast tribe, who had proved themselves worthless as soldiers; and these men were sent under escort to Assayboo to be employed as carriers.

Captain Huyshe's mission was only partially successful; and in order to obtain even the small number of men now demanded, it became necessary to disarm a certain number of the natives.

The truth must be told about this matter of transport. Thousands of carriers were obtained for the Control Department by the exertions of staff and special-service officers, but they melted away. "Handing carriers over to the Control Department," wrote the Major-General in one of his despatches, "is like pouring water into a sieve; they run away after making a single journey." Under any circumstances it would always be difficult to insure regularity of transport with native carriers, to whom labour is distasteful, who cannot bear regular discipline, and who would rather live on the fruits gathered for them by their women, and lie on their backs in idleness all day, than work regularly for any amount of pay. Still, if from the first the tribes had been kept together, subdivided into gangs by villages under their own head-men, worked by regular stages, never overworked, regularly paid—if they had been registered and a proper system of checks established, they need never have melted away in this fashion. But this was not done. When Colonel Colley took over the transport in December, there were men of nine different tribes at Mansu alone; and the native head-men often had little connection with their companies, sometimes did not even belong to the same tribe, but had been selected because they spoke a little English. The payments had been irregular, and the carriers often overworked. The transport was, for these reasons, a failure. And this was not because the Control officers did not work energetically and without thought of their own comfort. Nothing could have exceeded their zeal. Commissary O'Connor, the Commissary of Transport stationed at Cape Coast, had more on his hands than he could well carry out, without thought of anything beyond Cape Coast itself. All the labour of unloading the ships, and of despatching stores from Cape Coast towards the front, fell on him. Few men could have stood the work. From earliest dawn to late at night he was incessantly busy, bearing exposure in the most marvellous way. But he could organise no system for transport generally in the midst of this work, nor had he the necessary authority. At Cape Coast itself he organised a boat transport to and from the ships, and kept it working thoroughly, for it was entirely in his own hands; so, too, he obtained women and children who would carry loads to Dunquah and return. These, too, he could personally superintend. So also at Mansu, Assistant-Commissary Elliot worked like a slave from long before dawn till long after sunset. But there was no general system. The Control officers at each station were eager to send on to the front as many loads as possible daily; but whence the carriers came who took the loads, or what became of them after the loads were delivered, was not sufficiently considered. Under a proper system it would have been impossible for the complaints to arise which were so frequent, of carriers sent from a station not returning; or of the sometimes well-founded complaints of carriers that, immediately on the completion of one journey, they were, without even time being allowed to eat, compelled to commence another. Under a proper system, engineer labourers would not have been taken by Control officers and used for transport purposes, as was the case more than once.

But, once more, how could it be expected to be otherwise? The transport service alone would have required all the energy—and did subsequently require it—of a large number of experienced officers, with no other work. How could it be properly superintended by the Control officers, who had supplies and issue of stores to attend to as well, on whom it depended to supply ammunition to one place, and food to another, to look after their own stores, and issue rations to the garrisons of their posts? How could they look after transport, organise carriers in gangs, pay them, count them, and care for their comforts? What wonder if, under these conditions, some carriers made double journeys without pay, while others presented themselves for pay without having carried a load?

Surely efficient transport is the vital spark of an army, whose life depends on it. Surely it is a hopeless task to make war with the transport placed in the hands of a civil department already overcharged with other duties. If only the breakdown of transport in the Ashanti war teach that one lesson, then there will be ample compensation for the anxieties from which we suffered so deeply.

Every one was doing his best to push loads to the front. On the 15th December, Colonel Wood wrote from Acoomfoodie: "Though it was 7.30 P.M. before they all got back, I sent off 369 loads yesterday, unassisted by any Control arrangements. This morning I have sent off 360 loads." But system was wanting. How can a General hope for success, how can he even make plans of campaign, if he cannot count on a certain system of supply? Is it not the very essence of all military systems of Intendance, Intendantur, Etappen, Control—call them what you will—that the General's mind shall be relieved of any supervision of details in this matter, and that he shall be able to obtain a definite answer to any question of supply or transport? Nor is it the business of the General in command to find the means of transport, as was done here. So long as the transport was conducted on the regulation system, the whole body of carriers, except such transport as we found on arrival, and such other as Mr O'Connor raised at Cape Coast, was raised for the Control by measures taken by the Chief of the Staff.

On the 8th of November, the total transport corps

THE ASHANTI WAR. 339

was reported as 1323,—scarcely 700 more than had been found on our arrival. And now commenced those active steps, some of which have been already related. Captain Huyshe was sent to the native kings— Captain Lanyon to the Cape Coast men at Beulah.

On the 22d, in consequence of the great difficulty of obtaining sufficient transport for forwarding supplies to the advanced depot at Mansu, orders were issued to the commanding officer at Dunquah to send daily 500 men from some of the tribes under his orders to Cape Coast, in order to carry ammunition back to Dunquah. For a time this answered, but before long it became a source of desertion. Colonel Festing wrote:—

"The 500 who arrived from Cape Coast, under Despard, had to be turned out by force this morning; they refused to go on to Mansu to-day, declaring they were tired; however, I got all of them off except 29, and I filled up this number by others, these men being sore-footed. Now there are at least 1500 men at this occupation, and I fear we shall be unable to send any to-morrow in consequence of not having them; but as I have ordered in the Inkoorsokooms and Abrahs from Darman and Wonkorsu, I hope at any rate to be able, if not to-morrow, to send a detachment next day. This carrying, like everything else they are ordered to do, goes very much against their grain. Russell is here now, and has got some recruits; but we have so few men that he has not been able to get men from sound tribes. We do not get men back again that we send away to Mansu; even if we send away armed men, keeping their arms here, we do not get the men again."

Other steps now taken to obtain carriers and labourers met with considerable success. On the 26th November the chiefs and head-men of the disaffected villages, west of Elmina and east of the Prah, came into Cape Coast to sue for peace; and they were told that though His Excellency had not time now to consider the question of future punishment for their rebellion, it would very much depend on their present conduct; meanwhile he required them, as an earnest of their desire for peace, to send 300 carriers within three days, and keep up this number during the war. On the 30th, these 300 men arrived at Cape Coast, and were handed over to the Engineers as labourers.

On the 1st December the Major-General proceeded with Major Baker, and the principal medical officer, on a tour of inspection up the road. Previous to his departure from Cape Coast, he sent Lieutenant Bolton to the Goomoah and adjacent countries to procure carriers. Major Brownell at Saltpond was also requested to use all his efforts; and the result was the arrival of large numbers of carriers from these districts. 650 had reached Dunquah by the 8th December.

During the first twelve days in December more than 3000 armed men were handed over to the Control as carriers, by orders of the Major-General; on the road up country 1400, and on the road down the remainder, the native allies being all disarmed for this purpose; On the 10th December the Major-General instructed the kings and chiefs at Dunquah that he would not land the European troops unless they handed over to him 5000 carriers by the end of the month; and the officers attached to the tribes as commissioners proceeded into the various districts to collect men.

On the 10th the Major-General returned to Cape Coast, and immediately despatched Dr O'Reilly, the colonial surgeon, who was well known at Elmina, to procure carriers by the offer of pardon to the disaffected chiefs if they now showed themselves in earnest. By his active exertions he succeeded in obtaining 700 in ten days from the villages which had already produced 300. Dr Gouldsbury also was requested to obtain carriers in the neighbourhood of the windward ports, and his first instalment of 146, of whom 130 had been furnished by King Blay, left Dixcove on the 27th December in H.M.S. Coquette. The officer commanding at Lagos was applied to, but without success.

To supplement the transport, all the Cape Coast levies at Beulah were disarmed on the 14th December, and marched to Mansu; and the unarmed men of the Abrah levy were moved from Abrakrampa to the front, to act as regimental transport for Russell's Regiment. A regular train of women carriers was also organised from Annamaboe.

By these various means, no plan which could be thought of having been omitted, a vast number of carriers had been obtained and handed over. But, as before related, "handing them over to the Control was like pouring water into a sieve." Still, at the date of the Major-General's return to Cape Coast, there were such numbers on the road that there was every reason to suppose that sufficient transport would be available for the campaign before us, and that the arrangements which the Major-General now proceeded to make in detail could be carried out with certainty. On the 22d December, when the transport was placed in the hands of Colonel Colley, the returns showed 6000 carriers working between Cape Coast and the Prah, and the Commissioners gave hopes of large additional numbers.

These facts and figures are a sufficient answer to those critics who have accused the Major-General of neglecting the question of transport.

On the night of the 9th December, while Sir Garnet Wolseley was absent at Dunquah, H.M.S. Himalaya arrived unexpectedly from England with the following troops on board :—30 officers, 652 N.C. officers and men 2d Battalion Rifle Brigade; 30 N.C. officers and men Army Service Corps; 4 officers and 68 N.C. officers and men Royal Engineers, of whom 12 were telegraphists and constructors; 2 officers and 26 N.C. officers and men Army Hospital Corps; 13 medical officers; and 2 chaplains. The officer commanding the troops was requested to retain all the officers and men on board ship until the Major-General's arrival.

On the 11th the mail steamer Senegal arrived from England with Assistant-Controller Healy and another Control officer and 3 medical officers. On the 12th, H.M.S. Tamar arrived, having on board 30 officers and 650 N.C. officers and men Royal Welsh Fusiliers; 3 officers and 61 N.C. officers and men Royal Artillery, being half of 1st Battery 17th Brigade; 2 sergeants 2d West India Regiment; 13 medical officers; and 2 chaplains. On the 17th the steam transport Sarmatian arrived from England with the following details on board :—Brigadier-General Sir Archibald Alison, Bart., C.B.; Colonel G. R. Greaves, Chief of the Staff; Captain Russell, 12th Lancers, Aide-de-Camp to the Brigadier-General; Lieutenant M. Fitzgerald, extra Aide-de-Camp; Brevet Lieutenant-Colonel Colley, 2d Queen's Regiment, and 10 other officers for special service; 1 officer and 12 N.C. officers and men Army Service

Corps; 26 N.C. officers and men Army Hospital Corps 1 Staff Clerk; 2 men Royal Engineers; 30 officers and 652 N.C. officers and men 42d Highlanders; and 15 medical officers.

The arrival of the Himalaya in port was the first notice received that European troops were to be sent out. The reader will not have forgotten that the despatching of these troops had been reserved for discussion as a Cabinet question; and although we had all been made aware, by private letters from England, that the 23d and the Rifle Brigade were being got into readiness for embarkation, some little doubt had been raised in our minds as to the intentions of the Government by the receipt of the following despatch from Lord Kimberley, which had reached Sir Garnet Wolseley while we were at Abrakrampa, and on receipt of which a Commander in any way afraid of responsibility would have suspended further operations, and considered enough had been done in chastising the Ashantis at Abrakrampa, as her Majesty's Government were apparently backing out of their previous orders.

The Earl of Kimberley to Sir G. Wolseley.

"DOWNING STREET, *October* 6, 1873.

"SIR,—The preparations which had been made by the Military and Naval Departments to place you in full possession of all the means necessary for success in your important mission, have given rise to very numerous conjectures and speculations as to the intentions entertained by her Majesty's Government.

"It is not necessary for me to warn you against being misled by expressions which will not fail to reach you, of these unauthorised anticipations, and to insist again upon the cautions which have been conveyed to you in former despatches. Her Majesty's Government are confident that you will avoid engaging in any desultory operations which can lead to no serious result if successful, and may give an oportunity to the Ashantis of inflicting losses which, though not in themselves considerable, are magnified into serious disasters to the British arms. At the same time they desire to impress upon you that they would be most reluctant to sanction any expedition which would require that European troops should be sent from this country to the Gold Coast. Previous instructions have given you authority as to the immediate use of the forces now under your command with a view to a speedy peace, or to striking an effective blow at the Ashantis.

"A satisfactory state of things will be attained if you can procure an honourable peace, or can inflict, in default of such peace, an effectual chastisement on the Ashanti force. Unless, and until one of these objects shall have been gained, you will understand that the primary purpose of military operations will be to drive the enemy from that district of country, their presence within which endangers, or seriously menaces, the security of the British settlements upon the Coast.

"To procure their withdrawal from the large and ill-defined territory which may be included within the loose designation of the Protectorate, is an object which, however desirable, is distinct from the former one. The pursuit of it by military means must depend upon a variety of considerations, among which a main one is the union and force of the tribes who inhabit that country. This question should be reserved for the determination of her Majesty's Government.

"Her Majesty's Government desire that the views I have thus stated should be present to your mind in framing any recommendation which you may find it necessary to submit to them.

"But this will, of course, not preclude you from reporting your opinion in favour of any course of action which, with the knowledge you will have acquired on the spot, you may conceive that the circumstances demand.—I have, &c.

(Signed) "KIMBERLEY."

If any doubt, however, had existed in the mind of the Government as to whether the troops should be sent out, Sir Garnet Wolseley's despatch of the 13th October, given in Chapter V., at once settled the question; and it would have been difficult for any Government, in the face of that despatch, to have refused the troops whom Sir Garnet Wolseley demanded as absolutely necessary for the success of the mission intrusted to him by her Majesty's Ministers.

Immediately upon the receipt of that despatch, which was received on the afternoon of the 17th of November, a Cabinet Council was held, and orders were telegraphed the same evening for the Himalaya and Tamar to start at once with the troops on board, who were already held in readiness for service. These ships left Plymouth on the 19th, and Queenstown on the 21st November. The Himalaya brought out 20 miles of overhead telegraph wire, with tools and apparatus complete.

On the 18th November, in compliance with Sir Garnet Wolseley's request for a 3d European battalion, the 42d Highlanders were placed under orders for the Coast; and the S.S. Sarmatian was engaged by the

Admiralty for their transport. The 42d Highlanders, made up to the strength of 650 by a draft of about 169 men from the 79th Highlanders, embarked on board the Sarmatian at Portsmouth on the 3d December, and sailed the following day, making the shortest passage that had ever been made to Cape Coast.

The European troops were all equipped, according to Sir Garnet Wolseley's request, in grey tweed suits and helmets, and were provided with water-bottles and pocket-filters; but the 23d and 42d still retained the long rifles and bayonets, the latter of which would have been utterly useless in bush-warfare, while the long rifle would only have added an extra weight, and extra difficulty in moving through the bush. Short rifles and sword-bayonets for these regiments were, however, sent out by Mr Cardwell in a transport, and the troops were armed with them before proceeding up country.

The Himalaya brought the information to Sir Garnet that the 3d battalion was being placed under orders; and the Sarmatian brought out the following despatch from Lord Kimberley:—

"DOWNING STREET, *November* 24, 1873.

"SIR,—I informed you, in my despatch of the 11th of November, that I should address you further when the statement which you proposed to send to the Secretary of State for War respecting the employment of a European force had been received.

"2. You will have learnt from the Secretary of State for War by the last mail that, after consideration of that statement, it had been determined to despatch at once the troops which had been held in readiness, and that the further battalion which you had asked for would follow.

"3. I have now to acquaint you with the views of her Majesty's Government respecting the employment of this force, and the general limits within which, as far as circumstances may admit, your action should be confined.

"4. You are aware, from previous despatches, both from the Secretary of State for War and from myself, that her Majesty's Government were most reluctant to send European troops to the Gold Coast. In the instructions conveyed to you in my letter of September 10, before your departure from this country, you were informed that, if you should find it necessary to ask for any considerable reinforcement of European troops, you were to enter into full explanations as to the circumstances in which you proposed to employ them, and the reasons which led you to believe that they could be employed without an unjustifiable exposure and with a well-grounded anticipation of success.

"5. You have now given it as your opinion that a certain force of European soldiers is indispensable, not only for the purpose of an advance into the enemy's territory, but also for the preliminary operations which you describe in your despatch to me of October 9, and you state that you have satisfied yourself that they can be employed during the more healthy season in the manner you propose, without serious risk from sickness.

"6. After carefully considering the arguments by which your proposals are supported, her Majesty's Government had no hesitation in determining to comply with your request, and orders were at once given accordingly for the despatch of the troops.

"7. Before the troops reach the coast you will, no doubt, as far as lies in your power, have made every preparation in advance, so that no European soldier may be landed until the time for decisive action has arrived; and her Majesty's Government rely with confidence that you will not employ this force, especially in the interior, a day longer than the paramount objects of your mission may require. The limit of their employment is fixed by the continuance of the more healthy season, and her Majesty's Government trust you may be able to re-embark the troops for return to England during the month of February, or at the very latest in March, before the end of which month, at all events, it will be absolutely necessary to withdraw them. This limit of time, which is imposed by the conditions of the climate, will, of course, of itself place a corresponding limit upon the operations which it will be prudent or possible for you to attempt. The nature and extent of the operations which it may, within this limit of time, be necessary to undertake in order to bring the war to a conclusion, must be left to your own judgment to determine; nor do her Majesty's Government wish to fetter the discretion which must always be placed in the hands of an officer commanding a force in the field; but they desire that, in forming your decision, you will bear in mind the following considerations:—

"8. You were informed in my despatch of October 6 that a satisfactory state of things would be obtained if you could procure an honourable peace, or could inflict, in default of such peace, an effectual chastisement on the Ashanti force.

"9. It is obvious that it will be the interest of the

Ashantis to gain time by negotiations, so as to delay the progress of the operations against them until the unhealthy season returns. They have abundantly proved their capacity for carrying on such illusory negotiations, and I have no fear that you will suffer yourself to be deceived by them. But it may be that the King of Ashanti, on learning the retreat of his army and the further preparations against him, will be ready to make reparation, and to conclude at once a peace on conditions acceptable to Her Majesty's Government, in order to avert the impending blow. Her Majesty's Government would view with much satisfaction such a termination of the existing difficulties.

"10. But if it should be necessary to advance far into the interior of the country, and even beyond the Prah, it appears to Her Majesty's Government by no means to follow that it would be advisable to occupy Coomassie.

"11. If you should inflict a severe defeat on the Ashanti army near or beyond the frontier, the occupation of the capital might, perhaps, be effected without much difficulty; but it is probable that the result might be a complete break up of the king's government and power. In such an event, you might find yourself in possession of Coomassie without any government or ruler to treat with; and as it would be wholly out of the question to keep European troops in a state of inactivity in the interior, you might be compelled to return without having obtained a full security for the establishment of a lasting peace.

"12. It seems probable that one of the main grounds of quarrel between the Ashantis and the coast tribes arises, as in other parts of Africa, from the impediments interposed by the latter to the free access and trade of the Ashantis with the coast. If the King of Ashanti were persuaded that our object would be to facilitate and protect the trade of the Ashantis, and that they might regard Elmina as in every respect as much open to them, now it is under our influence, as it was when under Dutch protection, or as it could be in any other circumstances, it is reasonable to suppose that it would effect a great change in his relations with the British settlements.

"13. In any communication which you may have with the king, you should lose no opportunity to impress upon him that our object is to promote, in every way, the intercourse of the Ashantis with the coast, and to protect the trade coming from the interior from interruption and annoyance. You cannot too strongly assure him that we desire to be on terms of friendship with the Ashanti nation, and that he has been completely deceived if he has been led to believe that our object in obtaining possession of the Dutch forts was to cut off his people from communication with the coast; that, on the contrary, if they come as peaceful traders, it is as much our interest as his that they should meet with no hindrance which it is in our power to remove.

"14. I have further to observe that, whilst the violent aggression of the King of Ashanti upon the Protectorate, at a time when he was professing to be in friendly negotiations with the British authorities, cannot be overlooked, much less the ravages and barbarities by which the progress of the invaders has been marked, it must not be forgotten that there is a reason to believe that the Ashantis received some provocation from the tribes of the Protectorate, and in negotiating the terms of peace, you will be careful to give fair consideration to any complaints which the king may urge against these tribes; and if you should be of opinion that they are to any extent well founded, you will give due weight to them in determining the amount of reparation which you may require.

"15. I may sum up by saying, that it is the wish of Her Majesty's Government that you should conclude a satisfactory peace as soon as it can be obtained; that you should advance no further into the interior than may be indispensable for the attainment of such a peace; and that, after concluding, if possible, a Treaty with the King of Ashanti, you should return with the least practicable delay to the sea-coast, and send home the European troops, keeping on foot only such other forces as you may consider necessary for the service of the settlements, and for holding the road to the Prah, so as to keep the communication with the interior open to trade.

"16. With respect to our relations after the war with the tribes of the Protectorate, considering that with some few exceptions the native tribes since their first defeats have made very little effort to defend themselves against the Ashantis, and that, practically, the whole burden of the war has fallen upon this country, it must be understood that when the present operations have been concluded, Her Majesty's Government will hold that they have discharged their obligations to the protected tribes, and that they are entirely free to review their relations with those tribes, and to place them on such footing as the interests of this country may seem to them to require.

"17. In desiring you, therefore, to leave the road to the Prah under the protection of such a force as you may deem necessary, they must not be understood as pledging this country to permanently maintain a force to keep the road open; and you will be careful not to enter into any stipulation with the Ashantis which may fetter the discretion of Her Majesty's Government in dealing hereafter with the relations between this country and the Gold Coast generally.

"18. You will, of course, give such instructions to Captain Glover as will insure his conforming strictly to the views of Her Majesty's Government as indicated in this despatch.—I have, &c.

(Signed) "KIMBERLEY."

The European troops whom the Government had sent out with such unexampled rapidity, arrived on the Gold Coast too late, and yet too soon. They arrived too late to take advantage of the proximity of the Ashanti army to the coast, and of that splendid strategical position which the Major-General had held while the enemy was at Mampon, and he was in possession of a fortified post on their main line of retreat at Mansu : they arrived too late to enable Sir Garnet Wolseley to destroy the whole Ashanti army, as he might have done had they been in his hands by the first or second week of November. On the other hand, they arrived too soon for an immediate advance upon Coomassie. The Major-General had pledged himself in his earlier despatches not to land the troops till the day they were to march; and he had guaranteed that the operations in which they were engaged on shore should not last more than two months. Had the

THE ASHANTI WAR. 353

troops been landed at once, neither of these promises could have been fulfilled. Accordingly, the ships were ordered to sea, to cruise until the last day of the year, by which date they were to return to the roads.

The Major-General's reasons for this course will be best explained by his own letter to the Secretary of State for War, written on the 15th December.

"In my despatch of the 13th October, I expressed my opinion that on the arrival of the troops in these roads about the middle of December, all would be ready for their immediate advance into the enemy's country. I regret that it has been impossible to have the necessary preparations completed at so early a date, and that I am compelled to postpone landing the troops till the first week in January.

"Two main causes have contributed to compel this delay. The first has been the movements of the enemy; the second, the enormous difficulties in regard to labour and transport.

"So long as the enemy remained within a short distance of Cape Coast Castle, it was impossible for me to advance on the road beyond Mansu, as reported to you in previous despatches. When the enemy retired after his defeat at Abrakrampa, he made for the main road at Sutah, and I had no force capable of attacking him, or preventing his occupying the road from that point to the Prah. His retreat was very slowly conducted, and I was thus much hindered in pushing on working parties to make the road.

"In the second place, the difficulties in obtaining and keeping labourers and carriers have been beyond all conception. Where I expected thousands of men, I have received only hundreds. Handing them over to the Control Department is like pouring water into a sieve: they run away after making a single journey. There is also great difficulty in retaining labourers at the head of the road. Plantains, the food to which they are accustomed, are not to be obtained there, owing to the devastation of the country by the enemy in his recent retreat; and as they do not like the biscuit and rice, which are the only food we can give them, their natural laziness and their habits of self-indulgence lead them to run away, rather than remain at work, although they are well paid.

"The Royal Engineers have worked admirably on the road, and the Control Department have made the most of their transport; but it will not be possible to have the several halting stages, including the depot at Prahsu, completed, and a sufficient quantity of food and ammunition in magazines at Prahsu, before the 15th January next.

"By that date I count upon being able to advance from the bridgehead which I shall have previously constructed on the northern bank of the Prah, with the Rifle Brigade, and the 23d Fusiliers, and a force of native troops.

"On the arrival of the vessel containing the 42d Highlanders, I propose sending her also to sea till the end of the year, or even later, and then to keep her cruising off the shore so as to be always within my reach.

"When I asked for a third battalion, it was, as you are aware, for the purpose of having an effective reserve; and I then anticipated having to fight a costly action on this side of the Prah, which might have seriously diminished my small European force for operations in the Ashanti territory. This contingency has no longer to be taken into account, and I shall therefore not land the battalion, but shall keep it as a reserve at sea, where I can always find it, so as to land it at any time should necessity for its employment arise, owing to the severity of the resistance on the other side of the Prah being greater than I at present anticipate.

"I shall not land one man more than I consider essential to the success of my operations, and I shall not detain any English troops on shore an hour longer than is absolutely necessary."

It will be seen by this despatch that the Major-General did not purpose landing the 42d Highlanders at all, but proposed to keep them at sea as a reserve in case of need. On careful consideration, however, he changed this intention, and on the 18th of December, after the arrival of the Sarmatian, he wrote as follows :—

"In my despatch of 15th inst. I stated that it was my intention not to land the 42d Regiment, but to keep the vessel containing it cruising off the shore, so as always to be within reach at short notice.

"I have now the honour to inform you that, upon reconsideration, I have decided to land the battalion, and to take it with me across the Prah as part of my fighting force.

"I had intended to take into Ashanti territory only the two English battalions originally asked for, together with the 1st and 2d West India Regiments, and Russell's and Wood's Regiments of native levies. But upon a careful examination of the question, I find that the one great obstacle to the employment of a third battalion of English troops, viz.—the difficulty of transport, is as great in the case of a West Indian regiment. The West Indian soldier has the same rations as the European soldier, and a West Indian regiment requires, man for man, exactly the same amount of transport as a European regiment. You are already aware, from my despatch asking for European troops, of my opinion as to the relative value in this country of English and native troops; and when so splendid a battalion as the 42d is ready to my hand, when I see the martial spirit which animates both officers and men, when I think of the vastly superior numbers of the enemy, and see myself entirely deprived of the large force of native auxiliaries upon which I had counted, when I remember how vitally important it is that the campaign should be short and decisive, I don't think I should be acting wisely in keeping the 42d Regiment at sea while employing in the field the 1st West India Regiment, who, however excellent their officers and men, must, from the very nature of their material, be inferior to a regiment with such traditions and in so fine a state of discipline as her Majesty's 42d Highlanders. I shall therefore employ this latter regiment in the field, and retain the 1st West India Regiment in Cape Coast Castle and Elmina, as a reserve which can be called upon in case of urgent need.

"In thus announcing my resolve to land the 42d Regiment, I wish again to assure you of my strong hope, bordering upon conviction, that in about six weeks from the date of our crossing the Prah, I shall be able to embark the European troops, having suffered but little loss from the effects of the climate."

The 1st West India Regiment, as mentioned in this despatch, had been ordered from Jamaica to Cape

Coast, in compliance with Sir Garnet Wolseley's request; and on the 4th December the hired transport Manitoban left Jamaica with 21 officers and 455 men, and took in 3 more officers and 99 men at Barbadoes, whence she sailed for Cape Coast Castle on the 9th December, arriving on the 27th, and disembarking her troops on the 29th.

The Major-General's intention to cross the Prah on the 15th January, and his determination to have by that time the halting stages, including the depot at Prahsu, completed, and a sufficient quantity of food and ammunition in magazines at Prahsu, has been already stated in his despatch. The following memorandum will show what the Major-General considered to be these sufficient quantities:—

"The following munitions of war will be at Prahsu on the 31st inst.—

    6 Rocket-troughs and 200 rockets.
    3 7-pounder guns, and 100 rounds per gun.
    2 4⅖ howitzers, and 100 rounds   "
    300,000 Rounds of Snider ammunition, besides the 70 rounds in possession of each man, and the reserve of 100 rounds per arm.

"To be at Prahsu on the 15th January 1874, in addition to the above—

    300 Rockets.
    100 Rounds per gun for the three 7-pounder guns.
    800,000 Rounds of Snider ammunition.

"To be at Mansu by 20th January 1874—

    200 Rockets.
    100 Rounds per gun for 7-pounder guns.
    50   "   for each 4⅖ howitzer.
    300,000 "   of Snider ammunition.

"*Camp Equipment.*

"250 Bell-tents to be sent to the Prah by the 1st January next, it being notified at the time to Lieutenant-Colonel Evelyn Wood, V.C., and the commanding Royal Engineer, relative to their disposal between the camps of Barraco and Prahsu.

"*Supplies.*

"Provisions to be at the Prah to feed the following details from the end of this month—

Blue jackets and Marines,	250
Royal Artillery and Royal Engineers (English),	30
2d West India Regiment,	400
Rait's Artillery,	50
Wood's and Russell's Regiments,	800
English officers,	30
Carriers,	1000

"This force will remain at Prahsu until the concentration of all our troops there on or about the 13th January 1874.

"Provisions to be at Prahsu on the 15th January 1874 for 30 days for the following details—

English Infantry,	1360
Blue jackets and Marines,	250
Royal Artillery,	60
Royal Engineers,	50
1st West India Regiment,	500
2d West India Regiment,	400
Native Artillery,	50
Staff and other officers,	50
Wood's and Russell's regiments,	800
Carriers and workmen,	3000
	6520 "

Before despatching the ships to sea, the following detachments were landed from the Himalaya on the 12th December :—Lieuts. Jekyll and Skinner, and 20 N.C. officers and men Royal Engineers ;* 30 N.C. officers and men Army Service Corps ; Capt. Collin, Lieut. Dillon, and 21 N.C. officers and men Army Hospital Corps ; and Surgeon-Major Woolfreys and 5 other medical officers. From the Tamar on the 13th—Lieut. Fruth, R.A., and 12 N.C. officers ; 2 sergeants 2d West India Regiment ; 7 medical officers, including Surgeon-Major Surton, who was appointed sanitary officer in succession to Surgeon-Major Gore ; and Capt. Robinson, Rifle Brigade, who was appointed Brigade-Major to the European Brigade on the application of Sir Archibald Alison. From the Sarmatian on the 17th— Sir A. Alison, with his Staff, and Colonel Greaves, landed; as did also the special-service officers, who were disposed of as follows :—Capts. The Hon. Paul Methuen, Scots Fusilier Guards, F. Russell, 14th Hussars— Wood's Regiment; Lieut. De Hoghton, 10th Regiment —Russell's Regiment ; Lieut. Knox, R.A., to Rait's Artillery ; Capt. Paget, Scots Fusilier Guards, Lieut. MacGregor, 50th Regiment, and Capt. Brabazon, late of the Grenadier Guards (who, though now a civilian, had volunteered for service on this expedition), were attached to Capt. Butler for service on that expedition in Western Akim, of which we shall presently have to speak. An officer from each regiment was also landed

* As it has been stated that a blunder was committed in not landing the whole detachment of Royal Engineers, it may be well to remark that, in the absence of Major Home at Prahsu, the Commanding Royal Engineer at Cape Coast, Captain Buckle, was officially called upon to enumerate the details to be now landed, and the above party was disembarked at his request.

for the purpose of making arrangements on shore before the arrival of his corps, procuring servants for officers, &c.

Before the troops sailed, orders were issued as to the kit which they were to carry. On his person the soldier was to carry helmet, tweed frock, trousers, gaiters, boots, one pair of socks, shirt, cholera-belt, pouch-belt, and sixty rounds of ammunition, havresack with filter and ten rounds, water-bottle, tin-pot on waist-belt, a bandage, and a clasp-knife. The following articles in excess of those actually on the man were to form the field-kit, and to be packed with the greatcoat in the waterproof-sheet belonging to each man, and there secured by the coat-straps:—one pair of trousers, woollen night-cap, pair of socks, cholera-belt, flannel shirt, towel, housewife, pot of dubbing, piece of soap, piece of tobacco, a knife, fork, and spoon, a respirator, veil, greatcoat and waterproof sheet, mess-tin and strap, and half a shelter-tent. These kits were to be made up in packages of three, one carrier being allowed for every three men. As a shelter-tent would contain three men, only two packages in each load contained a half tent. The mess-tins were to be attached to the bundles, the poles of the shelter-tent to lie between the packages. No package of officers' baggage, or any kind of store, was on any account to exceed 50 lb. One carrier was to be allowed to each officer, and one to each mess of three officers. It was decided not to take the men's blankets into the field, and a second pair of boots for each man was to be left at Prahsu, each pair having a canvas label with the owner's name attached to it.

Before the Sarmatian left the coast, the Major-General issued, and had printed, the following notes, of which

100 copies were sent by the Sarmatian, ordered to meet the other ships at a rendezvous named by the Commodore, for distribution to each regiment :—

"The Major-General commanding has made the following notes for the information and guidance of the soldiers and sailors about to take part in the operations north of the river Prah.

"*Health.*—The climate is much better and more pleasant in the interior than on the sea-shore; and if ordinary precautions are taken, there is no reason why any of the troops should suffer in health during the few weeks that they may have to remain in the country.

"The officers must see that tea or chocolate, with a little biscuit, is provided for their men every morning before marching, and quinine will be served out by the medical officers.

"During the heat of the day, or when marching late in the morning, commanding officers may, at their discretion, allow the patrol-jackets to be taken off and carried by the men. These can be easily carried slung behind under the waist-belt. Immediately that the march is over, or if any long halt takes place, these jackets must be put on; for a chill, when the body is heated, is above all things to be avoided.

"The following maxims should be impressed upon the men :—

"1. Never allow the body to suffer from a chill, and there will not be much chance of your ever being sick.

"2. Never expose the head uncovered to the sun; and when halting, or on sentry, get into the shade if possible.

" 3. When camping for the night, do your best to construct a raised sleeping-place, even a few inches off the ground. (Examine the camps of the Ashantis on the road to the Prah, and copy their plan of making bedsteads ; they are easily and quickly made, and sleeping off the ground is a great preservative of health.)

" 4. If any irregularity of the bowels is experienced, go at once to the doctor for a dose.

" 5. Never drink water until you have filtered it.

" The operations beyond the Prah will last only a few weeks, and the Major-General relies on the manliness of the soldiers and sailors to keep them out of hospital as long as they have strength to march. The battalion that is composed of the best men, and that is best looked after by its officers, will send the fewest sick men to the rear.

" *Mode of fighting.*—The theatre of operations will be a great forest of gigantic trees, with an undergrowth of bush varying in thickness. At some places men can get through the bush in skirmishing order, at others they will have to use their sword-bayonets to open paths for themselves. All the fighting will be in skirmishing order, the files being two, three, or four paces apart, according to circumstances.

" When once thus engaged in a fight in the bush, officers commanding battalions, and even officers commanding companies, will find it difficult to exercise much control over their men. For this reason it is essential that the tactical unit should be as small as possible. Every company will therefore be at once divided into four sections, and each section will be placed under the command of an officer or non-commissioned officer. These sections, once told off, are not on any account to be broken up during the war, nor are their commanders to be changed except under extraordinary circumstances, and then only by order of the officer commanding the battalion. All details of duty will be performed by sections, or, when only very small guards or picquets are required, by half-sections.

"In action, as a general rule, three sections only of each company will be extended, and the fourth will form a support in rear of the centre of the company's skirmishing line, and at from 40 to 80 yards from it. Care must be taken that the support never loses sight of its own skirmishers, and that it conforms to their movements; but its commander must never allow it to become mixed up with the skirmishers, unless it be ordered forward by the officer commanding the company. The captain will always be with the skirmishing line exercising a general control over it; and as the enemy only fight in loose skirmishing order, it will seldom be necessary to bring forward the support into the skirmishing line.

"Fighting in the bush is very much like fighting by twilight; no one can see further than a few files to his right or left. Great steadiness and self-confidence are therefore required from every one engaged. The Ashantis always employ the same tactics. Being superior in numbers, they encircle their enemy's flanks by long thin lines of skirmishers, hoping thereby to demoralise their opponents. The men engaged in our front line should not concern themselves about these flank attacks. They must have the same confidence in their General that he has in them, and depend upon him to take the necessary measures for meeting all such attacks either in flank or rear. Each soldier must remember that with his breech-loader he is equal to at least twenty Ashantis, wretchedly armed as they are with old flint-muskets, firing slugs or pieces of stone that do not hurt badly at more than 40 or 50 yards range. Our enemies have neither guns nor rockets, and have a superstitious dread of those used by us.

"In action, the two comrades forming each file must always keep together, and the officers and non-commissioned officers commanding sections will use their utmost endeavours to keep their sections from mixing up with those on their right and left.

"If, during the advance through the bush, fire is unexpectedly opened by the enemy concealed behind cover, the men will immediately drop on the knee behind trees or any cover that may be at hand, pausing well before delivering their fire, and taking care to fire low at the spots from which the enemy were seen to fire. All firing against a concealed enemy should be very slow, and officers and non-commissioned officers in command of sections must spare no efforts to prevent the men from wasting their ammunition. It must be explained to the men that, owing to the difficulties of transport, the supply of ammunition beyond the Prah will be very limited; and that every shot fired which is not deliberately aimed, not only encourages the enemy, who would soon learn to despise a fire that did them no injury, but seriously affects the efficiency of the force—for, if ammunition were to run short, a stop would be put to our further advance. The Major-General must rely upon the intelligence of the soldiers and sailors to husband their ammunition, without any efforts from their officers being required.

"The advance will be made along narrow paths, where the men can only march in file, and sometimes only in single file; when an action commences, the troops on the centre path will deploy to the front into skirmishing order, either to the right or left of the path as ordered, upon the leading file; the rear section of each company will always form the support, and officers commanding companies will be careful to lead these deployments so that their front may always be as nearly as possible at right angles to the path they had been marching upon. All officers must remember that the front line will, as a general rule, face north by west, and when at any distance from the path, they must guide the direction of their advance by compass.

"Officers commanding battalions and companies will not order any bugle-call to be sounded in camp or on the march north of the Prah, except to repeat those sounded on the main road by order of the Major-General commanding; and these, if preceded by any special regimental call, will be repeated only by the battalion concerned, and by any battalion that may be operating between the main road and the corps indicated by the call. When any call is not preceded by a regimental call, it will be repeated by every bugler within hearing, except those that may be on duty with the baggage-guard.

"Whenever the advance and double is sounded, it is to be understood to order a general advance of the whole front line upon the enemy. The men will then advance cheering at a fast walk, making short rushes whenever the nature of the ground will allow of their being made. All such advances will be preceded by a heavy fire of guns and rockets.

"On reaching a clearing in the course of an action, or when the enemy is in the immediate neighbourhood, the troops will not cross over the open space until the clearing has been turned and the bush on both sides of it has been occupied.

"When once a position has been gained, it is to be held resolutely. In warfare of this nature there must be no retreats.

"No village or camp is to be set on fire except by order of the Major-General commanding. Officers and men are reminded of the danger and delay which occur if a village is set on fire before all the ammunition and baggage have made their way through it.

"All plundering and unnecessary destruction of property are to be strictly repressed. Officers are held responsible that when a village or camp is occupied their men are kept together, and prevented from dispersing to seek plunder.

"The importance of kindness from all ranks to the friendly natives who are employed as carriers cannot be too strongly urged. If the carriers are ill-treated the troops run imminent risk of being left without food and ammunition.

"It must never be forgotten by our soldiers that Providence has implanted in the heart of every native of Africa a superstitious awe and dread of the white man that prevents the negro from daring to meet us face to face in combat. A steady advance or a charge, no matter how partial, if made with determination, always means the retreat of the enemy. Although when at a distance, and even when under a heavy fire, the Ashantis seem brave enough, from their practice of yelling, and singing, and beating drums, in order to frighten the enemies of their own colour, with whom they are accustomed to make war, they will not stand against the advance of the white man.

"English soldiers and sailors are accustomed to fight against immense odds in all parts of the world; it is scarcely necessary to remind them that when in our battles beyond the Prah they find themselves surrounded on all sides by hordes of howling enemies, they must rely upon their own British courage and discipline, and upon the courage of their comrades.

"Soldiers and sailors, remember that the black man holds you in superstitious awe; be cool; fire low, fire slow, and charge home.; and the more numerous your enemy the greater will be the loss inflicted upon him, and the greater your honour in defeating him.

"By order,
"G. R. GREAVES, *Colonel,*
Chief of the Staff.
"HEADQUARTERS, CAPE COAST CASTLE,
20*th December* 1873."

This memorandum, the writer ventures to think, contains in it the whole essence of modern tactics. Let those who think that warfare of this nature is not calculated to teach lessons useful for warfare on a grander scale read this order, and see whether it does not breathe in every line the spirit of the teaching of the war of 1870. It recognises, amongst other points, the vital importance of giving independence of action to small units, and proposes to carry out on this system exactly what had been done by our fathers, in the days when the Light Division in the Peninsula could beat all other troops in the world in skirmishing—a system which at one time became overlaid and lost sight of under the monotonous uniformity of the barrack-square and the flat parade-ground.

These orders having been issued, all was prepared, so far as it lay in the power of the Major-General, for landing the troops and the advance beyond the Prah on the 15th January. The Deputy-Controller had undertaken that the ammunition and supplies required should be at Prahsu at the given date; but the question of transport still most anxiously engaged the Major-General's attention. Amongst the officers who had arrived in the Sarmatian was one in whose remarkable knowledge and great ability the Major-General had the most complete confidence. Lieutenant-Colonel Colley, who had resigned his appointment as Professor of Military Administration at the Staff College in order to see service in this campaign, had not only considerable experience of native character and warfare in Kaffraria, and as a staff officer in England, but he had for some considerable time past most specially devoted his attention to questions of army organisation, including, of course, the vital questions of transport and supply; and the Major-General counted upon his true military spirit leading him to sacrifice for the good of the expedition that keen desire which he must have in common with all soldiers for a combatant position, in order to take upon him the arduous, responsible, and comparatively uninteresting duties of organisation and command of transport. Colonel Colley was spoken to on the subject, and the Deputy-Controller was asked whether he would wish for the services of this officer under him, to organise and superintend the transport to the campaign. Mr Irvine wisely accepted the opportunity, and Colonel Colley was appointed Director of Transport under the Deputy-Controller. Major Maclean, Rifle Brigade, Captain Duncan, Royal Artillery, and Lieutenant Vandermeulen, 50th Regiment, special-service officers, were immediately appointed to serve under him.

On the 19th December, Colonel Colley proceeded to Mansu; and the following memorandum, which he submitted to the Deputy-Controller, will show how he at once grasped the subject, and proceeded systematically to organise the transport.

"*Instructions for Organisation and Working of*
"*Transport Corps.*

" 1. The Transport Corps will be organised in two branches; the first to be termed Regimental Transport, the second Local Transport.

" 2. Regimental Transport will include all attached permanently to regiments, corps, departments; and will move with the troops.

" 3. Local Transport will include all employed in maintaining supplies and communications between Cape Coast and the front, and will work permanently between fixed stations.

" 4. For transport purposes the road from Cape Coast to the Prah will be divided into four districts:—

" 1st, Cape Coast to Dunquah.
" 2d, Dunquah to Mansu.
" 3d, Mansu to Yancoomassie Assin.
" 4th, Yancoomassie Assin to the Prah.

" The headquarters of these districts will be at Cape Coast, Dunquah, Mansu, Yancoomassie Assin respectively.

" 5. Further districts will be formed as required when the troops have crossed the Prah; each district will include all hospital or halting stations within it.

" 6. Headquarters of the corps will be at Mansu for the present. Major Maclean will supervise the Dunquah, Mansu, and Yancoomassie districts; Commissary O'Connor will remain in charge of the Cape Coast district, and surf-boat establishment.

" 7. The Regimental Transport will be organised from that now working on the road as follows :—That for Royal Artillery and Royal Engineers (at Cape Coast) headquarter, brigade, and departmental staffs, and hammock-bearers for Naval Brigade, at Cape Coast. For one European regiment, at Dunquah. For two European regiments, at Mansu. For 1st Reserve S.A. ammunition, Rait's Artillery, 2d West India Regiment, and Wood's and Russell's regiments, at Yancoomassie Assin and Barraco.

" Details of the transport required for each corps are given in annexed memorandum.

" 8. The officers appointed to the regimental transport will at once take over charge of the men as above at their present stations, but will continue to work them as local transport until required with the field army.

" 9. The dates on which the several detachments will proceed to join their regiments and corps will be notified hereafter.

" 10. On joining the regiments to which they are attached, the transport officers will pass entirely under the orders of the officer commanding the regiment, but will continue to pay and superintend their men.

" 11. After the troops are put in motion, the carriers remaining in the districts will form the local transport, and be divided between supply and ambulance duties.

" 12. At each of the six hospital stations—viz., Accroful, Yancoomassie Fanti, Mansu, Sutah, Yancoomassie Assin, and the Prah, 35 hammocks—with the necessary bearers, will be permanently maintained : of these, 15 will proceed daily, with or without sick, to the next station in rear, returning the following day; 5 will remain as a reserve at the disposal of the medical officer, and the return hammocks will be utilised for the carriage of supplies to the front.

" 13. Local transport will be worked entirely by districts, and officers will on no account detain or send forward men belonging to other districts unless under orders from the senior officer of the corps. In cases of emergency, when it is absolutely necessary to do so, a special report must be made immediately to the officer whose men are thus withdrawn.

" 14. All organisation will be by tribes as far as possible.

" 15. All men employed in the transport corps will be registered and given a number.

" 16. Transport officers will keep the supply officers at their stations informed of the number of carriers available.

" 17. Every headman of local transport will be supplied with a way-bill, made out by the transport officer, and stating the number of carriers and packages sent. The receipt given by the officer to whom the stores are delivered will be the voucher on which the men will receive their pay on return.

" 18. The men will be paid as far as possible on their return from each trip, and always personally by the officer in charge ; chiefs and headmen are on no account to be intrusted with the money for their men.

" 19. When circumstances admit, it will be desirable to allow a days' rest after four days' work.

"20. A state will be sent in every second day from all stations to headquarters, at Mansu, showing the number of chiefs, headmen, and carriers effective at the station, sick, deserters, the number of coats and hammocks available at the station, the number of loads awaiting transport, and the number of loads sent forward, or sick sent back in the two days.

"21. Cots and hammocks will always be returned to the districts to which they belong.

"22. Hammocks are only to be supplied to officers and men in accordance with the general orders, or on written requisition from the officer commanding the station, or medical officer.

"23. Transport officers will endeavour to make themselves acquainted with the men under their charge, and the nature of work for which they are best fitted, Special men should be selected as hammock-bearers. and so employed as far as possible.

"24. As a rule, complaints should be investigated in presence of the men of the party, and minor offences should be met by fines; as far as possible, corporal punishment should only be awarded for very serious offences, and should rarely exceed twenty-five lashes.

"25. Officers are earnestly requested to bear in mind that firmness and patience are the most essential qualities in dealing with natives, and that irreparable mischief may easily be caused by frightening those on whom we are dependent for our transport.

"Good-humoured encouragement generally does more than threats. Officers must therefore be very careful, not only to control their own tempers, but to prevent their subordinates and headmen ill-treating those placed under their charge."

As regards the road and encampments it was arranged, on the recommendation of Major Home, that Captain Jones, R.E., with the headquarters of the 28th Company R.E., should be placed at Mansu, and that this officer was to be instructed to look after the whole line from Cape Coast to the Prah.

It now remains to describe the plan of invasion of the Ashanti kingdom, formed by the Major-General. The plan, briefly stated, was to invade the Ashanti country on the 15th January from as many points as possible, the lines by which the different columns would advance converging on Coomassie, the objective point of the campaign. On the extreme right, Captain Glover's force was to cross the Prah near Assum, and to move upon Juabin. The main body, consisting of a European force of three battalions, the Naval Brigade, Wood's and Russell's Regiments, and Rait's Artillery, was to advance from Prahsu by the main Coomassie road. As a connecting link between Captain Glover and the main body, a column composed of Western Akims, under the command of Captain Butler, half-pay 69th Regiment, was to cross at Prahsu Akim; while, on the extreme left, it was hoped that a force of Wassaws, Denkeras, and Commendahs, would advance by the road known as the Wassaw path, on Coomassie. The command of this latter force was to be given to Captain Dalrymple of the 88th Regiment, with whom Captain Moore, of the same regiment, was to serve. These officers were expected to arrive in the steam-ship Thames, and were told off for this duty before the Major-General left Cape Coast.

It may be said by theorists that the Major-General was thus violating some of the first great strategical principles, by advancing in a number of columns from bases far apart, by lines of operation converging upon a common objective ; that he was dividing his force, losing the advantages of concentrated force at any one point, and giving his enemy the advantage of interior lines. It may be said that he was playing his adversary's game, and giving him the opportunity of bringing his concentrated mass to bear upon our fractions, and that his enemy had only to follow out the theory of the text-books, and to bring the bulk of his force against any one column, while containing the others with comparatively small detachments. But " interior lines" lose their advantage when roads of communication between the different lines of operation do not exist ; and there is a limit, very soon reached, to the number of troops which can advantageously be employed in a bush fight. Moreover, if there be one quality in a general greater than another, it is the power of estimating his enemy at his true value, and acting not according to any formulated laws or rules, but according to the circumstances of the individual case. Sir Garnet Wolseley rightly counted upon his enemy's political condition, and judged wisely that the effect of the simultaneous presence of these various columns would be the separation of the component parts of the Ashanti army, and the departure of the chiefs of the various principalities, of which the Ashanti kingdom is composed, to guard their own territories against invasion. He counted, if not upon his enemy's ignorance of strategy, at all events upon his inability to compel these powerful tributary chiefs to abandon their own countries when threatened with attack, and concentrate in one body. The sequel will show how wise this judgment was ; and for those readers who are fond of precedents, the writer would note only two—first, the inability of the Austrian Government in 1866 to induce its South German allies, other than the Saxons, to abandon their territories for the sake of concentration against Prussia; and, secondly, Blumenthal's reply to Ducrot after the battle of Sedan. Ducrot had criticised the Prussian division of forces on that day as being extremely rash, and received the following answer in reply :—" Rash, no; audacious, yes. But you know, general, that in war one must act according to the *morale* of one's adversaries. We knew you to be much demoralised, and therefore we could dare much."

This plan of operations having been confided to the officers about to command the various columns, and their instructions having been issued to them; the European troops being ordered to return to the Coast by the end of the year; the responsible department having promised that the supplies and ammunition considered necessary by the General should be stored at his depôt on the Prah at the required time; the transport being in most able hands, and apparently in sufficient quantities; the road and camps upon the road being so far advanced that their completion in sufficient time could be counted upon;—the Major-General considered himself justified in imparting his intentions to the authorities at home, and to the correspondents of the press; and on the 26th December he informed the Secretary of State for War of his intention to leave Cape Coast on the following day for Accroful, and thence march with his Headquarter Staff to the Prah, where he would arrive on the 2d January. "I do not," wrote the Major-General, "intend to return to this place until the military operations against the Ashantis are concluded."

CHAPTER VIII.

CAPTAIN GLOVER'S OPERATIONS TO THE END OF DECEMBER 1873.

CAPTAIN GLOVER arrived at Cape Coast on the 11th September, and proceeded immediately to Accra. Dr. Rowe was relieved from his duties as Colonial Surgeon, and followed on the 15th in H.M. Gunboat "Merlin," taking with him 200 Houssas armed with Snider rifles, and equipped for active service. Colonel Harley wrote at the same time to the Civil Commandant at Accra, directing him to co-operate fully with Captain Glover, and made arrangements to relieve Captain Goldsworthy in his duties as Colonial Secretary and Collector of Customs, by Captain Lanyon, of the 2d West India Regiment, in order that he might join Captain Glover as soon as possible. The 200 Houssas were landed at Accra on the 16th. Captain Goldsworthy, however, could not proceed till the 25th, when he took with him a further detachment of 117 Houssas, 100 of whom were armed with Sniders. Mr. Paul, Civil Commandant at Accra, was directed by Colonel Harley to summon the kings and chiefs of his district and Accra, to confer with Captain Glover, and was to intimate to them that H.M. Government desired that they should be guided by Captain Glover's advice, and that their efforts should be exclusively directed to an immediate movement against the Ashantis. He was told to receive the kings and chiefs in a suitable manner, and to make a present to each of them. On the 20th Captain Glover proceeded to Akropong to meet the kings and chiefs of Akropong, Croboe, and Addah, and notify to them the substance of the message from H.M. Government. A Crepee chief also visited Captain Glover, and was promised assistance to return to his country. The king of Addah would not attend the meeting at Akropong, in consequence, as Captain Glover reported, of the Ahwoonahs having commenced to seize his people, on account of the landing of provisions for the expedition at Addah Fork. On the 26th Captain Glover returned to Accra to meet the kings of Eastern and Western Akim, and the other kings and chiefs of the eastern districts, who, he hoped, would assemble there in a day or two. It should be observed that Captain Glover counted upon the services of the king of Western Akim, whom, however, Sir Garnet Wolseley did not consider as belonging to the eastern tribes.

Captain Glover's difficulties commenced early: already he remarked upon the indifference manifested by the kings Tackie and Solomon of Accra as compared with the conduct of the kings, chiefs, and people of Akropong, Croboe, and Crepee. It was evidently, he said, the intention of the king and chiefs of Accra that all communications and presents should pass through their hands. Captain Glover, however, showed them his determination not to permit this, and made them accompany him to Akropong, where he gave an assurance that each king, chief, or tribe, should deal directly with himself, or the commissioners under him, an assurance which was received with much satisfaction. Another difficulty soon arose, and one which threatened to be of considerable importance in connection with the raising of a Houssa force. The Houssas being all slaves, differences arose early with their owners as to their joining Captain Glover's force; and on the morning of the 1st October a serious disturbance took place on that subject between the Houssas and the natives of Accra, in which two of the chief men of Ussher Town were wounded. The people of Ussher Town then turned out armed, but were induced to return home; however, Captain Glover was afraid of another disturbance with more serious results, as there was not a single round of Snider ammunition in reserve at the place, and the Houssas were armed with Sniders. Captain Glover was afterwards obliged to pay £5 apiece for Houssa slave recruits, inasmuch as domestic slavery was a recognised institution in the courts of justice in the Protectorate. Government officials even claimed the slaves of their wives and sisters, and one, a clerk in the Customs, told Captain Glover that he wished to prevent his father's slaves from enlisting. One Houssa came in with the marks of irons on his wrists and legs, and the staple still on him, by which he had been fastened down to prevent his enlisting, and reported many others to be, to his knowledge, similarly chained for the same purpose.

Immediately on his arrival at Cape Coast, on the 3d October, Sir Garnet Wolseley addressed two letters to Captain Glover, of which the following extracts contain all that is of any importance:—

FIRST LETTER—dated Cape Coast, 3d October.

" As it is absolutely necessary to the success of the military operations in which the Major-General and yourself are engaged, that he should be always thoroughly informed of your proceedings, I am directed to express his desire that you will communicate with him at least once in seven days, giving him full information on all matters connected with your expedition.

" While trusting thoroughly to your omitting nothing which it is desirable that he should know, the Major-General wishes me to indicate the following points as those on which he specially desires to be regularly informed :—

" (1.) The numbers of the forces you have raised, and from what tribe obtained.
" (2.) The actual position of yourself and the forces under your command, and of all detachments from your main force.
" (3.) Your operations up to date, and the nature and direction of the further movements which you propose to make.
" (4.) Your relations with the tribes through whose territories you pass.
" (5.) Any information you may have obtained as to the movements and designs of the enemy, with your opinion as to the amount of trust which may be placed in the report.

" The Major-General desires that no difficulties which can possibly be surmounted, and no consideration of reasonable expense, be allowed to interfere with the regular despatch to him every seven days of this information.

"He is most anxious to afford you every possible assistance in your task; and he is convinced that you will see well the paramount importance of his possessing constant, full, and accurate information of your proceedings, without which there cannot be that complete co-operation between you which the interests of her Majesty and the nation demand."

SECOND LETTER—dated Cape Coast, 3d October, and marked "Confidential."

"In accordance with instructions received from the Right Honourable the Secretary of State for the Colonies, Major-General Sir Garnet Wolseley intends despatching a letter to the king of Ashanti, informing him that her Majesty has sent the Major-General to this coast for the purpose of establishing a lasting peace with him, but that as a preliminary to negotiations, the king must at once vacate all the territories belonging to her Majesty's allies, restore all those whom he has made captive, and make reparation for the injuries he has inflicted upon the people in alliance with England.

"Sir Garnet Wolseley therefore desires that no offensive operations upon any large scale may be undertaken by you against the Ashanti kingdom until you receive instructions from him on the subject, as it is essential that time should be allowed for a letter to reach the king, and for an answer to be received, before such operations are commenced.

"By Sir Garnet Wolseley's desire I have already written to you, requesting that he may be kept constantly informed in the fullest manner possible of your doings and intentions, and I have to request that in acknowledging the receipt of this you will be good enough to inform me, for the Major-General's information, of the date when you consider you will be able to establish yourself on the Volta as a preliminary measure to your carrying out the operation proposed by yourself to Lord Kimberley—viz. an advance from thence as a base into the Ashanti country.

"The Major-General considers it needless to impress upon you the great importance of his movements and yours being undertaken in concert, and of the final advance towards the Ashanti capital, in the event of such a movement hereafter becoming necessary, being simultaneous."

Both these letters were signed by Colonel M'Neill, the chief of the Staff. To these letters replies were received, dated 4th October, to the effect, as regards the first, that the instructions contained in it had been duly noted, and would be cheerfully complied with; and as regards the second, a report to the following effect:—(1.) "That no offensive operations upon any large scale should be undertaken until such time as Captain Glover had the Major-General's authority to act. (2.) That Captain Glover's intentions were, on the arrival of the transport with provisions and ammunition, to conclude his preparations so as to enable him to be in motion on the 'Volta' in a fortnight's time." Captain Glover then proceeded to sketch his plan of operations as follows:—" From thence, aided by the Crepees, I shall proceed against the Ahwoonahs, who may probably engage my attention for a fortnight. Meanwhile stores will be conveyed to Pong. I then propose, with their assistance, to give a check to the

Aquamoo contingent, which it is well known is in alliance with the Ashantis, and from whom the Ashantis have been largely supplied with powder. It will be absolutely necessary to coerce these tribes, as from their position they could easily embarrass our communications with Pong. Having effected this I shall be enabled to halt on the Bayi, and open communication with the Adonkos and tribes to the north, perhaps even to Yaman on the north-west. It is probable, also, that I may make Chebi, Gyadan, or Bagoro a centre, but this will much depend upon the report of Captain Sartorius, who will probably proceed to the Akim country, in which these places are situated, about the same time as I take my departure for the Volta."

At the same period Captain Glover forwarded a report of the intelligence he had been enabled to gather from various sources with regard to the route to Coomassie and the feelings of the tribes; and he considered that the country north of the Bayi should be reached by him with as little delay as possible. This intelligence, gathered from natives who knew the country to the north, testified generally to the fact that the best way to reach the Ashanti country was by way of Sara or Salaga. They united in saying that if white men once safely established themselves there, the subjected tribes, who bore most unwillingly the Ashanti yoke, and on whom the king of Ashanti chiefly depends, would rise and join against that power; and that the Houssas and other tribes from the north would come down and join cheerfully in the war. Captain Glover was gravely warned by one man that at Currachee he must consult the fetish, which is powerful, otherwise it would stop his progress; and that if it were gained over, then the Ashantis must be destroyed. He was told that in this country water was plentiful, provisions likewise plentiful and cheap, and that he could go up as far as Currachee in a steamer, and would find there everything suited for a large encampment. Captain Glover's intention was at this time evidently to make his main movement from a point on the Volta far to the north of Pong, to raise the tribes in that district, and possibly to make an additional movement from Akim, if Captain Sartorius should be successful there. That officer, with Lieutenant Barnard, fifty Houssas, a master gunner, one 7-pounder gun, one howitzer, and some rockets, was to proceed to Western and Eastern Akim, and a road was to be cut from Pong, four days' journey, to Gyadan, Chibi, or Bagoro, close up to the Prah in Eastern Akim. The Eastern Akim depôt was to be the base of Captain Glover's centre column, while he himself hoped from the Bayi river to enter into friendly relations with the tribes to the north and east, feel their pulse, and decide upon the route to be taken to Coomassie.

At this time the Aquapims, Croboes, and Crepees, were showing a most friendly feeling, and a good spirit for work. The two latter tribes wished the left bank of the Volta dealt with first, and this coincided with Captain Glover's views. He was sanguine at this early time as to results, and expected 30,000 men to turn out.

Many minor difficulties were at this time felt by Captain Glover. No medical officer had been attached to his expedition, and he was unwilling to send Captain Sartorius and other officers into Akim with no possibility of medical assistance there. Four thousand five hundred stand of percussion arms, demanded by him to complete an equipment for 10,000 men before leaving England, were not sent out to him, and he had great difficulty in procuring small silver coin for immediate payments. He found also that the gin which he intended to use largely for presents to kings, chiefs, and native forces, was charged at 18s. a case at Accra, though it could be purchased for about 4s. a case in England; and he requested that a thousand cases might be sent to him from England for the service of his expedition. Two hundred and fifty cases only were sent out by the Government, who appeared to consider this enough. Still worse, however, was the condition of the Snider ammunition which he received from Cape Coast, 15,000 rounds being reported quite unserviceable. The detention of the "Gertrude" by Sir Garnet Wolseley, in order to remove from her 300 Snider rifles, may also have caused three or four days' delay in Captain Glover's early movements; unfortunately, too, Captain Glover was taken ill with fever, which for a short time laid him low.

Captain Glover counted on the services of the Western Akims; but Sir Garnet Wolseley, not considering them to come within the description of the Eastern tribes to whom Captain Glover was commissioned, and, moreover, absolutely requiring them for his own movements, sent to their kings and chiefs immediately on his arrival at Cape Coast, and informed Captain Glover of his having done so, requesting him at the same time to explain to these people that they were not to join the camp at Accra for operations on the Volta, but the camp at Dunquah for operations with the Fantis. As early as the 5th October Sir Garnet informed Captain Glover of his intention to cross a force from the Akim country, by way of Swaidroo, into the Ashanti territory, and of his wish that Captain Glover should cross the Prah at the point indicated by himself, at the same time that Sir Garnet's force would cross at Prahsu and Swaidroo; and it will be seen that this plan, now confided to Captain Glover, formed the basis of all the Major-General's subsequent operations. "Should it become necessary," wrote the Major-General, "for us to make an advance hereafter upon Coomassie, I sincerely trust that our efforts may be so well timed, and made so thoroughly in concert, that we may both arrive before the place at the same time. This I consider to be essential in the public interests, and for the purpose of securing a happy issue to our undertaking, and for properly giving effect to the policy of our Government."

In the most friendly and cordial spirit Captain Glover fell into Sir Garnet Wolseley's plans. "I anticipated," he wrote, "that you would make an advance from Western Akim, and am glad, with so small a staff as mine is, to be relieved of a part of so extended a frontier, though I believe the Western Akims to be the best fighting men in the Protectorate; but to have taken Eastern Akim would have deprived me of the only other frontier tribe." Captain Glover also fully concurred in Sir Garnet's view that their approach to Coomassie should be simultaneous after crossing the Prah.

On the 7th October Captain Glover wrote to the effect that the Ahwoonahs were already on the offensive, and asked for the services of a man-of-war. Several factories at Quittah had been set on fire, and this was attributed to the desire of the Ahwoonahs to destroy and plunder the entire place, in consequence of their having heard of the preparations being made on the Volta. There were at this time four Ashanti captains in the Ahwoonah country within a day's journey of Quittah. There was dissatisfaction apparently at Melamfi, as well as at Blappah, and there was also an Ashanti captain on the right bank of the Volta, and a small force in Aquamoo. On receipt of this request, H.M.S. "Bittern" was sent to Accra.

On the 8th of October King Attah, of Eastern Akim, and the king of Aquapim arrived with their chiefs and captains at Accra, and having duly saluted the British flag in accordance with the usual practice, appeared before H.M. Special Commissioner, having bullets and flints in their mouths to denote that they came prepared for war, and took solemn oath, by the head of the late Governor, Sir Charles Macarthy, to be true and faithful allies and subjects to the Queen of England, to follow Captain Glover wherever he went, and to forfeit their heads if they refused to go where he went. "If," said the king of Akim, "you go to Coomassie, I must go before you." They swore this upon the red coat of Sir Charles Macarthy, and they swore it not only against the Ashantis, but all the Queen's enemies. On the same day Captain Glover forwarded to Sir Garnet the information as to the projected Ashanti attack upon Cape Coast, which has already been narrated in the fourth chapter.

Unfortunately for Captain Glover the 300 Sniders which Sir Garnet Wolseley took from the "Gertrude" were down at the bottom of the hold, and getting them out was a longer business than had been anticipated. Thus, to the great regret of the Major-General, she was not able to sail till the morning of the 8th, and reached Accra in the evening. In her sailed Major Stevens, to act as civil commandant at Accra, and relieve Mr. Goldsworthy of the office, the duties of which hindered his work as second in command of Captain Glover's force. Still, in spite of three or four days' delay, it was hoped that Captain Glover's operations on the Volta against the Ahwoonahs would commence within the fortnight, which he had fixed as the time required from the arrival of the transport, and that they would be concluded within the second fortnight named; so that by the end of the first week of November Captain Glover, by his own calculations, would be able to proceed northwards up the Volta.

After the arrival of the transport, Captain Glover proposed to carry out his original intention to organise an eastern camp, clear the left bank of the Volta, push on to Salaga, and be able to sweep down on Coomassie from the north-east, when Sir Garnet should march up from the Coast; but Captain Glover, like Sir Garnet, was destined to find how worthless were the natives on whom he had ventured to trust.

On the 13th October a grand meeting was held at Accra between Captain Glover and the kings and chiefs of the eastern districts, at which were present—Attah, of Eastern Akim; Tackie, king of Accra; Asah, king of Aquapim, with his principal chiefs and captains; the kings of Eastern and Western Croboe; the king of Crepee, with his chiefs and captains; and the Caboceers of the towns and districts of Accra. The kings and chiefs all swore to be faithful, and to assist H.M. Commissioner; and King Attah, of Eastern Akim, again swore that he would forfeit his head if he did not precède the Special Commissioner in the advance against Coomassie. This oath upon the coat of Sir Charles Macarthy, upon the day of his death, and the manner of his death, signifies that whoever takes the oath and disregards it, testifies thereby that he is unmindful of the fact that Sir Charles sacrificed his life for him and his country; and it is held in the same veneration and awe by the natives in the Protectorate as the king's great oath in Ashanti is held by the Ashantis, the breaking of this oath being punished with death. Captain Glover estimated that the eastern district could put the following force into the field :—

Accra to Addah	12,000
Aquapim	7,000
Croboe	7,000
Eastern Akim	4,000
Crepee	14,000
Total	44,000

He proceeded to give the kings subsidies of gin and rum, tobacco, axes, cutlasses, and money to the extent of £200 or £300 apiece, and rations for their men at the rate of 3½d. per diem, together with £10 per month for every thousand men reported actually at work at road-making or fighting. On the 22d Captain Glover got rid of the kings and chiefs from Accra, it being then arranged that the Eastern Akims and Aquapims were to assemble their force and watch the north-west frontier, and that the Crepees and Croboes were to meet Captain Glover on the left bank of the Volta in a fortnight.

Thus already it was evident that the operations

against the Ahwoonahs and the Aquamoos could not possibly commence at the date that Captain Glover had hoped that they would be finished; and even this possible commencement was entirely dependent upon the punctuality of the native kings. It should be stated that Sir Garnet Wolseley had quite approved of Captain Glover's intention to organise a force in Eastern Akim, and to take steps to clear out the Volta district, so that his post might be safe and secure from attack when he was in the interior. It should of course be observed in addition that this approval was based upon Captain Glover's estimate of time.

Towards the end of October Captain Glover reported that the Ahwoonahs were clearing out from the beach, and he hoped soon to put his troops at them from Jellahcoffee. He intended to break ground as soon as he could get the allies in motion. He proposed to form his first camp on the Melamfi hills, to act against the Ahwoonahs; and after having driven the latter over the lagoon from the beach, he would then leave the native tribes, whom he would supply with guns and ammunition, to finish with the Ahwoonahs, while he would march north to the Bayi river. He heard that the king of Aquamoo was desirous of giving himself up, and Captain Glover anticipated no fighting, after once dealing with the Ahwoonahs, until the troops should knock at the gates of Coomassie. As regards these Ahwoonahs, information had been obtained from Jellahcoffee to the effect that an Ashanti captain and four Ocrahs, with several subordinate captains, were at Jellahcoffee, and had directed the Ahwoonahs to prepare for war, which they had done. Drums had been beaten throughout the whole of Ahwoonah, and orders had been given that any boats attempting to land with white men should be fired into at once. It was said that the Ashantis and Ahwoonahs had eaten fetish together, and that the Ahwoonahs were removing all their effects inland across the Lagoon.

Captain Glover himself remained at Accra till the 6th of November, waiting for Quabina Fuah, the king of Western Akim, who was in great difficulty of mind between his desire to go to Captain Glover for the sake of the handsome present which Captain Glover had given to the kings, and his orders from Sir Garnet Wolseley to act in another direction. The Accra kings and chiefs had led Captain Glover just such a life as all the unfortunate officers sent by Sir Garnet Wolseley to the native kings had experienced. Even when he left Accra he had not got the names of the Accra captains of companies. A good deal of trouble had been caused by the conduct of Sakkity, one of the chiefs of Eastern Croboe, who not only positively refused to take the oath of allegiance, but left the meeting of the kings and chiefs, and used words of disloyalty and exasperation. He had with difficulty been rescued from the hands of the mob, and lodged in jail under a Houssa guard. It was now decided to keep him a prisoner for safety. Nor were Captain Glover's difficulties only of a moral nature; they were material also. He was supplied with shot and shell for some $2\frac{4}{5}$-inch howitzers, which he got from store at Accra, but not with fuses; he had equipped his force to move in three columns, but had only one medical officer; the boiler of his steam-launch had to be condemned; the "Gertrude" store-ship grounded at every sandbank she could find inside the river Volta; one of his staff had to be

THE ASHANTI WAR.

removed on account of a predisposition to brandy; and other minor incidents occurred, which, slight as they may appear reviewed in this way, are of the most serious nature when they occur in the midst of important affairs.

On the 3d November the disciplined force at Captain Glover's command amounted to 937, being distributed as follows :—

Houssas at Accra	. . .	50
,, ,, Addah	. . .	433
,, ,, Akim	. . .	50
Yorubas at Addah	. . .	352
,, ,, Accra	. . .	52

Before accompanying Captain Glover from Accra it may be well to describe the orders which had been given by him to Captain Sartorius. This officer was sent as commissioner to the kings and chiefs of Eastern Akim and Aquapim, for the purpose of organising the native forces in those districts, and watching the Ashanti frontier along the banks of the river Prah. He was ordered to move from Akropong to Odoomassie and Pong. He was to take such measures as might be necessary in Eastern Croboe consequent upon the arrest of Sakkity, and was to explain to the people there that in keeping Sakkity he was protecting his life from the mob. He was to ascertain if there was a good defensible position in the neighbourhood of Pong for a camp and depôt, and such other information as might be useful in carrying out Captain Glover's plans of operation. He was to cut off all communication between Croboe and Aquamoo, and was to impress upon the people of Croboe that they would not be allowed to break this blockade. If the king of Aquamoo should wish to deliver himself up, he might be received unconditionally in camp. He was to ascertain the best site for a fortified camp and depôt, from which to draw supplies after crossing the Prah, and to organise the native forces of Akim and Aquapim. He was to consider this the chief object of his mission. He was to impress on the kings and chiefs that roads cleared to their rear as well as to their front were essential to the success of a rapid movement on Coomassie, and was to direct his attention to the cutting of a road from the depôt which he might select in Akim to the depôt on the Volta, taking the necessary precautions against attack on this road until the Aquamoos should be reduced. A native gentleman, Mr. Hesse, well versed in the affairs of the eastern district, was to accompany Captain Sartorius. A discretionary power was given as to payments to kings, chiefs, captains, and fighting men, but he was to impress upon the natives that aid would not be continued from England unless they helped themselves to the utmost of their own resources. He was to use every effort to recruit Houssas, and he was supplied with some artillery and ammunition. Twenty permanent transport men were attached to him, and two months' provisions for his detachment were placed at his disposal at Accra. "You have," said one paragraph of these able instructions, "a great trial of patience before you. From a long experience of the African character, I have found that quiet determination, with a certain degree of conciliation, always carries your point."

Captain Sartorius was instructed to endeavour to ascertain the best points for crossing the Prah from the depôt, and all possible information as to the country between that point and Coomassie. He was told to confine his operations strictly within the limits prescribed by Sir Garnet Wolseley's confidential instructions; and that if the king of Western Akim would not proceed to Prahsu without assistance in men from the king of Eastern Akim, he was to permit the king of Eastern Akim to detach "the usual portion of his force" to Western Akim, and to urge him to do so quickly. He was not to interfere with Captain Butler, who was already despatched to Western Akim by Sir Garnet Wolseley, and he was told that his services with the Eastern Akims and Aquapims would probably be required against the Aquamoos, and possibly on the eastern bank of the Volta. Such was the purport of the instructions with which Captain Sartorius started on one of those missions, which did indeed, as Captain Glover had said, involve a great trial of patience.

On the 6th November Captain Glover proceeded in the "Lady of the Lake," with the transport "Gertrude," arrived at Addah Fork on the 7th, and entered the river Volta on the morning of the 8th. On the 9th he again embarked with the intention of proceeding up the river for the purpose of meeting the kings and chiefs of Crepee, Shai, and other places, whom he had appointed to meet at Melamfi, but was detained by an accident to the boiler until the 10th, when he proceeded up the river as far as Battor. The Crepees, however, did not keep their rendezvous, but went by mistake to Medica, some twenty miles higher up the river. Not finding them, Captain Glover returned to Addah on the 14th. In the meantime Captain Glover had met Captain Sartorius, and had learnt from him the steps he had taken in Akim and Aquapim. Captain Sartorius was now sent back in a steam-launch to Medica, and was ordered there to collect as strong a force of Aquapims as possible, and as many Croboes as could be spared from operations against Aquamoo. As soon as he was ready to descend the river as far as Battor, he was to inform Captain Glover, in order that ammunition might be sent to meet him at that point. He was then to descend the river, and clear its right bank from Battor to Hoomey, burning to the ground the villages of Battor, Miffie, Melamfi, Blappah, and Hoomey, compelling their inhabitants to cross to the left bank. At the landing places of all these villages he was to collect and store the produce of the farms on the right bank, which was then to be shipped to Addah, provisions being scarce. He was to effect these measures without bloodshed, if possible, but to run no risk from treachery or useless negotiations. It being most important also that some movement should be effected in the assembling of the force promised by the kings and chiefs at Addah, Captain Sartorius was to collect on his line of march as many of the Shais, Ossoodokoos, and Essacharis as possible, and having carried out his orders, was to bring the whole of his force into camp at Addah.

On the 17th November Captain Glover reported from Addah that the kings of Accra had left their towns, and were on their road to join him in camp, and that on their arrival with their force, he proposed crossing the Volta, and at once commencing active operations against the Ahwoonahs and Aquamoos. Captain Glover had now present in camp at Addah about 1450 men, of whom 500 were Houssas, and 500 Yorubas, the rest being Staff and Transport. No friendly allies were yet in camp, though several thousand were promised in a few days, on whose arrival the operations on the other side of the Volta were to commence, Captain Sartorius in the meantime clearing the right bank of hostile natives.

On the 20th November the king of Accra arrived in camp at Addah, and announced his people to be following; but on the 22d only 160 had arrived. On the 26th Captain Sartorius had still not started from Medica, but announced his intention of starting on the following morning for Battor with a force as under :—

Champagne Charlie, Chief of Adoomang	1000 men.
The Demon, Boarfi Ansah	500 ,,
Sakkity of Croboe	400 ,,
Lam, under his brother	200 ,,
Shais	600 ,,
Crepees	500 ,,
Ossoodokoos	200 ,,
Total	3400 men.

He had again heard that half the men of Battor were on the enemy's side, and had sent a messenger ordering them to bring 200 carriers to his camp, in default of which he should burn their town. He found the greatest possible difficulty in getting carriers; as every man wanted to carry a gun, though the pay of a carrier was 1s. a day, and that of fighting men only 3d. Captain Sartorius had sent a force of Akims, Aquapims, and Croboes sufficient to guard the N.E. frontier against the Ashantis, who had possession of Janketty in conjunction with the Aquamoos. He had also established a line of Croboe outposts along the river Volta.

On the 29th of November, Captain Glover reported about 1150 in camp at Addah, but only 224 Accras had as yet come into camp, and of these he had sent 145 to the camps at Gravie and Sofie, preparatory to crossing into the Ahwoonah country. He now expressed his intention of acting against the Ahwoonahs first from Melamfi, and after destroying their principal towns north of the Lagoon, where all their cattle and valuables were stored, sweeping the beach from east to west. Considering it, however, quite possible that many hundreds might seek shelter in the swampy islands, and that much valuable time might be lost in hunting them out, he requested that a small gunboat might be stationed inside the bar of the Volta, for the protection of the ammunition, stores, provisions, sick, and women, who must necessarily remain at Addah Fork for some time after Captain Glover's subsequent movement into the Crepee and Aquamoo country. His own steamer and steam-launches would be engaged in removing stores to the depôt near Pong. The commodore was unable to comply with Captain Glover's request, having no gunboat of sufficiently light draught to admit of her being sent up the Volta.

On the 6th December, Captain Sartorius having, it is to be presumed, completed the destruction of the villages between Battor and Hoomey, had assembled his force in camp at Blappah, and reported that he had 3800 men under his command, the majority of whom had been tried on the occasion of a false alarm, and found to be very good men. A force of 5000 Akims, 3000 Aquapims, and 3000 Croboes, was reported by him to be "still in their towns, and encamped at Janketty, a village on our north-eastern frontier, and supposed to be occupied by Ashantis." The numbers given by Captain Sartorius were within the computations of the chiefs themselves, and according to his own judgment of the different towns and villages which he had visited. "The total amount of fighting men in the field," he said, "will be about 15,000 men, and, with the exception of the Crepees, all good men. Carriers are almost impossible to get. I have only 103; most of them were taken from villages destroyed, and have to be guarded." About the same date Captain Glover forwarded an estimate of his monthly expenditure to the Secretary of State for the Colonies, and estimated for 9000 fighting native levies in the field, and additional forces arriving from time to time up to 5000.

On the 13th December, Captain Glover reported 5000 present at Addah, 4000 at Blappah, and 500 at Gravie; and on this day his "state" showed a total force of 20,649.

It will be observed that exactly two months had now elapsed since the arrival of the s.s. "Gertrude" with Captain Glover's stores, within one fortnight of whose arrival he had intended to commence operations against the Ahwoonahs, and within one month of whose arrival he had intended to have finished with the Ahwoonahs, and be marching north against the Crepees and Aquamoos. Two months had elapsed instead of a fortnight, and yet the operations against the Ahwoonahs had not even commenced, while in the meantime Sir Garnet Wolseley from Cape Coast had cleared the Protectorate of the Ashanti army, and reached with his advance the banks of the Prah.

Captain Glover was still, even after this, considerably detained. Coals were a necessity for his later progress up the river, and the coal vessel which arrived was chartered to land her coal outside the Volta, in consequence of which all his canoes were now employed in discharging her. The Volta at Blappah was too wide to bridge and too deep to wade. Blappah was decided on as Captain Glover's base of operations against the Ahwoonah country; and he collected supplies of provisions and ammunition there, intending to use Medica as his base while in Aquamoo, and to move on the remaining stores from Blappah to that place. Even now, at this date, the 9th December, very few Accras had come in; it was the same old story with them as with the other Fantis; Captain Glover was constantly writing that he hoped to have in a few days a force of 4000 or 8000 Accras; but the days passed away, and still it was only the hope and not the fulfilment of the promise.

On the 11th December, the day following that on which Captain Butler reached Prahsu from Western Akim, Sir Garnet Wolseley addressed instructions to Captain Glover to the following effect:—After informing him that the Ashantis had recrossed the river Prah into their own territory, and that by the 15th December a road would be cut to Prahsu, and a small force assembled at that point; he announced the arrival of the Rifle Brigade, and the immediate expected arrival of the other battalions, at the same time stating that they would be sent to cruise at sea and return on the 1st of January. The Major-General further stated that under no circumstances could his force be ready to advance any distance beyond the banks of the Prah into the Ashanti country before the 15th January at earliest. The despatch continued as follows:—

"The Major-General commanding does not wish to interfere with the operations you are now engaged in, but he considers it desirable that you should be established with all your available force on the river Prah by the above-named date (15th prox.), ready to advance in the direction of Coomassie when you receive orders from him to that effect. In acknowledging the receipt of this you will have the goodness to report whether you will be able to co-operate in this movement by the date given above. The Major-General wishes to leave you the fullest latitude in the selection of the points on the river Prah where you will cross that river, as your local knowledge of the eastern districts (the information possessed by the Major-General regarding their topography being very meagre) enables you to be the best judge of where you can co-operate most effectively in his projected advance along the Prahsu-Coomassie line. I have to request you will be good enough to give, for the Major-General's information, the fullest details of the route by which you intend to co-operate, giving the probable strength of each of your columns in Houssas and in natives."

To this despatch Captain Glover replied as follows on the 14th December:—" In reply to despatch dated 11th December 1873, received this morning, I have the honour to inform your Excellency that I shall be established on the banks of the river Prah by the 15th January with all the available force that I may be enabled to assemble.

" Bagoro, in Eastern Akim, one day's journey in rear of river Prah, will be my principal depôt, from which my advance will be made on Juabin.

" It had been my intention to have endeavoured to

move on Coomassie from a point on the Volta farther north; but the delay in my movements, occasioned by the Accras and seaboard towns, may possibly prevent me from crossing farther north than Aquamoo. It is therefore doubtful how far I may be enabled to influence the tribes to the north.

"I informed the kings and chiefs of Accra this morning that unless they were prepared to cross the Volta from Sofie and Gravie in four days, I would relinquish all co-operation with them in Ahwoonah, and proceed northward with the Houssas, Yorubas, and force collected at Blappah.

"I estimate that the distance from Bagoro to Juabin will be fourteen marches of six miles per diem; that the force with which I shall cross the Prah from Eastern Akim will be, at the lowest estimate, 16,000 effectives,—possibly 30,000 men, all told.

"The Accras received, up to 4th November, 795 guns, 4300 lbs. powder, 1590 flints, 863 lead bars, £656 : 12 : 6, and 8 casks of rum, to enable them to put themselves in motion to proceed to the camp at Addah Fork, and it was not until the 9th December that 1000 men had presented themselves in camp.

"The inhabitants of the seaboard towns very naturally remained until the Accras had passed, in order to prevent their towns and villages being plundered.

"Lieutenant Cameron, 19th Regiment, and Mr. Cleland, native gentleman, returned last evening, having been sent by me on the 8th inst. to turn the Accras out of the seaboard town in which they were loitering until I should have crossed the Volta, where they intended to come up to share plunder.

"They are now fast flocking in, and I trust in four

days to get them over the Volta into the Ahwoonah country.

"It must, however, be borne in mind that the supply of coal only reached me on the 5th inst., and is now discharging. None could have been obtained from the Squadron, and but for the sixty tons I obtained from the Government store at Accra, I should have been helpless so far as regards transport by steam on Volta.

"I will not detain transport 'Gertrude' while map of Eastern Akim and Juabin is in preparation, but will send it by first opportunity."

Captain Glover's intention at this time was—having formed, as he hoped to do, 10,000 or 15,000 men in four days in two camps, one at Gravie, and the other at Sofie—to cross over the Gravie force first, and form a junction with the Sofie force which would be crossed from Sofie to Rock Point. These forces were to move in rear of the hills opposite Blappah, and engage the enemy's attention while a force was crossed over from Blappah; and he thought the Ahwoonahs would detain him for a week before he could march north. He estimated the force opposite to him on the other side of the Volta as 10,000 strong, who were of opinion that he would cross first from Blappah, and not, as his intention was, from Sofie; and his great object was to sweep Ahwoonah, because a first success would influence the number of men he would probably be enabled to bring up across the Prah. On the 11th December Captain Glover reported 2878 present at Addah, 627 at Gravie, 4672 at Sofie, 5818 at Blappah, and 11,072 at Janketty. His total force he estimated at upwards of 25,000. On the same day he wrote "I shall have crossed a force of 13,000 men into the Ahwoonah country in three or four days, and anticipate that Mr. Goldsworthy will reach Elmina Chica in ten days from this date, when I would request that H.M.S. 'Decoy' co-operate with the force under his command in clearing the beach from that point to the mouth of the river Volta. After subduing the chief inland towns of Ahwoonah, I proceed northward to Aquamoo, detaching Mr. Goldsworthy with sufficient force to the seaboard. If H.M.S. 'Decoy' returns to Addah Fork the day after to-morrow, I propose requesting Lieutenant Hext to take charge of the depôt at that place, and will detach two steam-launches to cover the depôt when he proceeds to co-operate with Mr. Goldsworthy."

Thus then all seemed to be at last going well on the Volta. It was true that two months and a half had passed since the Major-General's arrival, and that Captain Glover had not as yet commenced his movements; but the train was now laid, and the confident tone of his despatches left no doubt at head-quarters that most valuable assistance would be received from him. The operation of clearing his base had certainly seemed to be a long time in preparation, but now the promises made were distinct. In three or four days from the 17th Captain Glover "would have crossed a force of 13,000 men into the Ahwoonah country"; and he would "be established on the banks of the river Prah by the 15th January," with a force which he estimated "as at the lowest 16,000 effectives, possibly 30,000 men, all told."

The arrangements for the invasion of Ashanti were all planned, and the Head-Quarter Staff was to leave Cape Coast on the 26th December for Prahsu, when, on Christmas Eve, to the dismay of the Major-General,

H.M.S. "Decoy" arrived from the Volta, with the despatch of which the following extract contains the pith :—

"Twenty-four days from to-morrow should enable me to reach the Prah, but, after reading the above report of the last few days, I think your Excellency will agree with me, that I should be misleading you if I stated that I saw any possibility of my reaching that point before forty days."

This sudden collapse of Captain Glover's promises is so grave and so serious a matter, that it is only justice to him to give in full the despatch in which he related the cause of his inability to fulfil the engagement which he had undertaken.

"I returned from inspecting the camp at Blappah on the 11th inst., where I found the native allies assembled there in the best possible spirit, and ready to cross over at any moment; and their demeanour fully bore out Captain Sartorius' report of them under date of 6th inst.

"2. I therefore felt myself fully justified in reckoning upon their ready obedience, and informed your Excellency that I would most certainly be on the banks of the Prah, with a force of not less than 15,000, on the 15th proximo.

"On the morning of the 15th I assembled the kings and chiefs in camp at Addah, and the tenor of your Excellency's letter of 11th inst. was made known to them, as well as my reply thereto.

"3. I proceeded at noon in the 'Lady of the Lake,' taking with me Lieutenant Cameron, 19th Regiment, with fifty Houssas, and King Tackie and his immediate followers, and landed them at Sofie, the place agreed upon by the kings and chiefs from which to cross; the remaining kings and chiefs in camp with their people, numbering some 2000 men, promising to start next day.

"4. I reached the camp at Blappah, with provisions, stores, and ammunition, and acquainted the kings and chiefs there of your Excellency's letter, and informed them that King Tackie was in camp at Sofie, and that I would cross him with his force in four days, and they all expressed themselves ready and willing to co-operate.

"5. I left them in the evening, and anchored for the night at Sofie; and, leaving there early in the morning, arrived at noon at Addah Fork.

"6. Finding no movement had taken place during my absence, I rode out to Addah Fork and visited the kings of James Town and Christianborg, and their captains at their separate quarters, and endeavoured to shame them into joining their king at Sofie.

"7. A movement did commence next morning; King Solomon of James Town Accra setting a tardy example, but not reaching the camp at Sofie until the evening of the 20th inst., occupying three days in a march of one.

"8. I remained in camp, endeavouring to hurry the movement of the Accras, and arranging that 300 Accras, together with 57 Houssas, 50 Yorubas, and 100 Addahs, should garrison the depôt at Addah Fork.

"The 100 Addahs never appeared, nor has their king, up to this date, appeared in camp at Sofie.

"9. In the meanwhile the 'Lady of the Lake' proceeded to camp at Blappah with stores, ammunition, and 50 Houssas for camp at Sofie, returning to Addah Fork on the afternoon of the 18th.

"Having despatched the remaining Houssas and Yorubas by land to Sofie, I left at noon on the 19th, and on arriving at Sofie, and finding only 300 men of the native allies had arrived there, I proceeded to Blappah with the intention of withdrawing 100 Houssas, 100 Yorubas, and 1000 of the native allies, and with them, and those encamped at Sofie, to cross the next afternoon, and, marching the next day eastward on the Blappah hills, to fall on the rear of the enemy's camp and divert his attention, whilst Captain Sartorius crossed from Blappah.

"Captain Sartorius proceeded to carry out these arrangements, and reported that Chief Ababue, with 1000 Aquapims, would be ready to march next morning at daylight.

"10. At 8 o'clock that evening Ababue and his captains were assembled in my tent, when I pointed out to them that the enemy were in large force on the opposite bank, having made up their minds that the river would be crossed from Blappah; that there was no force opposite Sofie, and that if he would march his men next morning to Sofie I would at once cross them with Houssas, Yorubas, and a corps of Accras.

"They all expressed themselves satisfied with these arrangements.

"11. At 3 in the morning I heard drums beating in the rear of the camp, and going in the direction of Sofie, and I concluded that Ababue had started.

"The Houssas and Yorubas left at daylight, when Captain Sartorius reported to me that the Aquapims had left at 3 A.M.

"12. At 7 o'clock the king of Aquapim and his captains and stated in the plainest terms, which could admit of no mistake, and which they reiterated again and again, to my repeated appeals to induce them to march at once, was as follows: 'That they could not allow Ababue to leave their camp with his followers, and thus weaken their force, and that they would not be in a position to cross the Volta until Wednesday the 24th, on which day they hoped that the whole of their forces would have joined them at Blappah.'

"13. They further stated that they desired to be assured that the Accras would be in their proper position, and would co-operate in any movement across the Volta.

"14. They added that, if Ababue marched to Sofie with his force, or, if I insisted upon their crossing the Volta before the remainder of their forces had joined them, they would leave the camp and return home.

"15. I stated that it was in consequence of the Accras not having come up to take their position in time that I applied to them for a part or the whole of their force of 1700 men on account of the high character Captain Sartorius had given of their willingness to move, and desire to punish the Ahwoonahs and Aquamoos.

"16. They again stated that the remainder of their force having come up, they would cross on Wednesday the 24th at Blappah, and that at no other place would they cross.

"17. I thanked them for the very plain terms, and the decided tone in which they had made known their intentions; that hitherto I had reckoned on them only through Captain Sartorius' report of them, but that now I judged and appreciated them from my own personal observation. With that I left for the camp at Sofie.

"At an assembly yesterday morning of the kings and chiefs encamped at Sofie, they informed me that they had then only about 500 men present, and that they would not risk crossing with such a small force, and insisted upon delaying the operation until more had come in from Addah, and the places between Addah and Sofie.

"19. The chiefs of Croboe and Crepee encamped with the Aquapims at Blappah, on being requested to furnish a portion of their men to march to Sofie, displayed a similar disinclination to carry out my wishes in this respect.

"20. I beg to enclose copy of report received from Captain Sartorius late on the day of my leaving Blappah.

"21. A force of the enemy is now assembled opposite Sofie, and, on passing yesterday afternoon, I threw a rocket into their camp, 1800 yards from the bank.

"22. I cross to-morrow morning with 300 Houssas, 300 Yorubas, and 300 Accras, and trust I may be enabled to induce the remainder of the Accras to follow.

"23. Dr. Rowe, who left me yesterday, reports this morning:—'From Addah town I have hunted out from their holes 270 men, who have promised to start in the morning. In Addah Fork I find Pram Pram king and people 263, and many more are at Footey, a village six miles up the beach. Ningo people, 1015, counted this morning; they start now; they have more people at Footey. There are also at 200 Teshies, and the whole of Labaddy people. I start in an hour for Footey, and return here to sleep. Addah Fork 5 A.M.—I have just returned from Footey, which I left at 11 P.M. last night. I can guarantee you 2000 fresh men by Tuesday night, 23d; they have come up with me in the dark from Footey, and are the best men I have yet seen.'

"24. From the accompanying report your Excellency will be enabled to judge how far it is possible for me to be certain that I can be at any particular place on any particular day, when a hurried movement may be necessary.

"25. It had been my intention, after crossing the Volta, to have left Mr. Goldsworthy to finish the Ahwoonahs on the beach with part of the Accras and seaboard people, who should have numbered 15,000 men, and, with the rest, turning rapidly north, to have crossed a force into Ashanti territory from Aquamoo; at the same time Captain Sartorius, with Eastern Akims and Aquapims, would have reached the Prah at a point before Bagoro.

"26. Until the receipt of your Excellency's letter, acquainting me of the arrival of the English regiments, I was not aware that they had left England, and did not anticipate their arrival here until 15th January, or that, from the reported failure of the native allies, you would so successfully have driven the enemy across the Prah at so early a date.

"27. Captain Sartorius has not yet furnished me with a copy of his map of Akim and Croboe; but I send a map with tracing of the routes I have proposed for two columns to Prah, 35 to 40 miles north-east of Prahsu, and thence to Juabin, on Lake Echuy, 20 miles north-east of Prahsu, and 20 miles south-east of Coomassie, in three columns.

"28. Twenty-four days from to-morrow should

enable me to reach the Prah; but, after reading the above report of the last few days, I think your Excellency will agree with me, that I should be misleading you if I stated that I saw any possibility of my reaching that point before forty days; but I beg to assure you that no effort shall be left untried to carry a force to the point indicated.

"A report has reached me that the Aquamoos contemplate giving in their submission, and furnishing the kings and chiefs of the Accra and other eastern tribes with suitable guarantees for their good faith, on being permitted to join the expedition, and to lead the way to Coomassie.

"9. If this be true my movements may be somewhat hastened.

"I take this opportunity of acquainting your Excellency of the able assistance that the several commissioners under me have on all occasions afforded."

Inclosure to above.

"The native chiefs have met, and, after a short discussion, have informed me that they would camp with me at Blappah on Tuesday next, and cross the river on Wednesday morning, but not before.

"Messengers have been sent by them to King Tackie at Sofie.   REG. SARTORIUS, *Captn.*"

Captain Glover had at last found that, in trusting to the natives, he was leaning on a broken reed. In the despatch in which he offered his services on the 30th July, he had stated that he had acquired in action the confidence of the eastern tribes of the protectorate, and he spoke of his capability to organise and discipline irregular levies for the field. In using these expressions Captain Glover had not gone one whit beyond the truth ; but no power of inspiring confidence, no energy, no capability, can overcome or eradicate the apathy of the West African coast tribes. Nowhere could a man be found more thoroughly and completely capable of dealing with these men than Captain Glover. His indomitable energy, his personal courage, his tact, and knowledge of native character, make him unrivalled in such a task; but all these qualities were spent in vain, and broken to pieces, like waves upon a rock, when they encountered the hopeless character with which they were now brought into contact. An effort to cross 1000 men six miles to the right of where they fancied they were to cross was resented by the whole force; and why ? Because money had been spent in fetish for that particular crossing, and to change the point would have been to them so much money lost.

What, in the face of this startling news, was the course to be adopted by the Major-General? Was he to go on for ever hearing the same tale of intended movements against the Ahwoonahs, whom Captain Glover had hoped to attack early in October, and had not yet moved against three days before Christmas? If he were to delay for a few days his intended movements at the cost of great inconvenience and extra risk to the European troops, was there any guarantee whatever that, at the expiration of these few days, Captain Glover would not demand a few more, and that these demands would not go on till the rainy season? None. Captain Glover had himself settled that in writing, " From the accompanying report your Excellency will be enabled to judge *how far it is possible for me to be certain that I can be at any particular place on any particular day*, when a hurried movement may be necessary." Was the Major-General to abandon the idea of all assistance from Captain Glover, and leave him to conduct his operations against the Ahwoonahs, while he marched on to Coomassie? To do this would have been to fling away the whole results of all the labour and all the money expended in Captain Glover's expedition, and to give up the chance of lessening the dangers of the task about to be committed to the European force entrusted to the Major-General's care. There was but one course open; the original orders to Captain Glover must be enforced, his miserable, worthless, native allies must be left to do as they could, and Captain Glover, or one of his officers, with such disciplined force as could be trusted, must be told to cross the Prah on the day originally named. The following despatch was therefore addressed to Captain Glover on Christmas Eve.

"I am directed by Major-General Sir Garnet Wolseley to acknowledge the receipt of your despatch of 22d inst., reporting your proceedings up to that date, and stating that you do not see any possibility of your being able to reach the Prah before forty days.

"In reply, I am to inform you that Sir Garnet Wolseley desires that you will, immediately upon receipt of this letter, move the Houssas and any other disciplined troops under your command, by the shortest route, to the point indicated by you in your despatch of 14th ult., as that where you would be established on the banks of the river Prah by the 15th January, with a force which you estimated as at the lowest 16,000 effectives.

"You will also immediately take steps to move to the same point the force of 11,000 allies shown as present at Janketty in your state of 17th inst.

"In framing his plan of campaign, the Major-General has counted upon your undertaking to be on the Prah on the 15th January; and it is absolutely essential that a force composed of the disciplined troops under your command, and such natives of the eastern tribes as can be induced to proceed, should cross the Prah on the 15th proximo at the point which you selected and indicated to the Major-General.

"You will therefore make this your one object. If necessary to its attainment, you will break off all operations on the east bank of the Volta which have no direct bearing on the main issue; and if it should appear to you that your own presence for a longer period upon the lower Volta is necessary, you will detach officers to accompany the disciplined troops at your command and the Eastern Akims at Janketty in their march to the Prah, which river must be crossed by a column from the forces under your command on the 15th January, the day on which the Major-General will cross at Prahsu Assin."

At the same time that this despatch was sent to Captain Glover, the Major-General wrote to him privately, explaining fully his views. He pointed out that the English Government looked to him to get the British regiments away from the Coast with the least possible delay, and that next to beating or humbling the Ashantis, the removal of the English troops from the Coast was the object most desired at home. "I cannot," wrote the Major-General, "let them leave until I have finally settled with King Koffee; whereas with you at Juabin, which place I believe you could reach easily in about eight marches, and without much opposition, and the enemy having been previously defeated by the English troops near the Adansi hills, I could make what terms I like. With the Ashanti army beaten by my white troops, I should then, if I thought it necessary to occupy or destroy Coomassie, be able to send you forward to that place from Juabin, whilst I sent all, or at least the bulk, of my Europeans back to England. To enable you to carry out your engagement, I have run myself tolerably dry as regards money here, and am now compelled to use the authority confided to me, and to order you in the despatch which accompanies this letter to march all your disciplined troops to the Prah, and to cross that river on the 15th next month with them and the 11,000 Akims now collected at Janketty. The quarrels between the tribes to the east of the Volta can be settled at any time, but the Ashanti war, to prosecute which both you and I have been sent to this country, can only be disposed of *now; it* won't wait, the Ahwoonah business will. I speak at a distance from your theatre of operations, but I never believed that the Accras would join you on the Prah. Let them settle their own business on the Volta; or, should you feel bound to remain with them to assist them, of course you can do so, but I must have your disciplined men, and the Akims from Janketty, across the Prah on the 15th proximo. Unless you can accomplish this, no matter what may be your success with the Ahwoonahs, you must clearly see that, as far as this wretched war between England and Ashanti is concerned, you might just as well be operating on the Zanzibar coast of Africa as in the Ahwoonah district.

Having spoken thus plainly to you, and told you my views as to the military exigencies of the moment, I shall rest satisfied that if you do not cross the Prah as originally intended, it is because you could not. From what I know of you, I feel that if what I require of you could be accomplished by any one it will be so by you."

After writing his despatch of the 22d, stating his inability to be on the Prah before forty days, Captain Glover had on the 23d shelled and rocketed three or four villages a few hundred yards from the bank of the river in front of his intended landing place, opposite Sofie. At noon, no movement having taken place on the part of the Accras, over 3000 strong, he embarked the Houssas and Yorubas, 600, in the "Lady of the Lake," steam-launches, and canoes, and steaming a mile down the river, landed them, after first searching the bank with rockets and shells. The Accras then began to come down for embarkation, and the crossing continued until 3 P.M. the next day, by which time 5000 had crossed. Captain Glover then proceeded to Blappah, and on the following morning landed a force under Captain Sartorius of 50 Houssas, 100 Yorubas, 50 Aquapims, 50 Crepees, 50 Croboes, and 80 native Christians, after shelling the bush at the place of landing with two 7-pounder guns, and firing rockets, so as to search the bank to both sides of the landing-place. The enemy occupied the village of Adedomey, and armed men being observed in the bush on the right flank, Gatling guns opened fire from the bridge of the "Lady of the Lake," and cleared them away. A skirmish ensued, when our troops were extended on the upper side of the bank, and the enemy very soon gave way; but Captain Sartorius found it impossible to keep his men in hand, and lost sight of them; however, they subsequently returned. Captain Glover then occupied, with native detachments, Adedomey and the enemy's camp, and on the evening of the 25th was joined by Mr. Goldsworthy with the Houssas and Yorubas who had been landed opposite Sofie. Mr. Goldsworthy had marched with the intention of proceeding to Idafaille, but the guides took the wrong road, and he was obliged to halt for the night at a cross road. His left flank was attacked by the enemy, whom he threw back upon their villages which he burnt. He computed the number of the enemy as about 350, and he lost one Houssa killed and one wounded, several Ahwoonahs being placed *hors-de-combat*. Captain Sartorius had estimated the force opposed to him at 1000, his loss being one Houssa killed and one wounded, two Yorubas and two native allies wounded. On the 26th Captain Glover found both officers and men too much done up to move, and the native allies were not prepared, having to forage for provisions.

On the 27th, while preparations were making to advance, Sir Garnet Wolseley's despatch of the 24th arrived. Immediately on the receipt of it, Captain Glover summoned a meeting of the kings and chiefs in camp at Adedomey, and urged upom them the necessity of proceeding with him to the Prah. At seven in the evening they informed him that, after having subdued the Ahwoonahs they would accompany him to the Prah; and half-an-hour later the Aquapims promised to recross the Volta with him the following morning at daylight. On the 28th Captain Glover commenced to recross with Houssas, Yorubas, Croboes, guns, and stores. On reaching the camp at Blappah the Aquapims said that they must first destroy a village one and a half day's journey distant, and would then join him at the Prah. In the middle of the day Lieutenant Cameron left for Medica with 320 Houssas, 250 Yorubas, and 300 Croboes; he returned sick in the evening, and the force proceeded under the command of Dr. Bale. Captain Glover followed on the 29th with Houssas, guns, stores, and provisions in steam-launches and canoes. Captain Sartorius had previously started for Eastern Akim with 20 Houssas. Captain Glover sent to Addah Fork for the remaining Houssas and Yorubas, leaving the depôt at Blappah in command of Dr. Rowe, with 180 Christians, and 300 Accras under Mr. Adamson, R.N., to defend the depôt at Addah Fork.

As in a previous war the Ahwoonahs had burnt both Addah and Addah Fork, Captain Glover expressed great anxiety as to the magazines there and at Medica being left to the care of these unreliable allies, most unwillingly kept from the front; and said he could not be answerable for any untoward events. He wrote that his rear and right flank were liable to attack until the Ahwoonahs and Aquamoos should be subdued. Captain Glover's despatch continued thus :—

"This I have reported to your Excellency in a previous despatch, and my present proceedings had received your Excellency's approval, and you now inform me that these operations on left bank have no direct bearing on main issue.

"At Accra, the Aquapims, Croboes, Crepees, and Akims stipulated on the destruction of Aquamoo being accomplished before they would proceed to Coomassie; and the

THE ASHANTI WAR. 417

Accras and people of the seaboard likewise made it a point of the first necessity that the Ahwoonahs should be subdued before they could leave their country in safety from the attack of tribes unfaithful to their engagements and in alliance with the Ashantis, to whom they are large powder suppliers.

"I have left Mr. Goldsworthy, having with him Lieutenant Moore, R.N., Dr. Parkes, a gunner of Royal Marine Artillery, one 7-pounder, and one rocket-trough, with 11,780 men, to proceed against Ahwoonah, directing Lieutenant Moore to bring up the Aquapims and remaining Croboes, numbering 2460 men, as soon as they have fought or won their first engagement; it is possible some part of this force may be on the Prah by the 1st February.

"That I may induce the 11,000 men who are watching the Ashantis in the neighbourhood of Janketty to leave their country before the Aquamoos have been defeated, is most improbable.

"Eastern Akim may possibly furnish a contingent, and Western Akim, if not detached from their old fighting force, would have furnished your Excellency with a reliable and good contingent.

"In Quabina Fuah I lost the one chief whose influence could have placed the Eastern tribes earlier in the field than I and the Commissioners with me have, with all our efforts, been enabled to do.

"I am not aware that I have in any way deviated from the programme marked out for my guidance and following in Lord Kimberley's instructions; nor can I be responsible for the results which may attend the following out of your Excellency's instructions I now receive.

VOL. I.   2 D

"I expect to be on the Prah by the 10th proximo, with a force of Houssas and Yorubas numbering 700 men.

"It appears to me that, in withdrawing myself and the small number of disciplined men from the force I have succeeded in placing in the field, you have taken from its usefulness in the effect its advance would have in coming to your Excellency's assistance. In advancing from the Prah with only 700 reliable men, that number must necessarily be considerably diminished if it meets with any opposition before it reaches Juabin.

"This, therefore, must be the result to be anticipated. On the other hand, two days' successful fighting in the Ahwoonah country would have enabled me to put such confidence and spirit into the force from which your Excellency has withdrawn the heart or core, as would have given you a large force flushed with success on the banks of the Prah by the 1st February.

"In the position in which I find myself, I cannot but anticipate probable disaster to my magazines in rear, and small prospect of bringing to your Excellency essential aid in the point."

Captain Glover enclosed a report from Dr. Rowe, to the effect that he could not count on a greater force of Houssas and Yorubas at Bagoro than 700 on the 10th, and another letter from Mr. Goldsworthy, protesting against his position in being left alone with the native allies.

This last despatch from Captain Glover, dated at Camp Blappah, 28th December, was received by Sir Garnet Wolseley at Yancoomassie Assin on the last day of the year, whilst marching up the country. The

Major-General acknowledged its receipt, and then proceeded to give Captain Glover an outline of his plan of campaign. His despatch continued thus:—

"The information conveyed in your despatch of the 28th inst. shows the Major-General that the assistance which, by your despatch of the 14th ultimo, he had been led to expect from you, can be no longer counted on, or that the nature of that assistance is altered. But the Major-General considers that, even should it be impossible for you to cross the Prah on the 15th proximo with a larger force than the 700 Houssas and Yorubas named in your last despatch, you will still be able to do much towards carrying out the general object of your operations, as stated in your original instructions of the 18th August last from the Secretary of State for the Colonies, namely, 'to so far harass and alarm them (the Ashantis), as to enable an attack to be made on them in front with better prospects of success.'

"The Major-General is still in hopes that, through your influence with the kings and chiefs of the Eastern districts to whom you have been commissioned, you may be able to induce the 11,000 Akims in camp at Janketty to cross the Prah with you, or that at least a few thousands of your other native levies may consent to follow you.

"After crossing the Prah, you will operate in the direction of Juabin; but your mode of advance, and the distance to which you can penetrate into the enemy's country previously to any decisive engagements that may be fought by the column under the Major-General's immediate command with the main body of the enemy, must depend upon the strength of the force with which you are to cross the Prah. Should you only have with you the 700 Houssas and Yorubas of whom you speak, it will of course be essential that you should operate with the greatest caution, lest your communications with your base should be cut. Still, should this unfortunate event at any time befall you, it is to be remembered, that by a cross road (and cross roads probably exist north of the Prah as they do south of it), you can always move westward to join the Major-General on the Prahsu-Coomassie road.

"Should you consider yourself sufficiently strong to advance far into Ashanti territory, I am to request that you will march to Juabin as quickly as you may feel yourself justified in doing so, and that you will halt there until you receive further instructions from the Major-General.

"There will be, as already said, a force north of the Prah, at Prahsu, about the 5th January, when, if unopposed, a post will be established a few miles farther forward. You are therefore authorised to begin your advance north of the Prah as soon as you may think fit after your arrival on that river on the 10th of January, the date named in your despatch, No. 221, of 28th inst. Owing to the distance that will intervene between your force and the Major-General on the Prahsu-Coomassie road, and to the difficulties of communication in this country, it will be impossible for the Major-General to decide whether the force under your command will or will not warrant your pushing on directly and without halting to Juabin; but he relies entirely upon your own good judgment to decide this point correctly,—your decision being, of course, greatly influenced by the intelligence you may receive of the enemy's movements.

"Under no circumstances whatever will you allow any men of the force under your command to cross the 'Dah' river, which flows to the westward of Juabin, or to advance from Juabin towards Coomassie, without distinct orders to that effect from the Major-General. It is the Major-General's object to bring the king of Ashanti to terms, and, if possible, to do this without taking Coomassie; for, if taken, especially by a column composed entirely of natives, as that under your command, it would inevitably be pillaged; and were Coomassie pillaged, there would be no chance of obtaining from the king of Ashanti the sum that the Major-General intends to demand as a partial indemnity to her Majesty for the expenses that the English nation has been put to by this war having been forced upon it by the king.

"Should any attempt be made by the enemy to open negotiations with you, you will be so good as to refer the messengers or ambassadors to Major-General Sir Garnet Wolseley, telling them to approach his troops on the main Prahsu-Coomassie road, with a white flag flying, so that the object of their mission may be known; but you will not, on any account whatever, yourself enter into any negotiations with the enemy.

"As, in your despatch of the 28th inst., you seem to express a doubt as to the security of your magazines on the Volta, the Major-General has requested the Commodore to take such measures as he may deem advisable for their protection. I have the honour to forward for your information a copy of the letter which has been addressed to him on this subject.

"The Major-General hopes that Mr. Goldsworthy may, with the 11,780 men left under his command, be speedily able to bring the Ahwoonahs to terms, when it is presumed the whole, or a portion, of this large native force will be available to guard your communications.

"I am directed to request that you will be so good as at once to acknowledge the receipt of this letter; and that, immediately upon your arrival on the Prah, you will report to the Major-General your presence there, and the exact strength of the force present with you.

"You will also be so good as to state your opinion as to whether you can safely carry out the further advance conditionally ordered by the Major-General.

"While the Major-General is fully prepared to accept the responsibility of the directions issued by him to you, he must count upon your using the ordinary precautions of a military commander of troops in the field. The Major-General's headquarters will be at Prahsu-Assin until the 15th of January."

It is impossible to pass on without commenting upon the loyal spirit which Captain Glover had from first to last shown in carrying out the instructions of the Major-General. His task had been a hard and a bitter one; and the gloomy view which he now took of his prospects was but the natural result of disappointment. It is not difficult to understand why it was that he had been disappointed in beginning his march to Coomassie at the early date anticipated by him when Sir Garnet arrived at the beginning of October, and no one who knows how hard he and the officers under his command worked could ever think that the delay in beginning operations was in any way attributable to want of energy on their part. The nature of the tribes of Western Africa, which was formerly known to but a few travellers, and even by them scarcely appreciated to its full extent, has now, by the Ashanti expedition, become known to the whole world; and Captain Glover's position can be easily understood by all who have thus learnt the utter and complete futility of relying upon native promises. Now, Captain Glover was about to depend on these promises no more, but to act on his own account with his few disciplined troops; and the successful operations which he had already carried out in the few days between the 23d and the 28th were an earnest of the skill which he would show in his advance into the enemy's territory. As regards his magazines on the Volta, our experience in the Protectorate had taught us that there was no danger for them, as any fortified post (and of course Captain Glover had fortified his magazines during the two months at his disposal) can hold out indefinitely, as long as food lasts, against the attack of an enemy armed with flint guns, and without artillery. Besides, Mr. Goldsworthy had nearly 12,000 men remaining, a greater force than the Ahwoonahs were supposed to have in their whole country; and, as Captain Glover had an armed steamer and steam-launches, and as, moreover, Sir Garnet knew that he could rely upon the Commodore to take steps to make the magazines more secure should it be necessary, he felt no anxiety. Even supposing some risk were run by these magazines, the Major-General considered it well worth incurring for the accomplishment of the object for which Captain Glover had been sent out—namely, not to fight the Ahwoonahs, and act on the defensive on the Volta, but, in the words of Captain Glover's original instructions, —" To create such a diversion on the flank and rear of the Ashantis as may force them to retreat from the Protectorate, or, at all events, to so far harass and alarm them as to enable an attack to be made on them in front with better prospect of success."

The one great object now set before the mind of the Major-General was to defeat the Ashanti army in the field, to march his Europeans to Coomassie, to compel a treaty from the king, and to remove the British soldiers from the country before the commencement of the rainy season should make imminent the risk of disaster; all other operations of secondary importance must be subordinated to this one supreme end.

APPENDIX.

No. I. (Page 15, Chap. I.)

TREATY OF PEACE, 27th April 1831.

WE, the undersigned—namely, the Governor of Cape Coast Castle and British Settlements, on the part of his Majesty the King of England; the Princess of "Akianvah," and the Chief "Quagua," on the part of the King of Ashantee; "Aggery," King of Cape Coast; "Adookoo," King of Fantee; "Amonoo," King of Annamaboe; "Chibboe," King of Denkara; "Ossoo Okoo," King of Tufel; "Aminniee," King of Wassaw; "Chibboo," King of Assin; the Chiefs of Adjumacon and Essacoomah, and the other Chiefs in alliance with the King of Great Britain, whose names are hereunto appended—do consent to, and hereby ratify the following Treaty of Peace, and of free commerce between ourselves and such other Chiefs as may hereafter adhere to it :—

1. The King of Ashantee having deposited in Cape Coast Castle, in the presence of the above-mentioned parties, the sum of 600 ounces of gold, and having delivered into the hands of the Governor two young men of the royal family of Ashantee, named "Ossor Ansah" and "Ossoo In Quantamissah," as security that he will keep peace with the said parties in all time coming, peace is hereby declared betwixt the said King of Ashantee and all and each of the parties aforesaid, to continue in all time coming. The above securities shall remain in Cape Coast Castle for the space of six years from this date.

2. In order to prevent all quarrels in future which might lead to the infraction of this Treaty of Peace, we the parties aforesaid have agreed to the following rules and regulations for the better protection of lawful commerce :—

The paths shall be perfectly open and free to all persons engaged in lawful traffic; and persons molesting them in any way whatever, or forcing them to purchase at any particular market, or influencing them by any unfair means whatever, shall be declared guilty of infringing this Treaty, and be liable to the severest punishment.

Panyarring, denouncing, and swearing, on or by any person or thing whatever, are hereby strictly forbidden, and all persons infringing this rule shall be rigorously punished; and no masters or chief shall be answerable for the crimes of his servants, unless done by his orders or consent, or when under his control.

As the King of Ashantee has renounced all right or title to any tribute or homage from the Kings of Dinkara, Assin, and others formerly his subjects, so, on the other hand, these parties are strictly prohibited from insulting, by improper speaking, or in any other way, their former master, such conduct being calculated to produce quarrels and wars.

All "palavers" are to be decided in the manner mentioned in the terms and conditions of peace already agreed to by the parties to this Treaty.

Signed in the Great Hall of Cape Coast Castle, this 27th day of April 1831, by the parties to this Treaty, and sealed with the Great Seal of the Colony in their presence.

(Signed) GEO. MACLEAN, *Governor.*

Their marks.

X	AKIANVAH,	Princess of Ashantee.
X	QUAGUA,	Chief of Ashantee.
X	AGGERY,	King of Cape Coast.
X	ADOOKOO,	King of Fantee.
X	AMONOO,	King of Annamaboe.
X	ABOOKOO,	Chief of Acomfee.
X	OTTOO,	Chief of Abrah,
X	CHIBBOO,	King of Assin.
X	CUDJOE CHIBBOO,	King of Dinkera.
X	GEHAL,	Assin Chief.
X	OSSO OKOO,	King of Tufel.
X	APPOLONIA,	Chiefs.
X	AKINNIE,	Chief of Agah.

APPENDIX. 427

No. II. (Page 182, Chap. IV.)

RETURN OF CASUALTIES amongst the Troops, Marines, and Seamen from her Majesty's ships, in action at Essaman, 14th October 1873.

General Staff.

Colonel M'Neill, V.C., C.M.G. (Colonel on the Staff), gunshot wound, left forearm, very severe.

2d West India Regiment.

Captain Forbes, wounded by slug, right hand, slight.

Royal Navy.

Captain Fremantle, gunshot wound, right upper arm, severe.
Non-commissioned officers and men, 2 wounded, Royal Marines.
Non-commissioned officers and men, 2 wounded, Royal Navy.
Houssa levy, 16 wounded (1 since dead).
Coolies, 3 wounded.

No. III.

West African Settlements Command.

Weekly Percentage of Sick for the 13 weeks ending January 2, 1874.

Period in Weeks.	White Troops.	Black Troops.	Seamen and Royal Marines.
Week ending 10th Oct. 1873,	11	3	0
,, 17th ,,	21	4	28
,, 24th ,,	0	3	0
,, 31st ,,	3	3	0
,, 7th Nov.	16	5	4
,, 14th ,,	9	4	5
,, 21st ,,	7	5	13
,, 28th ,,	3	4	55
,, 5th Dec.	9	3	3
,, 12th ,,	7	3	7
,, 19th ,,	5	4	11
,, 26th ,,	8	4	27
,, 2d Jan. 1874,	4	3	1

END OF THE FIRST VOLUME.

PRINTED BY WILLIAM BLACKWOOD AND SONS, EDINBURGH

www.ingramcontent.com/pod-product-compliance
Lightning Source LLC
Chambersburg PA
CBHW070306230426
43664CB00015B/2646